"This debut effort offers the true-to-life story of a young girl's longing to connect with the mother she lost to cancer and to find love amidst loss and isolation in an unjust world. Haqq brings to life the challenges facing a newly arrived immigrant family in small-town Minnesota in the 1970s. In doing so, she gives us a tale filled with humor and poignancy, offering a testimony to resilience, strength, and forgiveness."

—JEFFERY RENARD ALLEN, AWARD-WINNING AUTHOR OF THE NOVELS, *SONG OF THE SHANK* AND *RAILS UNDER MY BACK*

"An ode to family and motherhood, Haqq's words carry pain and devastation, grief and solitude, courage and integrity. The palpable sadness from Haqq and her siblings consume the pages and brings the reader to crevices of the past."

—ANUSHREE SREEDHAR, BROWN GIRL MAGAZINE

Elisheba Haqq deftly weaves the loss of her beloved mother throughout this coming of age memoir. It takes courage to tell as it is, and Haqq does not waver from the truth. Ultimately what comes across is the deep sense of loss and the longing for times bygone, yet forging ahead in the face of injustice and a yearning for love. The fierce attachment to her family gives Haqq strength and humor to get through life, and she infuses her writing with these. What an absolutely delightful read!

—SUPRIYA BHATNAGAR, AUTHOR OF ...*AND THEN THERE WERE THREE*

Elisheba has a way of transporting you to another time and place that is unmatched. Mamaji will make you yearn for innocence that made you believe that parents are invincible beings.

—NINA FOXX, AUTHOR, MOMMA: GONE, NAACP IMAGE AWARD FINALIST

Elisheba Haqq's Mamaji pushes against the boundaries of memoir; her text pulsating with a novel's energy. Papaji, Mamaji, and their seven children move from India to the frozen wastes of Minnesota. Soon after their arrival Mamaji falls ill and tragically dies within months of her cancer diagnosis, when Haqq was only three years old. Haqq's yearning for Mamaji is deeply poignant–. "Was her voice like mine—deep and intense? Or was it soft and calm?" Mamaji's absence remains a lingering music in Haqq's childhood spent as The Other, as she tries to win the affection of a stepmother whose cruelty knows no bounds. Against the stepmother's locked heart the love between the masterfully-drawn siblings shines. Haqq's childhood self is as delightful and irresistible as Jane Eyre. Mamaji sweeps you away from yourself and into its pages.

—STEPHANIE DICKINSON, AUTHOR OF *GIRL BEHIND THE DOOR: A MEMOIR OF DELIRIUM AND DEMENTIA*

MAMAJI

MAMAJI

a memoir

ELISHEBA HAQQ

Published by Serving House Books

Copenhagen, Denmark and South Orange, NJ

www.servinghousebooks.com

ISBN: 978-1-947175-24-2

Library of Congress Control Number: 2020935479

Member of The Independent Book Publishers Association

First Serving House Books Edition 2020

Cover Design: Peter Selgin

Author Photograph: Sameer A. Khan

For Philip and Samuel,
because she would have loved you as much as I do
AND
For my siblings, because we saved we

"But as for you, ye devised against me evil—
God devised it for good"

—GENESIS 50:20

PREFACE

WHEN I WAS three, a younger sibling grew to kill my mother. And when I was six, the birth of my half-brother took another mother from me. The birth of a baby is supposed to be a life-giving event, but for me babies only signaled endings.

I suppose I should start at the beginning, but I am unsure as to what the beginning is. A doctor might say the beginning is the moment I took my first breath and squalled as I was released from the warm, slippery confines of my mother's womb. A minister might say it was the moment my parents conceived me. I am less sure. I cannot say I began life when I was born because so much happened before then that made me who I am today. How can I say my grandfather's life and my mother's childhood had no bearing on my life? I am entwined in the past lives of my ancestors. For me, there is no beginning—only a continuing story that joins me to people who have long ago vanished from this earth and whose whispers I hear when I close my eyes.

It is with these voices in my mind that I write. For a long time, I have tried to quell the desire to tell this story because I am afraid that it will offend and anger my family, my parents, my siblings, and even some of my friends. I have tried to tell it in a sanitized way, erasing all the pain, bitterness, and grief; but this is my truth.

Once, my friend, Thomas Kennedy, who is a mentor and fellow writer, allowed me to read an essay he wrote about his visit to a Pennsylvania prison. He quotes a writer whose name he cannot remember, "One of the most important jobs for a writer is to catch the policeman in your mind asleep." The policeman in my mind has been wide-awake and watching me for my entire life. But at this moment in time, he has fallen into a deep sleep and I am seizing the opportunity to write. I rush full speed ahead. This is my story.

A NOTE ABOUT THE TERM
MAMAJI

A S WITH ANY family, terms used to refer to relatives vary greatly. In my family, the term "Mamaji" (Maa-ma-gee) was translated as "respected mother". Indeed, the word "Mama" means mother in Urdu; a language my family members spoke along with Hindi and Punjabi. Some Indian families use the Hindi term "Mama" to refer to the mother's brother. In our home, we used the Urdu term "Mamu" (Maa-moo) for our mother's brothers.

PROLOGUE

I T's AUGUST 1996, and I'm back in my birthplace of Chandigarh, India, for the first time since Mamaji carried me out at the age of one. The people from my hometown look just like me and my family. I recognize their sturdy physiques, dark eyes, thick hair, and familiar bone structure. I see my strong nose on a lady in the flower stall, my brother's solid chin inside a rickshaw, and my sister's beautiful hands cradling a mango—it is as though I have walked into a huge family reunion of many-times-removed relatives. The language I hear is the same, a type of Hindi we speak at home in Minnesota which Papaji calls Hindustani. It's a mix of Hindi and Urdu. My parents also speak Punjabi but, while I recognize it, I cannot speak it. My trip from America was a long one and I am tired, but the moment I take my first step on Indian soil, I feel settled and relaxed in a way I have never felt before; a true sense of belonging. I heave a long, contented sigh that comes deep from within me. Mentally, I rejoice in the sea of black-haired heads and endless varieties of brown skin. I match the natural landscape, and blend seamlessly. *I'm like everyone else!* I repeat the reassuring words in my head. I have to lie to myself, because even I can see that I am still very different.

In preparation for the trip to Chandigarh, through a series of letters, I reconnected with Mamaji's younger sister, my Venetia Masi. She still lives in Chandigarh, and the last time she saw me, I was an infant. When we see each other we hug, kiss and exchange greetings. I am struck by the similarity she has to Mamaji. She looks as I imagine Mamaji would have looked had she lived. Venetia Masi is well into her 70s and walks briskly. I have her same pace and gait. Her high forehead, hands, and feet look similar to my own. She has pure white hair pulled into an elegant bun and her words are honest, animated, and strong. "You remind me so much of your mother," she says. Venetia Masi recalls funny incidents that happened long ago. I listen eagerly, desperate to remember, wanting so much to connect to the main character in the stories she is narrating, but I can't. I'm honored that I am the daughter of this wonderful person who had once known me, but I have almost no memory of her and virtually no relationship with her.

When we arrive at my childhood home, I recognize it, but only because I have seen pictures. A middle-aged lady answers the front door a moment after we knock. She listens as Venetia Masi explains that I lived here once. The lady is hospitable, offers us tea and allows us to look around. She notes the raw emotion on my face and she discreetly disappears, leaving Venetia Masi and me alone. I stand in the front room and take it in. Mamaji and I had the same tastes. I would have selected the same mantelpiece, wood trim, kitchen cabinets, countertops, and the open floor plan. Mamaji had even planned for a small window cut from the kitchen to the dining area, so dishes could be passed with efficiency.

As I walk through my once-upon-a-time home, the emotions are too great for me and I begin to sob. For the first time in my life, I have come home, to my real home—but Mamaji is not here to welcome me. I have arrived much too late. I stand still. I feel the shadows of my family here. I hear laughter and Hindi music, smell wonderful dahl or chicken tharkari simmering on the stove, and I even see my family members here and there. But I cannot hear Mamaji's voice.

People say the first thing an infant recognizes is the sound of her mother's voice, but I have no recollection of her timbre or tone. What did she sound like? Was her voice like mine—deep and intense? Or was it soft and calm? Did she sound like Venetia Masi? I hate that no matter how hard I try, I cannot hear her saying my name. I had not even known of her special nickname for me—Eeshee, until Papaji suddenly recalled it in 2017. And what's worse is that I cannot remember calling for her out loud. Many times I have longed for her and I reached out into the nothingness trying to connect, but since I did not know her, my hands remained empty.

I try to gain some control over my tears.

Venetia Masi, strokes my back and speaks softly to me in Hindi. "There, there," she says. "She loved you so much."

Did she? Instead of consoling me, this only brings fresh tears. How I want to feel her love for me! I have never known mother-love. *She loved me? Why? Is my love for her real? How can I love someone I did not know?*

We walk outside to the backyard into the warm sunshine. Amazingly, one of the wicker chairs I saw in old family photographs sits on the back veranda. On the floor are the white stones Mamaji had laid out among the dark flagstones to create each one of our names. I find all of them and then, finally, my family nickname—BABY. I click a photo and start to cry all over again. I cannot imagine being loved so much that my nickname was forever set in stone.

When this house was finished, it encompassed all Mamaji had wanted in life—home, family, stability, and roots. Our grandparents and aunts and uncles lived close by and her dream house became the hub of our family. My longing to know this time and to know her is so great. There is an empty cave in my soul when I think about Mamaji in Chandigarh.

Mamaji

PART
ONE

CHAPTER
ONE

I REMEMBER THE night Mamaji died. I've been told that I couldn't possibly remember, but for me the last time I saw her *was* the day she died. I was only three, but I distinctly remember the clear, red flashing light that flooded the sitting room. My sister Hannah and I were playing with toy cars near the staircase. We pushed them up and down the green carpeting that had a pattern cut into it. I saw the bottom of a stretcher first as it moved above me and then Mamaji's hand reached out. Her index finger had a Band-Aid wound around it and I wish so badly that I had taken her hand. It was her final goodbye to me, and I didn't know it. When I play that scene over in my head, I see her hand and then I reach up and grab it. Then I hug her and she kisses me and we have a mother–daughter moment—one that I could carry with me for the rest of my life. But that didn't happen. Instead, I have a faint, brief memory that she looked pale and worn out. I guess the cancer had fully taken hold, but I was busy playing. Somewhere over my head I heard, "Poor girls, they don't even know what's happening."

When you lose something, there is always the hope that perhaps that lost item will show up again. But Mamaji wasn't lost; she died. She was gone for good. The older I got, the more I missed her. I had more time on my hands to imagine the increasing list of "what if's."

As a three-year-old, I was innocent and protected. The pain that was to come was muffled in the trappings of playing and enjoying all the extra attention that Mamaji's death produced. Later, as a young adult, there were many months when I didn't even think about her. But when I became a mother, Mamaji or the absence of Mamaji, was ever present. Something would happen that I wanted to share with her, but then, WHAM! I remembered—*Oh yes! I have no mother. I have no mother to call, no mother to invite, no mother to give me a wise counsel or a reprimand, no mother to rejoice or cry with and, most of all, no mother to grow old with.*

I'm just starting to understand how important it is to grow old with your mother. Because, not only would Mamaji have been uniquely interested in me and my life, but also as she grew older, I would have had a chance to be with her and see my future self. Watching Mamaji age; her hair grow whiter, her face line and crease with the years of joy and sorrow, the skin on her hands grow translucent and paper thin—all this would have helped me know what to look for, what to expect. The idea of aging gracefully, Mamaji could have taught me that.

And I could have taken care of Mamaji. She would have taught me her recipes and then I would have reproduced them for her in her older years—less spicy, of course, to protect her aging system, but still her recipes. I could have taken her for a drive, just to get some fresh air; hand-washed her salwars and nightgowns and returned them to her fresh-smelling and sweet. I could have helped manicure her nails, pluck an errant hair around her eyebrow, groom her scalp with neem oil, or perhaps we could have enjoyed a massage or facial. I could have taken her to the doctor and been her most vocal advocate because I speak health-care language and know the routine. I could have assessed her condition, perhaps by auscultating her lungs or putting my hand to her forehead, my brow furrowed with worry, and then bundled her off to the doctor and to the nearby pharmacy for some decongestant. Mamaji could have traveled with us on our sister trips, all five of us enjoying India or Europe together, learning and appreciating a new food or just laughing at a joke. She could have been with me when my boys were born, counseled me through their growing years and then, much later, she could have enjoyed their baraat and danced at their weddings. Or I could have simply sat next to her, close and sheltered in her company, saying nothing, but just being near her—reassured by the regular patterns of her breath, her sighs, perhaps a small cough now and then. Maybe we could have gone through the old family photos, and I would finally learn who the heck were those people at her wedding, because Papaji has no clue, and everyone else who might have known is already dead.

It's been said that it's unnatural for parents to bury their children and it's true. But it's just as unnatural for seven young children to have to bury their mother. It's shattering. Yet none of us children were at Mamaji's burial. She was not buried in Minnesota or in India but in Fairlawn, New Jersey. She shared a headstone with my paternal grandmother, my Dadhi, who had died years earlier. Both their graves are marked with a double headstone that bears the scripture, "Blessed are they that die in the Lord." Only Papaji attended the burial, and maybe a few uncles living in New Jersey as well. About a half decade later, my relatives who lived in New Jersey moved out of the state. I saw the gravesite for the first time at age 26, after I had married. It's a good thing that none of us really placed too much importance on visiting a

MAMAJI

grave, or maybe *because* Mamaji was buried so far away we had learned to put it out of our minds. In any case, the fact that her grave was inaccessible was convenient and helpful in aiding her successor to put her name, her memory, and the fact that she ever existed, out of our lives. And out of Papaji's life.

When I finally realized how little I knew of Mamaji, I began researching to find out who she had been. Her friends, whom she met during the two years she lived in Minnesota, loved her so much that even more than 50 years after her death, they still check on me and my siblings, sending cards and letters, attending weddings and celebrating our milestones with us. From hearing them speak of her, I knew she must have been a wonderful friend. I gleaned bits of information here and there from Papaji and my siblings. I learned she was a wonderful mother—not perfect of course, but still a loving, concerned, and caring mother.

The death of Mamaji was, by current standards and medical advances, a mistake. If it happened today, there would have been a million-dollar lawsuit filed and my family would have won. While Mamaji was living in Hopkins, Minnesota, she contracted a rare form of cancer called a hydatidiform mole. This "mole," which was really just a nice euphemism for a tumor, began as a fetus within her womb, which morphed and grew into cancer.

The way I see it, is that once upon a time I had a sibling that was so selfish that it was not satisfied to join me and the rest of my siblings in the living world. For this greedy, tiny being, it was not enough to drink up my mother's life blood and juices. No, there came a moment that it rose up, changed form and grew into an invasive, life-sapping, killing, tumor. It did not want to share Mamaji with me or any of us. It gave up whatever chance it had at life and took Mamaji with it as well.

A hydatidiform mole is quite rare. In the 1960s it occurred in about only 1 in 100,000 pregnancies. The ob-gyn in charge did not have the benefit of modern ultrasounds and the tumor began to spread quickly. A hysterectomy would have removed the evil baby-tumor and completely cured Mamaji. But without the benefit of modern technology and knowledge, the doctor was not able to diagnose her early enough, nor was he able to properly advise my parents of the danger of saving the uterus and ovaries. Mamaji did not realize the extent of her illness until it was much too late. As the cancer spread throughout her body she was ever hopeful, anticipating a full recovery and making plans for her future. She underwent chemotherapy and radiation. She rapidly lost weight and large chunks of her hair. While the medical team provided her with palliative treatments, the cancer moved swiftly through her system, spreading to her brain and killing her. Six months after writing an optimistic letter to her closest friend, Gloria, she was gone. She would never again feel the coolness of Mussoorie mountain air as she slept, marvel at the rhythms of a new song, or laugh while running through the monsoon rains. Worst of all, I would never be a part of her life.

There is a photo that was taken of our family during those last days of Mamaji's life. A photographer arrived to take our picture and captured a memory for me: The Family We Once Were. In the photo, we are sitting outside in the expansive empty land that surrounded our rental home in Hopkins, long before Minnesota ceased to be the Land of 10,000 Lakes and became the Land of 10,000 Big Boxes. The trees behind us are in the peak of their vivid autumnal splendor. We are together but sitting in what seems to be three groups. To the right of the photo, Papaji's unmarried sister Rashida sits ramrod straight in a pink sari and is the only one looking directly into the camera. Next to her are my two oldest siblings, Miriam, 17, and Gideon, 16, who are both grinning broadly—which were most likely fake smiles, given that they were the only children who completely understood the gravity of our situation. Miriam is holding me in her lap. I had just woken from a nap. I was grumpy and no matter what the photographer tried, I refused to cooperate. I am stubbornly looking down into my lap, my dress bunched up around me. In the middle group is my sister Hannah, 4, just a year older than me. She is looking toward Mamaji, and it is hard to tell if she is smiling or ready to cry. My brother Emmanuel, 12, is behind her and he is kneeling with his hands in his pockets, face serious, his eyes intent on Papaji. Next to him is Deborah, 10, who is looking rather confused. She is nearly touching Mamaji, but her shoulders are shrugged as she grasps her knees, hugging herself. The last group is my brother David, 7, with my parents. His hair is mussed and he is sitting contentedly next to Mamaji. My father sits close by, strong and handsome, and impeccably dressed in his Ricky Ricardo black suit and tie, his dark pompadour shining. He is pointing at something in the distance and is smiling a half smile. And there is Mamaji—my beautiful, graceful mother, who could not disguise the ravages of her disease. Despite her careful makeup and lipstick, she is pale and frighteningly thin. Her hair is sparse and her dark eyes have sunken into her face. She is wearing a lovely silk sari and her left collarbone juts through her lilac blouse. Her face is full of pain and sadness.

A month later Mamaji was dead.

On the day Mamaji died, Hannah remembers that she was in her room with Deborah and heard some loud commotion downstairs. Deborah told her, "Wait here, I'll go check." When she returned, her face was filled with tears and she told Hannah, "Mamaji died." Hannah went down and saw Miriam sobbing, Emmanuel sitting on the sofa, his arm around David, both of their heads bowed. But even then she was unsure of what had happened. Just a few weeks earlier, Hannah had been ill with pneumonia in the hospital. Mamaji was in the hospital at the same time and, even though she was weak and in great pain, she went to the pediatric ward and held Hannah until she stopped crying and could fall asleep.

David knew Mamaji was sick but didn't understand the severity of her illness. Shortly before her death, he sat down at the kitchen table, waiting for his dinner. Mamaji put his dinner in front of him. He was disappointed because, instead of her usually tasty Indian food, she had made an American dish, something with noodles. David protested and pushed the plate away.

"I don't want this! I want Indian food, some *murgi tharkari*!"

Mamaji didn't say anything.

After she left the kitchen, Emmanuel scolded David, "Don't you know she's sick? She got out of bed to make food for you and all you can do is complain."

David didn't understand what was happening. It was much later, when he was older that he realized what he had done and the guilt washed over him. Deborah remembers playing with Emmanuel outside her room the day Mamaji was taken to the hospital and hearing her shout for them to be quiet because she had agonizing headaches and seizures as the cancer spread to her brain. Emmanuel recalls being upstairs in bed when he was woken in the early morning hours by the sound of crying. He rushed downstairs and saw one of Mamaji's dearest friends, Mrs. Zipf, crying. She said, "You poor kids." No one told him Mamaji was dead; he just knew. The last time he had seen her, she said to him, "Emmanuel be a good boy." My oldest brother, Gideon, told her goodbye and Mamaji told him she would see him soon, as she often did when she was not feeling well and going to the hospital.

Only Miriam was old enough to be with Mamaji in the hospital, since the rules did not allow anyone under 17 to visit. Many years later, Miriam told me how in the days before Mamaji's death, she had stayed at her bedside, caring for her the best she could. Mamaji struggled to even urinate and asked Miriam to run water to assist. Mamaji usually did not complain or vocalize discomfort, but her fortitude was no match for the evil cancer and she cried out in pain. The ordered medication had almost no effect. Miriam was frightened and ran out to the nurse's station to beg for a stronger dose. The nurse was curt, "She can't have anything yet. She has to wait." I always remember Mamaji and the agony she bore when I treat patients in pain. I advocate and provide for their absolute comfort and rest. But Miriam was a teenager and didn't know what to do. She hurried back to the room, desperately rubbing Mamaji's temples with Vicks VapoRub. It wasn't until Mrs. Zipf arrived and spoke sternly to the nurses that something was done to ease the pain. Soon the prescribed visiting time was over, and Miriam leaned over to kiss Mamaji goodbye and promised to come back the following day. The next morning, Miriam waited anxiously by the window, a bag packed with a few items, watching for the car. When Mrs. Zipf arrived, she slowly walked to the front door.

"Let's go. Mamaji is waiting!" Miriam said.

But Mrs. Zipf sat down, not sure of how to deliver the next piece of news, "Oh Miriam—your mother died. She's gone to be with the Lord."

It was the last thing Miriam expected to hear, and the news quickly spread throughout the house. Miriam and Gideon conferred in the hallway. What should they do now? How would they tell the other kids? How would they contact Papaji? It seems outrageous to think that a 17 and 16-year-old would be faced with such a grave situation. I cannot imagine a modern-day teenager having the courage to face such a situation as my brother and sister had.

But for me, on that day, everything seemed to be going along just fine. I do not remember that Mamaji had been unusually sick. I heard commotion and crying around me, but I did not understand what had happened. I am uncertain at what age I fully understood that she had died. No one came out and just told me, "Mamaji is dead." How do you explain such a thing to someone of my age?

Papaji was in India at the time of her death. I have been told that this was Mamaji's wish—that his work in India should not be hampered due to her illness. Indeed, she had always been his greatest support. She had written his monthly newsletters, and helped him manage his office from our home in Chandigarh. She had traveled to Chicago so he could complete his PhD, at the same time finishing her master's degree while she was pregnant with Emmanuel. She had agreed to live in Minneapolis for a year or two to further his work as a preacher. She had raised seven children, largely on her own, so he could concentrate on his passion. So, perhaps, it is understandable that she would have made such a request. But what is difficult to understand is that Papaji actually upheld her wish. She had been ill for a long time and he had gone on many trips. During this trip, he heard of her death through a telegram and rushed back to Minneapolis but it was too late. Mamaji died without her husband or children beside her.

In the days that followed her death, all sorts of wonderful things happened to David, Hannah, and me. Another one of Mamaji's best friends, Aunt Helen (we called her "aunt" out of respect), arrived to take us out. She wore a gold and white brocade dress, shiny patent leather shoes with square heels and told us she was taking us to our first movie. We arrived at the Mann Southtown Theatre. The state of the art theater featured windows of colored glass on the outside of the building. I had never seen a movie before. Watching Julie Andrews as Maria Von Trapp, traipsing through the Alps, singing along with the seven motherless Von Trapp children in *The Sound of Music* thrilled and excited the three of us. We laughed and thoroughly enjoyed the antics of the children as they tried to sabotage the Baroness' plan to capture the Captain. But Aunt Helen's eyes remained red before and after the movie. The irony of the story was lost on us—as it turned out, *The Sound of Music* was to play a role in the outcome of my life.

A few days later, I was dressed in a scratchy frock and left in the church nursery with Hannah. Everyone else was gathered in the sanctuary and we could hear talking and singing going on inside. It was the day of Mamaji's funeral, but for me it was just another day in which I could play unsupervised without rules or any grownups telling me to be quiet. It was great fun. David came in during the service and reported that the church was full of people. Later on, after the church was empty, he said he saw Papaji kneeling and crying next to Mamaji's coffin. I don't recall if Papaji was sad or lonely, because he was basically absent during this time as he continued to travel the way he always had. Many years later, he told us that he had been so wracked with grief that after the burial he walked for hours and hours, mourning his first love and wondering how he was going to raise the seven children that were now left solely in his care.

Hopkins, Minnesota October, 1965
The Family We Once Were (Left to right Papaji, David, Mamaji, Deborah,
Emmanuel, Hannah, Miriam, Elisheba, Gideon and Rashida Chachi)

Minneapolis, November, 1965
At Mamaji's funeral (clockwise from the top—Papaji, Miriam, Emmanuel, Han-
nah, Elisheba, David, Deborah and Gideon)

CHAPTER
TWO

U SUALLY WHEN CHILDREN ask about the history of their parents' initial meeting, their life as a young couple, their first home, and the family history, there are two perspectives that are offered. Over the years, I have been able to glean a bit more from friends and family but, I have never known Mamaji's version.

In the summer of 2013, I was given a miraculous gift. Mamaji's close friend, Gloria, had saved a packet of letters Mamaji had written to her from the year 1961 up until the time of her death. Through these 21 letters, I was finally able to hear a first-hand account from Mamaji herself. I had never seen her handwriting before. I was captivated by her style, her choice of words, her little Mamaji-isms. Instead of commas she preferred to use ellipses. Her sentences were scattered with arrows, plus signs, and dashes. She wrote with great conviction and honesty. And she wrote about me. For the first time in my life, I heard what Mamaji thought of me when she and I first met each other. She wrote to Gloria, *You know mother was here for my confinement. Our baby came at 1 AM (night) 24TH + Dr. left the same evening. So he saw her just a few* *hours old. She is very sweet + I think will be the prettiest of all the girls. She resembles all the boys in some way or the other.* I had not known the time of my birth until I read this letter. I was relieved that I had been a, "sweet baby" and that Mamaji and I had a happy beginning. I wanted more, but that was the only sentence in her letters that pertained to just me. Her letters created as many questions for me as they answered.

On the other hand, I had heard Papaji's perspective of our family history many times. He met Mamaji in 1941 at the Christian Movement Camp; according to him, it was love at first sight. Papaji was a tall, handsome student at Murray College at the University of Punjab. Mamaji had a high forehead, wide smile, large eyes and was studying at Kinnaird College for Women in Lahore. They began to discuss their faith and politics and Mamaji was so impressed with Papaji's responses that the two began to correspond. The friendship quickly deepened into love and a courtship that lasted five years. They wrote letters using their pet names for each other, "Pyari" and "Pyara" which means "beloved." I have always liked this story because I believe that there can be an instant connection between two people. And it showed a softer side of Papaji—one I rarely saw; even he was capable of passion, love, and desire. During this time in India, parents selected their child's spouse and it was unusual for two people to make an open declaration of love. But my parents promised their love to each other, and it was to be the first marriage in their generation for both families. Papaji was the oldest of ten children and Mamaji was the oldest of five. When my paternal grandfather, my Dadha, first met Mamaji, he was against the marriage because he mistakenly thought Mamaji was a foreigner as she was very light-skinned. Eventually, my parents married in Hoshiarpur, Punjab, on April 12, 1947. Papaji was always foggy about this date, and it was Mamaji's letters that clarified it. There is just one blurry family photograph of the event. Papaji is wearing a light-colored suit and tie. He is looking seriously into the camera but there is love and desire in his eyes. Mamaji is wearing a white sari with a silk chunni over her head. She is carrying a large bouquet of flowers. Her eyes are filled with hope, innocence, and adoration. They are surrounded by family and friends, dressed in their finest. My Vera Masi is in the front as the flower girl.

After the wedding, Papaji began teaching at Forman Christian College in Lahore, Punjab, which at the time was a part of undivided India. Four months later, on August 15, 1947, my parents experienced the horror of the Indian–Pakistan Partition. This war had a profound impact on my parents. It was a moment in time in which they were brought even closer together because they faced the daily prospect of death. Indeed, when they went to sleep each night, instead of wishing each other, "good night," they said, "goodbye" for fear that they might be killed in their sleep.

During the violence of the Partition, my parents lived near the borders and saw brutality unlike anything they had ever seen. In a matter of hours, many of their friends were forced to leave the lands of their ancestors because of their religious beliefs. Muslims, who lived in India, took what they could carry and crossed into Pakistan, and Hindus living in what had become Pakistan, fled into India. Some survived the exchange; many did not. Houses were looted and property stolen. Women and girls were raped and murdered. Dead bodies were strewn everywhere as the borders were crossed. Papaji recalled that the blood from the killings darkened the dusty roads with an intense, vivid shade of maroon. Fires raged and smoke filled the air. He heard stories of trains arriving from Pakistan with disembodied torsos, chopped off breasts, lone arms and legs, or severed heads of Hindus their faces twisted in horror and blood. In the same way trains filled with the massacred bodies of Muslims left India and arrived in the newly born Pakistan. He remembered screams of agony and cries for help that filled the air. The final death toll from the Partition was never clear. Some estimated it to be as high as one million deaths in those few weeks. At least ten million people became refugees.

Papaji's most vivid memory of this terrible time is of his encounter with a pretty, little girl about nine or ten years old. She was sitting alone in an abandoned village, surrounded by burning buildings, dead bodies, and bloodied streets. Papaji approached her. She had a small blue bowl in her hands and rain water dripped from the roof into the bowl. She was strangely still.

As Papaji got closer, he asked her, "What is it? Why are you just sitting here?"

The little girl looked up at him with huge tearful eyes and said, "I don't know, Uncle. I have been sitting here for two days and I am so thirsty. I want to drink but I just can't seem to take a drink."

Then Papaji looked at the girl closely. A long thin stick was protruding from her stomach. It entered from her abdomen and exited from her back. He shouted for assistance but no one was close enough to hear. As he bent over to help her, she looked up at him, closed her eyes and died. Her little bowl of water clattered to the floor, splashing water on his legs and feet.

Eventually, the massacre ended and my parents, like many others, looked hopefully to the future. They rented a house in Chandigarh, and my eldest sister Miriam was born in 1948, and my brother Gideon followed a year later. Papaji always told us of Gideon's birth with great drama. Gideon was born premature and was blue with cold. The doctor thought he was dead and, "threw him out" as Papaji described. An astute nurse retrieved my brother, wrapped him warmly and gave him to Mamaji.

Later that year, Papaji decided the family would travel to America so he could obtain his PhD, and he bought four tickets on the Queen Elizabeth. In Chicago, both Papaji and Mamaji became students at the same university. It was a bit more difficult for Mamaji to study as she was looking after Miriam and Gideon and was expecting my brother Emmanuel, but she still managed to earn her master's with honors from Northwestern University in 1952. The family story is that Emmanuel acquired his intelligence because he received the benefit of her education while in her womb. Two weeks after returning to Chandigarh, Emmanuel was born. Two years later, Deborah rounded our family out. For a brief time, we moved to the quiet and beautiful hill station of Mussoorie where David was born in 1958. Both Mamaji and Papaji wanted more children and returned to Chandigarh to begin the construction of what would be Mamaji's dream home. We moved into the house in 1959. Two years later, Hannah was born and I arrived a year after.

Shortly after my birth, Papaji was asked to spend some time in America to further his work as an itinerant preacher. Mamaji was reluctant to leave her friends, family, and home, but she wanted to encourage and support Papaji. She was insistent that they only remain in Minnesota for two years, as she did not want to raise her children in America, far from all she knew and loved. On the day she left India, she gave the keys of her beloved home to her mother, our Nani, who promised to take care of it until we came back. The family gathered for a tearful goodbye at the train station.

On Thanksgiving weekend of 1963, our family arrived in Minneapolis, Minnesota. The weather had already turned quite cold and we all shivered in our inadequate sweaters, thin dresses, and suits. Papaji rented a small house in Hopkins. The house was dilapidated, leaky, and isolated. It was a far cry from the warm, comfortable home in Chandigarh, but Mamaji made the best of the situation as she always had. She made new friends—Glenice Zipf, Helen Wilson and others—but she was still lonely. In her letter she wrote: *Gloria I get very lonely here and miss home very much. I don't feel at home here at all. If my eyes don't cry my heart cries + yearns to be back...I have got some of the Urdu records here that we used to play in Chandigarh. They remind me of you so often + of the time we were together in Chandigarh and the tears start flowing down.*

Soon after our move to America, Mamaji became ill; she was diagnosed with cancer and within a year she was dead. During her illness, Mamaji asked for Nani to come and be with her during her last days, but my maternal uncle, Vidyasagar Mamu, refused to let his mother travel such a long distance. Papaji and Vidyasagar Mamu argued and never spoke again. Mamaji died without her mother or siblings nearby. After Mamaji was buried, Papaji told his friend, "I am half dead; the springs of love have dried up."

In India, Nani, Venetia and Vera Masi were heartbroken. They worried and wondered what would happen to all of us. Venetia Masi had dreamt of her sister just days before her death. In her dream she spoke to Mamaji who was dressed in a woolen shawl and sari, and was carrying a bag. They were both standing at the train station waiting for a train to appear.

Venetia Masi asked, "Where are you going, elder sister—Bua?"

Mamaji did not answer her and continued to look down the railroad tracks, anticipating the arrival of the train.

Venetia Masi persisted and asked, "But Bua, who will take care of the children?"

Mamaji turned and looked squarely into Venetia Masi's eyes and responded, "The children will be fine."

Wedding Day April 12, 1947
Hoshiarpur, India
(Clockwise from front-Dadhi in sari, Papaji, Mamaji, Feroza Chachi,
Vera Masi with arms crossed)

CHAPTER
THREE

THE HOME THAT Mamaji made for us in India was, from my older siblings' accounts, a paradise. For me it was only a fantasy. I heard them talk about the olden days; trips to Delhi for Christmas shopping, visits from relatives, helping Mamaji make sticky, marigold-colored jalebi in the kitchen, packing trunks with snacks or, "tucks" for boarding school and hundreds of other stories that seemed too good to be true. Sometimes I try very hard to imagine what a home like that must have felt like.

I can envision Mamaji wearing just one sari. It's the only one I know belonged to her, a pink leaf, block-printed silk she wore while lulling me to sleep. In my fantasy, I pretend that I know what Mamaji's cooking tastes like. I pretend I can see her opening the front door to welcome my Nani. I pretend that she is smiling and shooing me outside to play in our front yard. I pretend she is combing my hair and twisting it into braids. I hate that I cannot be granted even a small part of this dream. When I hear my older siblings recall the love, warmth, and smells of this home, I long to remember us in this place.

Chandigarh, India, is the capital of the state of Punjab. The town had been planned by the French architect, Le Corbusier, and it is a beautiful city with many gardens and trees. Mamaji had carefully planned her dream home, choosing stone flooring, wood trims, mantles and top-of-the-line bathroom finishes. Miriam, Gideon, Emmanuel, and Deborah remember the care Mamaji took in each selection she made. When it came time to build the stone wall and the floor of the veranda, she and my siblings spent hours rooting through piles of stones, casting aside the rough or misshapen ones. It was a large, double-story house, with open, airy verandas and housing for the extra help Mamaji needed.

When we left Chandigarh, Mamaji made it clear that she would be back. When she gave the keys to Nani, she left the house with all our family keepsakes inside—photos, knickknacks, books and furniture. When we arrived in Minneapolis, nothing could have prepared us for the cold November weather and I suspect nothing could have prepared Mamaji for the dreadful little house that greeted her. It was a small, white two-story farm house. The floors creaked, the basement was constantly flooded, and the house was generally falling apart. The boys used a toilet in the basement that sat in a corner surrounded by water, and they strategically placed tiles so they could use the toilet without sloshing through the foul water. It was a far cry from the palatial home we had left behind. While the land surrounding the house was beautiful, it was isolated and lonely. The only people nearby were an old couple that owned the house. They didn't particularly care for the loud group of wild banshees that had just moved in. Poor Mamaji—her new life in America was far removed from the home she had worked so hard to create. It must have been a terrible shock to her, even though she was somewhat accustomed to American culture.

I have two flash memories of Mamaji. I can see them in my

mind, and I have to believe that they happened. Our short time together was in a new, cold place, which was as foreign to her as it was to me. I feel cheated that I have no memories of her where she was at her happiest—in India. In 1965, milk was still delivered to the doorstep and the mailman would knock on the back door and hand the mail to Mamaji. On one of his deliveries, the mailman gave her a packet of letters as usual. It was windy and terribly cold outside and his face was bright red, eyelashes and nose hairs crusted over with ice. Some of his fingers poked out from his gloves and looked dry and chapped. The zipper on his jacket was frozen over with ice and he was unable to pull it all the way up. Mamaji put the mail on the table and beckoned him to come inside. The mailman protested, perhaps he didn't want to dirty her kitchen floor. But she insisted, and when he sat down in our warm kitchen, she brought him a steaming cup of chai, hot chapati and sabzi—a spicy, vegetable mixture. He looked surprised, but quickly took off his coat and gloves and began eating and drinking. I don't remember what they talked about, but I do remember the tone of gratefulness in his voice and the genuine care and concern Mamaji showed.

Mamaji had two great worries about me as a two-year old. One was that I was yet to be potty-trained. She despaired because in India potty-training is usually achieved by the time a child completes the first year. Another worry was that I had been born with a birthmark on my face. It was a white patch that covered the eyelid and skin under my left eyebrow. I wish that patch had never faded and she was still here to rub oil on it. She used to massage this area over and over, hoping to erase the whiteness of the patch. She walked around the house, humming and smoothing my eye, hoping I would soon fall asleep. I felt the warmth of her skin and softness of her sand-colored silk sari, block-printed with many rose-colored leaves. I laid my head on her shoulder and

Hannah followed behind, mirroring Mamaji by holding her doll on her shoulder, patting its back and humming. I felt safe, warm, and comfortable. I was with the person who loved me the most in the world.

✳✳✳

When she knew her death was inevitable, Mamaji made three requests to Papaji. The first was that she did not want to be buried in America. She asked Papaji to take her body back to India, where she could be buried in her home, next to her relatives and family. She loved India, and while she died in a cold, foreign country, she did not want to be buried there. I imagine she must have remembered the frigid Midwestern winters and longed for the warm breezes of her beloved home.

Her second request to Papaji was, "Don't ever sell the Chandigarh house." She knew it was the only childhood home we would have. When she died, she wanted us to return not only to the physical home she had made for us, but to the emotional stability that home would provide for us. In India, the grief the older children felt could have been lessened by our Nani, Masis, cousins, and all the loved ones we had left behind who knew and loved Mamaji so well. In that home, those of us who had been too young to know her would have learned of her love for us. To this day, I marvel that I had absolutely no contact with Mamaji's family from the time of her death until I got married. All I knew was that she was born, she married, she gave birth to her children, and she died. I knew no one who had known her before she had met my father.

Since Mamaji's death, I struggled to find a place to call home. In December, while everyone else is busily traveling, I want to say, "I'm going home for Christmas, too." But there is no home to go to. Of course, my siblings gather together for Thanksgiving,

Easter, a wedding or some other family event. And, we all have our own homes that we have made with our children. But it's not the same as going to your childhood home. Mamaji is not there to call us back. None of us has ever known that feeling, and she knew we would need the house in Chandigarh.

Mamaji's last request was one that, as an adult, I see the difficulty in fulfilling. She did not want Papaji to marry and told him to stay single in order to keep the family together. She knew what would happen if Papaji remarried. Even with seven children, they had both longed for another—indeed, it was this desire that had taken her life. She knew Papaji would have another child if he remarried. And she knew how that child would change my life. The truth is that the pull of mother-love is so great that the child who is The Other can never compete with the child from the mother's body. She did not want any of her children to be The Other. In a struggle between the two, a woman will show mother-love to the child of her womb and a watered-down sort of tolerance for The Other. Oh, it will be subtle, it will be discreet, it might even be imperceptible to her husband, but it will be there. And Mamaji was right. It was the one decision that changed my life forever and destroyed whatever semblance of a home I had. I have always been The Other. At the moment my father remarried, I lost all that was dear to me—the little I had left of Mamaji, a relationship with Papaji, and my hope for a real home.

I wonder about these last three requests Mamaji made. She could have written a will or even asked her older children to promise to carry out more selfish requests. She could have asked for a memorial in her honor or she could have given us some of her worldly belongings. But what she wanted for all of us was something only a mother could give—a home. In light of how things turned out, I feel an overwhelming sense of loss and devastation as I realize how well she knew me, and how each one of her requests took my well-being into account. She was able to con-sider not only what my needs were as a small child but she knew what they would be as a grown woman.

Mamaji's dream home in Chandigarh, India, 1959

CHAPTER
FOUR

M AMAJI WAS GONE. And without her we had all lost our
compass. There was no more discussion about moving
back to India. We were to be permanent strangers in the new
land. The school year commenced, meals were prepared and
eaten, and the usual noise and bedlam of a house filled with children continued. Miriam became Papaji's right hand and she was
put in charge of running the entire household. For a college freshman this was a huge task, but she managed it the best she could.
Papaji's unmarried sister, Rashida Chachi, who had arrived when
Mamaji became ill, moved in permanently to help. We all limped
along, much like a dog does with an injured hind leg, each of us
coping with our pain and finding our own way to manage our
great loss.

Miriam found solace by sitting alone in Mamaji's closet and
burying her face in her familiar saris, allowing the smell of Mamaji
to remind her of happier times. Gideon graduated from high
school and prepared to start his life over by moving to his own
apartment and removing himself from the reminders of his former life. Emmanuel took long walks in the woods surrounding

our house, sometimes twenty miles at a time, thinking and missing Mamaji. Deborah did her best to cope by helping take care of the younger kids and blocking out the painful loss the best she could. I don't remember much from the year or so which we lived without a mother. There were few tears or even sadness. The older ones protected me from much of what was going on. But there was a game that David, Hannah, and I played, and it amused us. It was called *Mamaji Died*. The object of the game was to exhibit control over our emotions. We sat cross-legged in a small circle and then David said, "Okay, ready?" Hannah and I nodded and then with great aplomb he took a deep breath and said, "And...(*pause*) Mamaji Died!" Whichever one of us could manage the next few minutes without crying, won the game. To control my tears, I held my breath, bit the inside of my lip, swallowed hard, and tried not to blink. The more we played it, the better we all became at it. Eventually, our control was so great that the game would end in helpless laughter. We had great fun playing this macabre, taboo game. It made the serious situation palatable.

That Christmas was our first one without Mamaji. The Christmas party organizers at Papaji's office asked us to entertain them at the company's annual Christmas party. They must have felt sorry for us, or maybe it was because there were so many of us, but in any case, just like the children in *The Sound of Music*, we were slated to sing for a large gala event. Under Miriam and Rashida Chachi's directions, we all rehearsed a Punjabi song. In addition, as the youngest, I was to have a starring role. Besides singing along with the Von Trapp à la Haqq Family Singers, I was to have the added pleasure of reciting Psalm 121 in front of the entire audience. I was told of the great honor that was bestowed upon me, and without really understanding what was expected, I began memorizing under the tutelage of Miriam. The psalm was filled with vivid images, and Miriam came up with the idea that not only should I recite from memory, but I should also add in actions to emphasize the descriptions.

On the night of the party, I put on my best frock. The skirt was full and pastel pink with a black velvet bodice. I wore shiny, black Mary Janes and white, lace-trimmed ankle socks. We reached the venue, and our song, *Khushi Khushi Manao* created quite a stir. It was rather different from the usual Anglo Christmas carols, with its infective bhangra beat and mysterious Urdu words accompanied by our rhythmic clapping. The song was about being joyful and happy because of God's love. I imagine the pink-skinned Midwesterners who boisterously clapped along must have been puzzled about who and what we were. After dinner it was my turn. I took my place at the huge podium; the microphone was adjusted and lowered so it was even with my mouth. I began my recitation of Psalm 121 in the King James Version, complete with hand movements.

I WILL LIFT UP MINE EYES UNTO THE HILLS, (*hand to forehead, shield eyes, look to a faraway place*)
FROM WHENCE COMETH MY HELP. (*both hands raised to the sky*)
HE WILL NOT SUFFER THY FOOT TO BE MOVED. (*take one step forward*)

Unfortunately, during our intense rehearsals, Miriam had not accounted for the heavy wooden podium that was in front of me. When I stepped forward, a loud, atomic boom echoed all over the auditorium as my foot struck the podium. The audience exploded in laughter and I blushed miserably. After the laughter died down, Miriam signaled me to continue:

HE THAT KEEPETH THEE WILL NOT SLUMBER.

BEHOLD, HE THAT KEEPETH ISRAEL, SHALL
NEITHER SLUMBER NOR SLEEP. (*close palms together,*
place on right cheek, tilt head to the right, close eyes)
FROM THIS TIME FORTH AND EVEN FOR
EVERMORE. (*hold hands open, wait, then curtsey and*
exit)

The loud applause caught me off guard and I stumbled to our
family table and into Miriam's lap. I hid my face in her soft sari,
embarrassed at my mistake and the attention. She held me and
stroked my back soothingly while telling me what a good job
I had done. Later, as the party broke up, many well-powdered
ladies, smelling wonderfully of flowers and fruit, bent down to
hug me and tell me how marvelous they thought I was. Men in
dark suits pinched my cheeks and clapped my brothers' backs.
They congratulated Papaji on what fantastic, brilliant, beautiful,
and delightful children he had. That evening when we arrived
home, we found a shiny, brown piano in our front room. It had
a huge, crisp red bow on it and was from Papaji's office. The
card read, "To the Haqq Children—Miriam, Gideon, Emmanuel,
Deborah, David, Hannah, and Elisheba. Merry Christmas!" The
magnificence of that gift took my breath away. Eventually, Deborah learned to play it by reading notes and Hannah played it by
ear. The music from that piano carried me through many difficult
times and I have always been so grateful for it.

The winter passed and the cold warmed into spring. Days were
filled with loud discussions, fights, smells of cooking garlic and
onions, screen doors slamming, and playing for hours outside in
the long grass. It was raucously loving and confusing and wonderful. We had only Miriam and Rashida Chachi to manage us,
so we learned all sorts of bad habits—banging on the table with
forks and spoons, shouting when we wanted food, going for days

without washing, and wearing the same underwear for weeks. It was like living in Neverland. I was only four but I learned fast and spent most of the time outside with David and Hannah until it was dark, and then played inside until I fell asleep with a smile on my grubby face.

That same summer, my two oldest brothers decided to rig up David's toy car to Gideon's black VW bug. The toy was an old metal car, the kind with the pedals inside to make it go. The right rear wheel had lost its pin and the only way to keep the wheel from falling off the axel while the car was in motion was to hit it with a hammer. This worked fine for David who drove the car only as fast as he could pedal it. He only needed to bang the wheel back into place once in a while. Gideon and Emmanuel decided to tie the toy car to the back of the VW with a rope to give David, and all of us, a fast ride. This plan was a great idea. We loved the thrilling entertainment, which became all the more daring because the high speed would cause the wheel to nearly fall off its axel. David was the first to try, and he developed a steady rhythm, steering with his left hand, while banging on the wheel with his right. Dust filled the air and we all begged for a turn.

Rashida Chachi came outside to see what all the shouting was about. She watched as Gideon drove David around. He showed off, taking a few extra turns for added excitement. When he came to a stop, she told him to take the rope off because it was much too dangerous. We all pleaded with her, trying to convince her of the relative safety. Finally, Gideon had an idea—why not try the ride herself? Then she could be assured that it was completely safe. After some hesitation, she gingerly squeezed herself into the small car. Gideon took his place behind the wheel. David and Emmanuel, just like any seasoned pit crew, came close and offered racing advice.

"Steer clear of that gutter."

"Keep your feet off the pedals," said Emmanuel.

"Don't forget to bang the wheel with your right hand, otherwise it'll fall off," said David.

At this last piece of advice, Rashida Chachi looked horrified. She tried to dislodge herself from the car but it was too late. Gideon revved the engine and smiled wickedly. As he hit the gas and took off, the tiny car and Rashida Chachi came to life. The car veered treacherously back and forth as she forgot to steer all together and concentrated only on hitting the back wheel with all her might. Ben Hur in all his glory could not have driven his chariot with greater skill. Through the clouds of dust, we saw long lengths of green sari, flapping furiously as Rashida, The Great Charioteer, screamed frantically for Gideon to stop. He pretended not to hear and drove around and around the Circus Maximus to the immense delight of us all. We cheered, clapped, and laughed until our sides ached. Finally, Gideon slowed the VW and stopped. Our champion, Rashida Chachi, pulled herself from the car and threw the hammer on the ground. Usually always neat, she was disheveled. Her sari was soiled and mussed, her neat bun was undone, and her hair was a tangled heap. We all gathered around her, congratulating her on her amazing driving skill, but she was angry. After a few choice words to Gideon and the boys, she stormed back into the house. From then on, she stayed inside no matter how much noise we made.

Papaji began dating a few American women. Mrs. Bater was one of them and, like the other women he dated, she brought over casseroles or hot dishes, hoping to impress us and win our approval. The elevated decibels of noise and confusion in our house must have scared the women off. Maybe the semi-mock switchblade fights my brothers orchestrated didn't help either. Eventually, news of a house full of wild Indian kids without a mother and a father who traveled frequently became a concern to the State of Minnesota Child and Family Services. I am not sure how they found out, but they were convinced that David, Hannah, and I would be better off living in another family with a father *and* mother. Papaji was alarmed at these threats and, as an immigrant, he did not understand his rights as a birth father. Miriam volunteered to give up her dreams of further education and even marriage to take care of all of us. She was horrified at the idea of being separated.

I cannot imagine what kind of social worker made such a terrible threat, but I am eternally grateful that I was not separated from my older siblings. I had already lost my mother and, to this day, I cannot imagine how losing any more of my family was considered a fitting solution. Papaji sought advice from friends who advised him to marry. He asked the three older children, "What kind of mother do you want? An American mother or an Indian one?" They stated their preference for an Indian mother. I had no recollection of this conversation but I was told that I would soon have a new mother. "Aren't you lucky little girls," the nice church ladies at Bloomington Baptist Church said to Hannah and me, as they bent down on their creaky knees. Getting a new mother was exciting—another big event, much like Mamaji's death and funeral had been. I couldn't wait to meet my mother. I had already almost forgotten what Mamaji looked like. To me this seemed normal. *Doesn't everyone get a new mother, now and then?*

Papaji was a man who needed to be married; he needed companionship. The idea of being a single father was an anomaly. He had been raised in a family where women were a necessity for the proper functioning of the home. Papaji's father had married his second wife at the age of 76, and when she died he was looking to marry again. Only a heart attack and then his death at age 92 prevented him from doing so. I was not told anything about Papaji's remarriage. It happened, despite us, in spite of us, and because of us. In all fairness, I think Papaji must have had us in mind when he married again. He certainly didn't want to separate us, as it had been suggested or threatened. He couldn't take care of all of us alone. But I like to believe that even though he married again, he still missed Mamaji, no—I desperately *need* to believe that he missed her. But his actions made me wonder.

Soon after Papaj and Mamaji met
Lahore, Undivided India, circa 1943

Mamaji saying goodbye at the train station
Chandigarh, India, November 1963
(Clockwise from the left-Mamaji, Feroza Chachi, Nani
and Vera Masi's back)

E ARLY WINTER MORNINGS in Minnesota are not for the frail. Winter often begins well before Halloween. One frigid December morning in 1966, Miriam gently shook me awake. With my hair frowsy and the sleep still in my eyes, I was told to dress quickly. For some reason the entire household was up and about, getting ready in the chilly air. After a dark ride in our light blue Pontiac Catalina station wagon we arrived at the Minneapolis-St. Paul Airport and went inside to wait at the gate. I dozed in Miriam's lap for what seemed like a long time. Suddenly, Miriam shook me awake, "Look, there she is!" I stood up and craned my neck. *Who am I looking for? Who is it?* There, walking through the gate alongside Papaji was a woman. She was wearing a blue and brown tweed coat with a round collar and oversized buttons over a sari. She had bright red lipstick and wore her hair smoothly back in a low bun. Oh, but her shoes! Her shoes were from my dreams. She wore the same high-heeled pumps that Barbie wore! For a long time I had wished for a Barbie. The doll's red lips and shoes fascinated me. And now, here was Barbie in the flesh. I was the luckiest girl in the world. Who else could say their new mother looked like Barbie? Immediately, I fell in love. Papaji hugged us all and then held me as my Barbie-doll mother smiled at me. I was in ecstasy. I don't know what she said but she sounded different when she spoke. There was something unusual about the way she said some words. But it didn't matter, she was my new mother and she was coming home with me. We all walked to the car together and she reached down and took my hand in hers. I had a feeling of contentment and peace and I didn't even notice the wintery cold.

✳✳✳

A few months prior to the arrival of my new mother, Papaji had travelled to India to meet her. Papaji's cousin Zorah, remembered this lady surgeon because she had once treated Zorah's husband for a growth on his neck. Zorah thought the doctor would be a good match and told Papaji. Much later, Zorah remarked that she always regretted her decision to make the introduction and, for her own reasons, referred to the surgeon as, "a cold-blooded woman."

On the couple's first meeting, Papaji brought his brother Ashraf or Babu as he was called, along with him. They asked the lady doctor to get them some tea so they could see how she walked. After some keen observation, Babu said, "She doesn't seem to be lame at least!" Papaji told me many years later that he was praying hard that she would at least, "not be too ugly." As it turned out, his new fiancée was a handsome woman. When Papaji asked her, "Well, when should we have the wedding?" She responded by saying, "You haven't even asked me to marry you!"—as if there was any doubt that she would say yes to a dashing Indian Ricky Ricardo. So Papaji took her to Rampur, a picturesque mountain village and the hometown of Sundar Singh, a famous man that he admired and there, he formally proposed.

Before Papaji traveled to my new mother's hometown to

remarry, he made a stop in Chandigarh and gathered the keys of his and Mamaji's home from my still-grieving Nani. He did not tell Nani or any of Mamaji's relatives of his plans to remarry. Later, when Nani learned of his marriage, she along with the rest of the family felt disheartened. In fact, Mamaji's family and Papaji did not speak again. This ended not only their relationship with Papaji but any connection my siblings and I could have with them.

In less than a year, I lost Mamaji and contact with her entire family. I was not to see or hear from any of Mamaji's family again until after I married. Papaji secured my once-upon-a-time family home in Chandigarh and then traveled to Jalandhar in the same state of Punjab to be married. The wedding took place in the family church. At the wedding, my new mother walked down the aisle wearing a simple white silk sari, veil, and long white gloves. She carried a huge bouquet with a long cascade of greenery and flowers. She said goodbye to her family, friends, and work colleagues as she left them for a new life in America as a wife and the mother of seven children.

What stands out the most about the marriage is the separateness of it all. None of us were present, none of us met my father's new wife or even spoke to her before they married. He saw her, he liked her, he wanted her, and he married her. Papaji went to India and like magic, one day, he returned with a factory-fresh, brand-new mother. Mamaji died on November 15, 1965. Papaji was remarried on November 21, 1966. In a little over a year, Mamaji's replacement had arrived.

In the weeks that followed, I learned to call my new Barbie-doll mother "Mama." The older children had a private conference and decided that it would be the right thing to say, "Mama" instead of "Aunty." When I think of this now, I know this was a crucial error. Because we gave Papaji's new wife respect with this term, instead of allowing her to *earn* it, she began to take liberties she did not deserve. If we had only called her Aunty, there is a good chance she would have always understood her position as one of a caretaker, rather than the honored position of mother.

There was another change in the terms we used. Instead of the respectful term of Mamaji, we now referred to my dead mother as only, "Purani Mama." We still spoke only Hindi in our home, and *purani* meant "former" or "previous." For some reason, I instinctively knew not to use the term "Mamaji" for my new mother. The term of respect was something I could not muster. In our conversations at home, we seldom spoke about Mamaji. Even at that young age, I knew that subject of Mamaji was closed and not to be discussed in the open. If there was some reason why we had to speak of the dead, we knew to refer to Mamaji as Purani Mama. At the time it wasn't objectionable to refer to Mamaji this way, but as I grew older, it first annoyed me and, then later, made me furious. Eventually, I stopped using the term Purani Mama.

But I didn't really begrudge using the term Mama for my new mother—my childish admiration of her makeup and shoes changed into a more grown-up admiration of her accomplishments. I was in awe of the fact that she had fought the odds and being a strong, capable, intelligent woman competing with a world of mostly racist, white men in a foreign land, she had come out at the top of her career. She was a surgeon during a time when women surgeons were almost unheard of. She had not cared that she was single even when it was considered terribly improper that she remain unmarried. If she had not been introduced to me as my mother and I had met her just by chance, I would have wanted her as a friend. And so, the transition to my new mother appeared to be a seamless one. I, along with everyone else, even Miriam, began to call my new mother "Mama." We continued to use the term "Papaji," and he did not protest or argue our silently agreed-upon terms for both our mothers. There was no discussion, no tears or arguments. It was a smooth and unbroken transition from one mother to the next. Mama was here to stay.

I thought Mama and I got along just fine. Many times, she held me on her lap and stroked my hair. Sometimes, I fell asleep and urinated in her lap, which was a recent development. Even then she didn't get angry at me. Now and then, I saw her wear the old printed silk with the pink leaves or other saris that Mamaji used to wear. Mama was horrified with our manners and stopped the table banging right away. Miriam and Deborah made sure Hannah and I took regular baths and changed our underwear. Sometimes I heard the boys snicker at some of the terms Mama used, words like, "pally, cheeky, dustbin, zed, plait." Mama often used British phrases and words. It was a time of adjustment for everyone.

When we were invited to dinner by our neighbors, the Wriggerson's, or any other family for that matter, Mama made sure we behaved properly. Mrs. Wriggerson made an extra table for David, Hannah, and me, simply by opening her oven door and having the three of us sit cross-legged around it. She made white and beige food with green Jell-O and was overwhelmed by the sheer amount of food we could consume, "My, your children, certainly have large appetites!" Upon hearing this, Mama's lips tightened and she leaned in and discretely whispered, "T-T-T." This meant "Tummy Touching Table." At this warning, we knew we had eaten enough. Indians view a remark about the amount of food a guest has eaten to be in extremely poor taste. Mama began to feed us dinner at home *before* we went to eat at someone's house. This way, when someone was brave enough to invite our entire family for dinner, they never commented on the Haqq children's large appetites. Thereafter, when eating at Mrs. Wriggerson's house, we ate less, and when she was faced with mounds of leftovers, she cheerfully exclaimed, "Don't worry! Whatever you don't eat, I just make into glue!" Since her husband's name was Elmer, I never figured out if she was teasing us, or if she really meant it—she was a strict waste-not-want-not sort of woman.

As a doctor, Mama was similarly a no-nonsense practitioner. When dealing with our illnesses, she was firm and clinical. She treated our ailments in a practical and detached manner. From something simple like a fever to an itchy rash, she was methodical and terse. She didn't explain what she was doing or how much it would hurt. Once, while removing a splinter that was deeply embedded, the pain from the needle she was using to dislodge the splinter become too intense for me to bear. She became angry when I moved my hand and then she refused to remove the splinter. If we had a fever or a cold, we would spend the day in bed with a glass of 7UP next to us. That was always something I enjoyed about being ill—we were allowed to drink soda. She rarely came up to check on us but if Papaji was home, he climbed the stairs every two or three hours, and with a concerned look asked, "Are you okay? Do you need anything?" His special attention was something I looked forward to on sick days. One summer Deborah, David, Hannah, and I all came down with mumps. I wailed and cried because my ears and throat were on fire. Many years later, Mama confessed to Hannah that she had given us a small dose of phenobarbital so we would all fall asleep.

But Mama didn't believe in using pharmaceuticals or visiting the family doctor unless it was absolutely necessary. Until I turned 21, I visited Dr. Wilson only twice—once when I had a rash that would not go away and another time when I had a bladder infection. My siblings and I developed fantastic immune systems and, even to this day, I rarely get ill. When I was about 12, I developed a recurring growth on my left wrist. It wasn't serious or life threatening, just an odd, strange ball on the bend of my wrist. Mama called it a ganglyion cyst or a Bible bump and didn't seem too concerned when I showed it to her. The lump annoyed me because sometimes it was the size of a large pea and other times it grew as big as a shooter marble. Occasionally when I bent my wrist, it caused pain. When I could no longer move my wrist without wincing in pain, Mama took notice. Without preamble or any warning, she grabbed my wrist firmly in one hand and with the other she swung Papaji's huge Bible and wacked the cyst. Surprised, I was unable to react. Was I being punished or was this an accident? But when I looked at my wrist, the lump had flattened. When I was in nursing school I learned about this strange treatment. The cyst was called a Bible bump because one treatment was to whack it with a large book such as a Bible. The nodule grew back about every six or seven months and Mama administered the same no-nonsense treatment. When I was working as a full-time nurse and had my own health insurance, I went to a surgeon and had it removed in an hour-long office procedure. Once it was removed, I never dealt with it again.

Sometimes, Mama's old colleagues, and even some surgical residents who had trained under her, visited our home. They all told us she was a demanding but highly skilled surgeon, an amazing diagnostician, and they all confessed to a great deal of fear when working with her. Amazingly, Mama had been the lady surgeon who had attended to my Dadhi at the time of her initial cancer diagnosis and she had recommended that Dadhi be taken to America for treatment. Once I found a cache of photos in the living room side table drawer. They were professional pre-operative photos of men and women with huge neck goiters. David, Hannah, and I had great fun mimicking the goiters with rolled up towels and small pillows, falling into fits of hysterics, then going back again and again to gawk at the anomalies pictured in the glossy 8' x 10's. Mama heard the commotion and snatched the photos away. We looked for the pictures later but we never saw them again.

✷✷✷

It was 1967 and Papaji and Mama decided that it was time to buy a house. After many rides to various suburbs surrounding Minneapolis, they decided to purchase a home about 15 miles south of the city in Burnsville. It was a small farming town in Dakota County. Just four years earlier, the community had been connected to the city by Interstate 35W. On a cold and snowy morning, we drove for what seemed to be hours and finally ended up in the middle of the flattest land I had ever seen. I got out of the car and looked around. The long, expanse of snow seemed to go on forever. In front of us were a group of four or five model homes next to a small trailer. While inside the biggest one, Papaji walked through each room, closely inspecting the size and shape. Then he told the lady he would buy the house but the builder would need to add on two feet to each room to accommodate our entire family. The lady repeated, "Seven Children? *SEVEN* children? SEVEN CHILDREN?" many times loudly, shaking her head. I felt ashamed at her reaction. *Why was seven such a bad number?*

We moved to Burnsville over the span of a few days. Our house was a big green colonial, much bigger than what we had been living in. It sat on the end of a cul-de-sac, had a large undeveloped park on one side, and a neighbor's house on the other. Papaji loved land and purchased extra so the lot totaled one acre. The new house had hardwood floors but my parents wanted wall-to-wall carpet which had been featured in the model house. To accommodate their budget, they brought in the carpet that had been used in the old rental house. It was a dark, emerald green and had a pebble-like pattern cut into its short pile. There was enough carpet for the living and dining room, the entire upstairs, and both sets of stairs. The carpet was one I was familiar with—I had driven a toy car in its pile the day Mamaji died. It was comforting, and I was glad to have it in the new room I shared with Miriam.

While we were still living in Chandigarh, Mamaji had decided on the buddy system for us. This way each of the three youngest had an older sibling to watch and care over them. While David, Hannah, and I called the four older siblings "The Biggers," Papaji called us younger three the "Three Stooges," after the famous vaudeville comedy act, because for the most part we were inseparable. Each Bigger got one Stooge. In India, Miriam and I had shared a pink bedroom and in the new house, we stayed with our roommates. Deborah got Hannah and since David was such a challenge as the Head Stooge, it was clear that he would need two Biggers to manage him. Rashida Chachi was to have her own room upstairs. The girls were on the second floor and the three boys were downstairs. My room, which I shared with Miriam, had two windows. She purchased two beds plus we added a dresser that had once been a part of the master bedroom set shared by Papaji and Mamaji. Deborah and Hannah's room had the full-size bed that had been in the set and the dressing table and mirror that went along with it. The boys had bunk beds which had been moved over from the old house and a collection of odds and ends. They moved into the large, cold unfinished basement. Other furniture that had been purchased for the old house, such as our old kitchen table made of yellow laminate and metal legs was put into the new, huge eat-in kitchen. White curtains with red and pink roses from were added to the picture window. We moved in other small pieces selected by Mamaji—iconic, white and gold 70s style lamps, a desk with a world map laminated on the surface, and coffee tables. A gleaming new dining room set, gold and green living room couches and a master bedroom set were purchased. The Haqq's had arrived to Keating Court.

While it was nice to be in a new house that didn't flood, didn't have lizards, had new windows that blocked the howling wind, and some normal neighbors, the house had two immediate complications. Sometime after the snow started to fall, we woke to freezing temperatures. We always wore sweaters and socks in our house but this was different. I could see my own breath and I began to tremble. As we got dressed, Papaji told us to put on winter jackets and hats. The Biggers sat at the kitchen table in coats and blankets, shivering as they studied. Mama and Papaji sat in the living room, talking seriously in low tones. Sometime later in the day there was a knock at the door and a man came in and was invited to sit in the chilly living room. He had graying hair, wore a sport coat and a clerical collar. He spoke to Papaji and they had a conversation that made no sense to me.

"I wanted to explain," the man began.

Papaji leaned forward in his chair, "Yes?"

"I wanted to apologize for this neighborhood and this community," the man said. I'm not sure who is responsible, but I am very sorry that you are going through all this difficulty. I'm very ashamed of what has happened."

Papaji was silent for a moment. "Well, I want to thank you for coming and speaking to us. We appreciate your concern."

"Please let me know if I can do anything to help," the man said.

Papaji stood up, shook his hand, and walked him to the door.

I didn't understand what had happened that day, until years later when Hannah asked Papaji about it. At that time, the electric and other cables were easily accessible, since the town had not yet buried them. During the night someone had come onto our property and sabotaged the main wires from the cable box to our home. Father Burns from Mary, Mother of the Church, the largest Catholic church in our town, had stopped by to offer his apologies. We were the only non-white family in the entire town. We did not think about the fact that to many of the people living there, our arrival to the community was not necessarily a welcome one.

The other complication had nothing to do with the town but, in its own way, had a similar sobering effect of facing the reality of our new situation. With the move to Burnsville, Mamaji's dream to have us all back in our family home in Chandigarh was officially dead. The new house was what Papaji had bought with Mama, it was *their* home together—and Mamaji's family members were not welcome there. While we lived at Keating Court, we were never again allowed to communicate in any way with Mamaji's family or our relatives who knew us and loved us so much. Any connection to Mamaji was officially over.

In the summer of 1974, my Nani came to America via England to visit her children and grandchildren. In London, she briefly met Vincent Mamu, Farina Masi, and their two children, my cousins Sandeep and Anita. Then she traveled to Ohio and stayed with Vidyasagar Mamu and Shirley Masi and my cousins Joel, Joanna, and Jonathan for a month. Nani had dental work done and then traveled with the family to Disney World and Niagara Falls. She also went to Fairlawn, New Jersey, and visited Mamaji's grave for the first time. She wept and asked for details from my uncle about not only my life but all my siblings as well. Outliving your own child goes against the law of nature. Nani had not only lost her oldest daughter but seven of her grandchildren too.

While Nani was in America, we did not know she was there and we were unable to meet her. I am not sure of the exact reason why but depending on who was asked, the answer would be different. If I had asked Papaji, he might have said that he was not speaking with his former brother-in-law. If I had asked

Vidyasagar Mamu, he might have said that he had cut off his relationship with Papaji after his sister died. I am more inclined to believe that Joel or even Nani must have called our house, but were told we could not see her. In any case, the end result was the same—we children were the ones who had to pay the price for the petty behaviors of the adults. We were unable to see our Nani. For me this is a personal disappointment of enormous proportions. I often imagine how wonderful it would have been to spend time with the one person who knew and loved Mamaji better than anyone in the whole world.

A short while after Nani returned back to India, Vidyasagar Mamu and my cousin Joel experienced a great tragedy. Joel was summoned home from his first year at college after an electrical short ignited a fire in his family home. Vidyasagar Mamu suffered third degree burns over 80% of his body and was not expected to live. Tragically, my Shirley Masi, and my cousins Joanna and Jonathan (who I had never met), all perished in the fire. Shirley Masi and Mamaji had been great friends and had loved each other as sisters. Although Papaji was called with the news, none of us attended the funerals, except Gideon who was married by that time and living in Chicago. Eventually, Vidyasagar Mamu made a full recovery and returned to his work as the pastor of a local church. It was not until I was married that I was able to reconnect with my uncle and cousin.

In 1976, Nani died. She had been living with her youngest daughter, my Vera Masi, in Hoshiarpur, Punjab. I knew almost nothing of my Nani. My older siblings told me some stories, but when I looked at her pictures, I longed to know more about her. In 2016, I took a trip along with Miriam and my oldest son Philip, and we went back to the church where my parents had been married. We also visited Nani's old home that was on the same church campus. There, by pure chance, we met Pastor J.B. Mathews. He had known both my maternal and paternal grandparents and, when he was 18, he had played the organ at my parents' wedding. Among other stories, he recalled the day of Nani's burial. Her death occurred on a scorching hot summer day. Since all her children lived far away, there was great concern about how to preserve the body until the service and burial could be held. There were no funeral homes that could preserve the body for more than a day or so. As they contemplated this problem, the skies grew gray and then black. It began to rain and sleet. Before long, huge fist-sized hail fell from the sky and covered the ground with layers of ice. Nani's friends gathered the ice to keep her body cool until her children and family could arrive. It was the only time the townspeople and Pastor Mathews ever recalled seeing ice or hail falling from the sky. After the burial service, Vera Masi went to live with her older married sister Venetia Masi who lived in Polladpur, Maharashtra. The following year, in 1977, Vera Masi died of infective hepatitis. I never knew my Nani, Vera and Shirley Masis, Vincent Mamu or my cousins Joanna and Jonathan. I had to find their stories on my own. I only learned the details of Nani's visit and of her death at the time I began my research for this memoir.

✳✳✳

Soon it was Christmas again, and this year, as a newly repaired family, we planned to attend Aunt Helen's annual Christmas open house at her home on Humboldt Avenue in Minneapolis. That Christmas one of Mamaji's best friends met the woman who had taken her place. Aunt Helen and Mama hit it off right away and began chatting about the wedding, the cold Minnesota winters and the children. Aunt Helen's home was different from our home because it was one of the stately, historic houses in a beautiful, old neighborhood of Minneapolis. It reminded me of the tree-lined streets featured in Disney's animated movie *The Lady and the Tramp*. Perhaps it was the Christmas lights or the beautiful decorations, but Aunt Helen and Uncle George's annual Christmas open house was always a magical part of the season. The inside of the home was characteristically American. It had thick wall-to-wall shag carpet, televisions in every room, nylons drying in the bathroom, rock music, smell of lemon Pledge, slick issues of *Seventeen* tossed carelessly on the coffee table, and American snacks like Coke and sour cream potato chips. For Christmas, they gave us stiff red envelopes—mine had a new, woodsy smelling $10 bill in it. They gave the Three Stooges new octagon-shaped ornaments with a small figure inside for our first Christmas tree in the new house. David's was blue. Hannah's was green with a clown wearing a harlequin costume, and mine was rose-colored with a beautiful blond, pink robed angel nestled inside.

I loved Aunt Helen and Uncle George and their family. They had always been good to me and I was fascinated whenever they would talk of "the cabin." They often invited us to, "come up north to the cabin." It seemed so wonderful and mysterious to me and I longed to see a real Abe Lincoln–style log cabin. One summer, we visited the famous cabin and I was sorely disappointed to learn it was nothing but a white, two-storied house situated on a lake. Aunt Helen and Uncle George's children were about the same age as my older siblings. There was a girl named Janet who was Deborah's age. I couldn't take my eyes off her blond hair. I longed to touch it, to find out if it felt the same as mine. Their children water skied, wore shorts and bathing suits. My family dressed in saris, dresses, long pants, formal shirts and watched the carefree Americans enjoy a Minnesota summer.

In the days leading up to Christmas, the mountain of gifts piling up under our tree grew. Presents were put out as they were wrapped. Since Santa didn't exist in our home, the presents didn't appear suddenly. We opened them on Christmas Eve because in the darkness, the splendor and lights of the tree could be most appreciated. Once I asked Papaji about Santa. He snorted, "Humph, why should that old, fat man get all the credit for my hard work?" It made sense to me. I would much rather get gifts from Papaji and Mama, anyway. That Christmas there was a special gift from Mama. She had noticed that neither Hannah nor I had pierced ears. Most Indian girls had their ears pierced as toddlers. Miriam and Deborah already wore earrings. Piercing ears was a simple procedure for a surgeon and Mama expertly sterilized a needle and pushed it through both Hannah's and my earlobes. She wanted the piercings to heal first before putting earrings in, so she kept the holes open with a bright scarlet thread. Hannah and I could barely contain our Christmas joy. We were delighted and showed off our new holey earlobes to the family.

The new house had lots of visitors. Papaji had nine brothers and sisters who had settled in America and one or more of them seemed to always be at our house. Papaji's brothers spent weekends with us, eating heavy Indian meals, talking, laughing, and debating. On weekends we all enjoyed mutton curry or spicy keema, which was made with chopped meat. We looked forward to visits from our Peter Chacha and his American wife, Maureen Chachi. They had no children and Maureen Chachi enjoyed spoiling us Three Stooges. She would always bring an extra treat or a toy for us. Once, when Papaji was entertaining his colleagues, Peter Chacha and Maureen Chachi took us to see *Mary Poppins*. Other Chachas came over as well. Agri Chacha lived out east, Arshad Chacha had settled in the west, Taj Chachi lived in Oklahoma with her family. I loved my Salim Chacha because, like his brothers, not only was he extremely handsome and a great dresser but he also drove a red Jaguar. He was a psychologist and was married to an American lady.

My Feroza Chachi lived in Ohio. By this time, Rashida Chachi had left our house and joined her sister. She left sometime after Mama arrived. I never knew why she left so abruptly, as she had been a member of our household since the time Mamaji died. When I began writing this memoir, I learned that Rashida Chachi and Mama had argued quite often about Mama's methods of child-rearing. Maureen Chachi recalled that the breaking point came one evening when Rashida Chachi reported Mama's repeated practice of having Hannah and me bathe in the same water in which she had already taken a bath. A huge fight erupted and Rashida Chachi left that very night. I only remember that when I awoke, she was gone.

Babu Chacha, was married but had left his wife and three children in India. He said he planned to go back and bring them to America, but most of the time he talked about the American women he was dating. Babu Chacha wore aviator sunglasses and gave me a quarter if I sat on his lap. One afternoon, when we were expecting a group of the Chachas to come, Mama took me and Hannah aside while Papaji was still upstairs showering.

"When Babu Chacha comes, I don't want you sitting on his lap. Is that understood?"

Hannah nodded obediently.

"Why?" I asked.

"Because I told you so. Don't let me see you near him," said Mama.

When Babu Chacha arrived, I forgot Mama's warning and after he handed me the quarter, I climbed on his lap. He stroked my bare leg under my dress.

When Mama came into the room, she shouted, "ELISHEBA!" She had never raised her voice before. Even when she disciplined us, her voice was calm and deadly serious, and I had never heard her scream. I was so startled at her voice that I jumped off Babu Chacha's lap and ran to the kitchen. She grabbed my ear and slapped me.

"Didn't I tell you?" Mama pinched my ear.

"I forgot." I sobbed.

I was sure Mama only wanted to keep me from getting the quarter. It was not until I was 12 or 13 that I remembered how Babu Chacha had touched me. I cannot recollect the extent of it, but I do know that if she had not put a stop to it, he would have done much more. She knew she couldn't tell Papaji—she was too new to the family, but she did what she had to and saved me from being abused. Deborah remembered that he had grabbed her breasts when she was 13 and he was abusive to Gideon as well. Since Babu Chacha did not have a license, he would ask Papaji to tell Gideon to drive him around. Gideon drove him to women's homes and then was forced to wait in the car while Babu Chacha went inside. Afterwards, he told Gideon in perverse detail what he had done, getting excited about spoiling a young boy. Gideon was only 16 and was thoroughly disgusted but wasn't able to tell Papaji. He carried it with him and was finally able to tell Papaji only when he was a grown man with grandchildren of his own. When they talked about it, they both cried together. Papaji called

Babu Chacha on the phone and shouted at him about his past actions. The two brothers never spoke again.

We had visitors from Mama's family too. In the summer, Mama's sister and her husband visited. We were told to call Mama's sister Sheela Masi and her husband was to be our new Uncle John. He looked like a horse—Mr. Ed, to be specific. He had large, yellow buck teeth, pasty white skin, a horrible comb-over, and thick glasses. He was pudgy, pale and his hands were slick with sweat. His wife was petite and looked like a miniature version of Mama. Sheela Masi and Uncle John were the first family members of Mama's to visit us. It was a puzzle why these two grossly unmatched people were together. He spoke in a thick British accent, wore shorts, half-sleeved dress shirts, socks, and sandals. He was jittery, stuttered horribly, spat when he spoke, had bright pink knees and elbows, and was terribly nervous about everything, in particular my mischievous brothers. During their visit, a terrible summer storm flashed across the sky. The skies turned black and a tornado was sighted on the prairie, not far from our home. Uncle John was the only grown man I had seen behave like a child. If there was a crack of lightning or a clap of thunder, he would squeal and tremble like a small girl. He was so afraid of the dark skies that he ran and hid. When the storm passed, my brothers found him shaking behind a group of trash cans, his face white as paper. After they left, we often played "Uncle John" and acted out this scene, exaggerating, and putting Uncle John not just behind the trash cans, but inside them, the lids clamped firmly on top. We spent hours mimicking his nervous habits and laughing until our stomachs hurt.

Our new house began to feel more familiar to me. To divide our yard from the park, Papaji had planted a long row of tall, thin poplar trees. On hot summer nights, when the wind blew, the leaves made a soothing rustling sound in the dark quiet. We also had ten to fifteen apple trees. Papaji took great pride in these apple trees and pruned them carefully while he waited from them to begin producing fruit. He told me of how he had tasted a crisp sweet apple during his first trip to America and the impression it had made on him. After that he had always longed for apples. He planted The Jonathan Apple, Macintosh, Crabapple, Red Delicious, Cortland, Red Rome, Japanese, and three or four other kinds of apple trees I have blocked from memory. Sadly, I did not share his love for growing apples. Eventually, the trees started literally producing bushels of apples, and this grew to be the cause of great angst. Peeling and cutting apples during the summers was one of the chores Hannah and I despised more than anything. Papaji was a preacher but deep in his heart he was a just aching to be a good old, Minnesota farm boy.

In the far left corner of the yard, there was a large, square, kitchen garden. Papaji specialized in tomatoes and cucumbers but also grew eggplant and two or three varieties of hot mirchee or chili peppers. I learned that by helping Papaji garden or water, I could spend time alone with him. Working in the sun was a small price to pay. Mama pretended to like gardening but after an hour she complained of a migraine or that her blood pressure was high and went inside. Papaji and I talked for hours in the garden. We discussed his work, his hopes and dreams, my school and friends. Sometimes we said nothing and I just enjoyed being next to him, listening to his exertions as he dug into the dirt or pulled weeds. He often talked about buying a hobby farm and not only raising crops but our own chickens. Sometimes he told me old stories of his boyhood in India, other times we laughed together at the antics of his Three Stooges. We talked about the beauty of the earth, God, politics, science, art, philosophy; Papaji could talk about anything. Our efforts in our Minnesota garden resulted in a bumper crop every year. The kitchen and garage would be filled with hundreds of tomatoes and cucumbers. I loved tomatoes and we made a delicious Indian version of tomato salad—tomato chaat. We cut up sun-warmed tomatoes, mixed in salt, pepper, red pepper powder, cumin, and a little lemon juice. It was a favorite summer treat.

Many years later, Papaji came to visit me in New Jersey and we strolled all around my acre-size yard, the vibrant leaves of turmeric, saffron, and pomegranate crunching underfoot. As we walked, he gave me hints and advice on how to increase my produce output the next season. He asked me about my life, my children, my writing. By the time we came to the end of our garden tour, I ached with sadness. I realized how much I missed all the talks I had with Papaji while I worked in the garden with him those many years ago.

✳✳✳

Food was always a discussion in our house. Someone was always eating, getting ready to eat, or finishing eating in our house. Papaji and Mama bought bags and bags of groceries each week—grocery shopping was no joke, and it was something they did alone. When they returned, Papaji honked the horn of our station wagon, and we ran down to help them unpack the mounds of groceries. He always seemed so happy as we unloaded the bags and put the food away. In the days before shopping in warehouses was common, Shoppers City knew him well and provided him with cardboard boxes to lug all the supplies. After one food shopping trip, there would be ten loaves of bread, four gallons of milk, eight pounds of butter, industrial-size packages of bologna and cheese, extra-large bottles of jam and peanut butter, 20 pounds of potatoes, six 24-pack hot dogs, six whole chickens, three plastic gallon buckets of Kemps vanilla ice cream, and much more. In the basement we had a huge sarcophagus-sized freezer, along with industrial gray shelves that were stocked with provisions. Papaji always joked about the amount of food that was required to feed us. The boys had a habit of making six open-faced peanut butter and jelly sandwiches at a time. Instead of using a plate, they would carry them by laying three on each arm. It was one of Papaji's favorite stories to parody. Sometimes, after a shopping trip, for no reason at all, he would give us huge bags of mixed candy, laughing and enjoying our delight.

In the fall, when the older kids went off to school, I enjoyed the long, quiet days at home. Hannah was in half-day kindergarten and reached home earlier than the others. She and I played with Papaji when he was home from his travels. One of our favorite games was to watch him when he exercised. He would stand on his hands for long periods of time, until the blood ran to his head. We would bend down to kiss him, laughing and taking turns, as he leaned up against a wall. On other days, he would ask us to walk on his back. This was wonderful fun. We held onto each other as we tried to walk without slipping off his broad back. Even though he had suffered a great loss, he seemed to be his same old self. During these days, he was fun, loving, and jolly, filled with good humor, jokes, and laughter.

Papaji was a big man. Even though he was not quite six feet, he was impressive. He was careful and meticulous in his grooming. One of my favorite pastimes was to sit on the floor of the master bedroom as he got ready in the mornings. He shaved carefully, applying shaving cream and shaving twice, deliberately and slowly, while singing a romantic Hindi movie song. He was clean-shaven except for his distinctive mustache, which looked like two capital letter Ls lying down on their sides. He dressed his hair carefully hair with Vitalis and then combed it into a perfect pompadour. The hair oil had a sharp, pungent, woodsy scent. He wore well-tailored, neatly pressed suits and shirts. He didn't wear jeans or casual clothing. When he wasn't wearing a suit and tie, he would wear his idea of informal clothing, which was a pair of pants and a short-sleeved dress shirt. Like most little girls, I thought my father was the handsomest man on the earth.

Some mornings I would go along with Papaji and Mama when they ran the many errands they had. The worst trip was a visit to the chiropractor of which Papaji was so fond. It was a long ride, what seemed to be hours and hours and I soon fell asleep in the back seat. Once, I was woken from a nap when the car stopped. My eyes still closed, I heard giggling. I opened my eyes just a small bit and saw Papaji kissing Mama. He kissed her slowly down her neck while she laughed softly, then he kissed her deeply on the mouth. I was fascinated, trespassing on a private moment. I closed my eyes until the car started to move again.

Sometimes, while I waited for Hannah to get home, I stayed in my room and played for hours with my bald-headed baby doll. I had given her a haircut and there were huge areas with only dots, amidst patches of pink plastic where her hair had been cut to the roots. David had used her head for a hammer and her left eye had dented into her hollow skull, causing it to remain forever open. When I laid her down for her nap, she stared eerily at me with her one dented blue eye. She was the ugliest doll in the world. Both Hannah and I longed for a Barbie doll, the same kind that Deborah had. Her Barbie doll had a sleek yellow ponytail still in in its original rubber band and, most importantly, she had large hard breasts. The Barbie had many beautiful and unmarred clothes. A red Japanese kimono complete with a samisen, a slinky, black dress with a pink scarf that left the top of her bosom uncovered, a drum majorette jacket with a skirt and flesh-colored nylons, a striped croquet dress including a tiny mallet and balls. I wanted to dress and undress that Barbie, take her hair out of the ponytail, and brush it with all my might, but Deborah would not allow me to touch it. She would only take out the Barbie on special occasions and show it from a distance. Hannah and I cried, begged, and pleaded for a Barbie, all day, every day and any day.

One evening, Papaji heard Hannah and me begging Deborah to let us play with her Barbie. He smiled and got his keys, "You girls want a Barbie? Let's go get you one." Just like that. It wasn't our birthday, Christmas or anything, just an ordinary day. He didn't hesitate to buy us a doll for no reason. Deborah came along to supervise the trip. When we got to the store, the display was dazzling. There were rows and rows of smiling red-lipped Barbies. Hannah touched package after package, unsure of how to choose the right one. But Deborah was quite sure of who our new Barbies should be. She reached over and plucked out two boxes. One doll had long blond hair, bangs, and was wearing a red swimsuit. The other doll had curly brown hair and was wearing a striped two-piece bathing suit. I didn't want the dolls. I couldn't quite recognize what it was, but something was wrong with these dolls. The fact that Deborah wanted us to choose them alerted my radar, but they also looked uglier. They looked like little girls, not grown women. Deborah held out the blond doll to me, "Look, Elisheba—she's got long hair! And Hannah, see this one? She has dark, curly hair just like you!" *Why was she being so nice to us?* Hannah and I feebly protested, but I already knew these were to be our new Barbies.

We left the store with a Skipper for me and a Scooter for Hannah. Something was not right, but I was still excited to have a new doll—and, after all, it was a Barbie! When we got home, Hannah and I raced upstairs with our purchases. In a flash, the dolls were released from their plastic confines and our combs and brushes raked through their hair. We stripped the two dolls and they lay naked in front of us, completely flat. No firm, proud breasts; just smooth pieces of hard plastic. My disappointment was so great that I pushed Skipper under my pillow. Now I understood why Deborah had chosen these dolls. Eventually, we did play with Skipper and Scooter again. But we scornfully referred to them as "Flatsies." That spring, David threw Scooter on to the roof. I chopped Skipper's hair and lost her clothes. When a gutter repairman finally found Scooter, years later, she was bleached bright white and her face had melted.

Despite the small ups and downs, it seemed that our adjustment to our new life was working out. The household was running as it should; meals were eaten, clothes were washed, baths were given, toys were played with, church was joined, laughter was heard, and school was attended. Even though Mamaji was never mentioned, things appeared to be as normal as they could be for a large, noisy, Indian family. Pungent aromas of spices, garlic and onions combined with the strains of Kishore Kumar and Lata Mangeshkar singing on the stereo spilled through the windows of our house in a small, dairy town in southeastern Minnesota. Life was peaceful and pleasant and I was happy.

Hoshiarpur, India at Nana and Nani's house, 1953
(Left to right Nana, Nani behind Miriam, Gideon, Vidyasagar Mamu,
Mamaji carrying Emmanuel and Vera Masi)

CHAPTER
SIX

O F   T H E   T W O   major occurrences that broke the serenity of
my new, readjusted world, the start of my formal education
was the first. One February, I was playing quietly in the kitchen,
minding my own business while Mama and Feroza Chachi, who
was visiting, were having tea. The two ladies chatted and sipped.

Suddenly, Feroza Chachi looked at me and said, "How old is
she now?"

"She's four, no wait, she must be five," Mama said.

"I think her birthday is in March," Feroza Chachi counted on
her fingers. "That means she'll be six. Why isn't she in school?"

And that was how it was decided that I should start my education. School was already in session, and the late entry required
a special trip to the principal's office with Mama. I would begin
kindergarten the next morning. I was eager to join Hannah and
David and I looked forward to school.

On my first day, Hannah accompanied me to the principal's
office. She quickly deposited me in a chair and left. I sat and
watched a lady type at a desk in front of me. She had gray hair
and wore horn-rimmed glasses dangling from a chain made from

tiny safety pins. She looked at me through hugely magnified eyes, came around her desk, kneeled next to me and said, "Welcome to William Byrne Elementary School! My name is Shirley." She must have said something else as well, but I was so fascinated with her, I didn't hear any more. She was the first adult who had introduced herself to me using her first name. *And what an unusual name she had. So agreeable! So positive! So can-do! "Surely, I can help you. Surely, I can take you to your class. Surely, I can make you feel comfortable. Surely, Shirley will do it!"* Before long I was skipping down the hallway, hand in hand with my new friend. School seemed like a wonderful place.

We arrived outside a classroom. Shirley looked down at me and put a finger to her lips. It was as though she and I were sharing a big secret. I nodded conspiringly. She opened the door and I walked in behind her. The room was filled with children, but I was too scared to look closely at them. She spoke to the teacher and handed her a white card. Then Shirley patted my head and walked out the door, leaving me alone with a room full of strangers.

The teacher read the card and looked at me, "My name is Mrs. Hill." Then she turned to the class, "Class, this is Aalla-She-ba Hawk. She's from Pakistan, India, and she will be joining our class." Then Mrs. Hill pointed her finger to the room full of children, "Why don't you take a seat in that empty one next to Laura?" She indicated a desk next to a girl with flaming red hair. I began the long walk.

It was at that precise moment I realized my world had entirely changed and that nothing would be the same again. Every single face that looked at me was white and had pale yellow or light brown hair. My surroundings were completely alien. When I reached my desk, I took note of Laura's red hair and then, on closer inspection, it was clear that she also had thousands of tan spots all over her face, arms, and legs. Horrified and intensely curious all at the same time, questions began to swirl in my head—*Was her hair warm? Would the spots get bigger? If I sat next to her, would I also get the same disease? What would Mama say if I came home sick? And where were Hannah and David? Weren't they in school too?* I sat down feeling miserable, making sure to keep as far as I could from Laura.

At the end of my first day of school, I was met by Hannah and David. Together we walked the four blocks home and I told Hannah about Laura's spots and her hair. Hannah told me there was a boy named Paul in her class who also had red hair. Her own curiosity had been so great that while walking past him in class, she ever so gently patted the top of his crisp, red crew cut. In a flash, Paul raised his hand, "Miss Jensen, Hannah's slapping me!" Hannah was shocked. Slapping? *Slapping?* Paul didn't know a thing about slapping. We laughed and laughed thinking about what would happen if Paul ever found himself at our house. If he spent one day with us, he'd learn exceedingly fast what *real* slapping was all about. Hannah made Laura's hair and skin seemed less daunting and after my initial fear wore off and I realized her spots were not contagious, Laura became my friend.

But an even greater change—one that would drastically change my relationship with Mama forever happened the following year. I had not noticed anything unusual during this time, but one day in late September, I came home from school and saw Mama holding a small bundle.

"What is it?" I asked.

"This is your brother, Joram," said Mama.

I was curious and reached out to touch the blue blanket, "Oh! He's so little."

"Don't touch him! Your hands are dirty!" Mama warned.

Joram's birth was viewed as a miracle. When I was a teenager

I learned that Mama had suffered a number of miscarriages while Miriam functioned as her nursemaid through all of them. Mama moaned and cried out in pain and Miriam helped her through the difficult process the best she could. Before Mama even knew she was pregnant with Joram, she was told she had possible uterine tumors or even fibroids. To treat this, the doctor placed small radiation seeds in her uterus. Later, when preforming an exploratory surgery, he learned that Mama was pregnant. When closing her abdomen, the surgeon was careful but warned my parents, "I can't be positive that I didn't stitch through the head." He recommended that they terminate the pregnancy. When Joram was born, it was fully expected that he would have some sort of deformity or anomaly. But Joram was perfect. His birth was a cause for great celebration. According to Indian tradition, we had to eat something sweet, and Mama made chooree, a delicious mixture made of small pieces of soft chapati combined with butter and brown sugar. With the birth of Joram, we had an even number of boys and girls in our family. "You have to be very quiet from now on, because Joram has to sleep," we were warned. His crib was set up inside the master bedroom.

It wasn't too difficult to keep quiet. It was nothing new and I was accustomed to hearing the word and observing it. I had been quiet when Mamaji was ill. Then I had been quiet because Mama got sick too. She suffered from malaria when she first came from India. After that, she had never been healthy. She had migraines and high blood pressure, and I was told to be quiet again. Being quiet for Joram was just another day at the office; I was an expert at it. We were warned that we should get ready for school in the mornings without making any noise. David, Hannah, and I learned to get up, dress, eat breakfast, and leave for school without making a sound. Mama did not get out of bed to see us off to school. Even during the dark, icy winter mornings which lasted at least five months, we got out of our beds, got ready in silence, and soundlessly exited the house while Mama slept. If there was noise, I was usually the culprit, and when we arrived home in the afternoons, we would receive a scolding.

"You were very noisy this morning. I've had a migraine all day."

"I'm sorry," I said.

"I'm sorry too," Mama said in an accusing tone.

This was to be her sardonic response to all my sorrys for the rest of my life. She wasn't apologizing to me or to any of us; she was only making certain that her anger was communicated. I never knew what the proper response to her statement was supposed to be. It was a riddle to which I never discovered an answer. But we apologized anyway.

"I'm sorry," said Hannah.

"I heard you opening the cereal box and it woke Joram up."

"I'm sorry," said David.

"I'm sorry too," said Mama.

In the mornings my stomach became too upset to eat and I began to throw up my breakfast before leaving for school. But David and Hannah had been given orders to make sure I ate. They finally gave in to my pleadings and secretly allowed me to skip breakfast. Then we dressed as warmly as we could and walked the half mile to school. This was not unusual in those days, although during the dark and cold winter months, most children were driven to school by their mothers. Mama didn't know how to drive and she hated the icy weather, so we walked. After school, we eagerly looked forward to our after-school snack. Usually, it was chocolate cake with chocolate icing and milk. When we reached home, three pieces of cake would be sitting on three plates with three glasses of milk. David claimed the largest piece by spitting on it. Until Joram was old enough to attend school, afternoons also had to be silent. We ate quickly and quietly and then went outside. In the yard, we loudly shouted the words "cake" and "milk" over and over, laughing and emphasizing the hard "K" sounds in the two words—the viscosity of the milk making the sounds even more distinct.

As we got older, the after-school snack was whatever treat Joram most craved. Thankfully, he had a massive sweet tooth and cake was still featured. Sometimes Mama made chocolate chip cookies and our snack was the cookies which had been over-cooked a bit and were too dark for Joram. Mama left a snack for us every day after school. It was something we looked forward to with great anticipation.

I enjoyed watching Mama make Joram's bottles, but when I became a mother, I found it strange that Mama had not nursed Joram. Indian women have a high regard for breastfeeding, not just for the nutritional value but for the bonding that occurs. For me, it had been such a wonderful part of being a mother and I wondered why Mama had refused to nurse her only child.

Eventually, much of Joram's care was given over to my two old-est sisters. They fed him, changed him, and put him to sleep in his crib in the master bedroom. The second floor bathroom was small and it became even smaller with the arrival of Joram. Our house had three bathrooms—a powder room on the main level, a full bathroom inside the master bedroom which only Papaji and Mama used, and a full bathroom on the second floor which the seven of us shared. Mama decided that our crowded, shared bath-room was the best place for the diaper pail. It was a large white bucket with a lid. It smelled strongly of disinfectant and con-tained Joram's soaking, soiled diapers. While Joram never used our bathroom, his dirty diapers were always stored and washed there.

About the time Joram was born, Hannah and I began taking

turns with Miriam and Deborah to make our lunch sandwiches. Lunch-making was a precise process. The boys had two sandwiches and the girls had one. Each one was made with two slices of bread and either peanut butter and jelly or one slim slice of shiny, processed cheese food or one skinny slice of bologna—never both and never more than one slice per sandwich. In addition, we packed one apple or one cookie. The cookie was not to be wrapped but just placed in the paper bag. There were no additions to be made to the lunches. We reused our plastic sandwich bags and brown bag all week. I felt wonderfully free on Fridays, when, with the other kids, I could throw carelessly and offhandedly the paper and plastic bag in the trash. When I was an adult, I visited my cousins in England and I was given a similar skinny cucumber sandwich for lunch. I finally understood that Mama was only drawing on her limited experiences with fancy English sandwiches when she gave instructions for our sandwich-making. She had no clue, nor did she inquire about the capabilities of these scrawny sandwiches to fill our stomachs or even fulfill the nutritional needs of full-grown teenage boys. One day, I decided to amend our plain single slice of cheese and mayo sandwiches. On our way to school I confessed my offense to David and Hannah.

"Guess what? I made lunches last night and I added lettuce to our sandwiches!"

"Whoa...really? Can't wait for lunch," David said.

"Good one, Elisheba," congratulated Hannah.

I felt happy that I had gained their approval and looked forward to a tasty meal. When lunchtime arrived, I bit eagerly into my sandwich, expecting the crunch of lettuce along with the cheese slice, but it never came. My sandwich had no lettuce, only cheese and mayonnaise. My disappointment was so great that I tossed the rest of it into the garbage. I assumed the lettuce had been removed the night before, and I couldn't figure out how my transgression had been discovered.

The master bedroom door that had once only been closed now became a locked door. It was a simple lock, one that was easy to pick with a hairpin. When Papaji, Mama, and Joram were inside we were not allowed to enter without knocking first and then waiting for permission to enter. When I waited outside the door, I heard whispers as Papaji and Mama scurried about. I became an expert eavesdropper and spent many hours listening at the door. Tasty snacks like cashews, almonds and Club crackers disappeared behind the locked door. All the fruit except for soft, mushy apples and black bananas disappeared as well. Obtaining fresh, luscious fruit was a complication. The only time I ever caught Miriam doing something against the rules was the one time I picked the lock and found her inside taking her first bite of a forbidden fruit.

Shocked and Eve-like, she held out a golden sphere, "Want some?" Her mouth was filled with juicy peach.

"Sure! I'll have some," I took a big bite and we grinned at each other as we shared the illicit fruit.

Miriam had always loved peaches and I enjoyed this moment in which she and I could conspire together. None of us ever thought to question why the fruit was locked up, why we could not eat it, and why it was only given to Joram. I would have understood a rule that was made to exclude *all* the children, an adults-only rule, but I could not fathom why Joram was allowed privileges that we were not.

Television was also restricted. The color TV was in the master bedroom and, only available to Papaji, Mama, and Joram. The large black-and-white set sat downstairs in the basement and we were not allowed to watch it, except for one hour of *The Wonderful World of Disney* on Sundays. My imagination was vast and so play-acting was a large part of my free time. We all acted out stories we had read or we put on plays for the adults and Joram. Sometimes we dramatized the story of Moses in the bulrushes or other Bible stories. Other times we created our own. Once, when Papaji was leaving for India, the Biggers wrote a melodrama which culminated with Miriam and Deborah dramatically crying and grabbing Papaji's legs, begging him not to go. Then the boys came and pulled them off Papaji's legs as they continued to sob while being dragged away. Hannah and I cried alongside. We made up songs set to familiar tunes. We used the tune from "C-is for the Christ Child" by Jim Reeves to sing a song for Father's Day.

F is for the father that we love so much
A is for the airplane that takes him far
T is for the tomatoes that he loves to grow
H is for the humor that you always have
E is for everything that he does for us
R is for reading the book you'll write
And that's why there's a Father's Day!

Any story or even any adult visitor could be the subject for a long afternoon of play-acting. Once, I decided to act out the story of Hansel and Gretel. In my version I decided that I would use my ugly, dented baby doll to play Gretel and that only Hansel would make it out of the witch's house. I put the doll inside our cold oven and soon forgot about her and became occupied in another activity. Later, I heard a commotion in the kitchen.

"Elisheba? *Beti*? Come here," Papaji called.

When he used the term for daughter—Beti, I knew he was not angry. But when I came into the kitchen I saw Mama looking at me with horror.

"What is this?" Papaji looked confused as he held up my baby doll.

"That's Gretel. The witch is cooking her."

Mama broke down and sobbed to Papaji in Punjabi, "I knew she was jealous but I never thought she would do something like this!"

I was confused, "Whad I do?"

Papaji looked concerned, "Why did you put her in the oven?"

"To cook her," I said.

Mama eyes widened with terror, "If she can do this, imagine what would happen if she ever...oh, I don't want her to ever be alone with him!" She clutched Joram close to her.

After that, I was always accused of being jealous of Joram. I was viewed as someone who wanted things that did not belong to her. I was suddenly seen as unstable and so jealous that I would do anything to even the score, even murder my own brother. I was only seven or eight but I earned the label of "neurotic" and "disturbed" forever. The story was told over and over again to anyone who had not heard it. I understood that Mama actually believed I was capable of burning my own brother alive. Each time I heard it told, I felt ashamed and boiled with anger that she had twisted my innocent game into something so depraved. No matter how much I proved my love for my brother, there was nothing I could do to change what happened that day.

THE THREE STOOGES
David, 7 years old;
Hannah, 4 years old;
Elisheba, 3 years old

CHAPTER
SEVEN

L IVING IN MINNESOTA meant learning how to acclimate to
the long, frozen winters. A Minnesota winter could take my
breath away with its cruel cold and delicate beauty. At night the
wind blew hard and the house creaked and shifted in the chilly
air. Early morning, the hoarfrost traced its delicate lacy pattern
on the windows, while coating even the wood on the panes with
a thick layer of rime. It tasted of freezer burn when I scraped it off
with my fingernails and licked it. The walk to school was made
longer by the frigid temperatures. Long expanses of vast, blank
plains stretched as far as my eyes could see. The fierce wind blew
the snow into hard, swirling waves. Papaji and Mama were not
knowledgeable about appropriate winter attire or how cold a
Minnesota winter could be. After Christmas, Papaji regularly
traveled to India for his work, for at least six to eight weeks and
Mama rarely went outside. To keep warm, David, Hannah, and I
wore extra socks with plastic bread bags on top to prevent our feet
from getting wet and then added more socks over our mittens. As
was the case with all our clothing, we wore hand-me-down coats
and scarves. By the time I got an article of clothing, it had already

been worn by all three of my sisters. Hannah even wore David's old loafers as her school shoes one year because, she was told, "all loafers looked the same." We went to school with kids who bought brand-new school clothes and shoes every fall. We got one set of new clothes at Christmas and occasionally, one on our birthday.

One winter both Hannah and I had outgrown our boots. For Christmas that year I asked for some nice snow boots, maybe the kind that looked like the fashionable, laced-up, granny-style boots. Hannah just prayed for some of any sort. We were growing so fast that even the hand-me-downs didn't fit. We never got our boots. Hannah wore Deborah's and I had to wear the dark brown, fur-trimmed, pointed ankle ones that Mama had worn in London in the 1950s. I cringed wearing these. Right or wrong, I wanted to wear fashionable clothing. I learned to hide my 1950 exclusives by quickly switching to my shoes while I was still 800 feet or so from my school. By then we had grown accustomed to the sort of presents given to all of us. A large bag of candy was usual, or sometimes it was the same T-shirt for all of us, just in different sizes. New clothes were usually Kmart blue-light specials—ugly and cheap but, somehow, we made them work by adding or subtracting to the clothes to make them wearable.

The gifts that were carefully chosen for me were usually given to me by one of the Biggers, David or Hannah. For instance, in Christmas of 1974, I remember Emmanuel had given me a necklace and earring set. Hannah had sewn a fabric purse for me and Deborah's present was a wood-finish radio alarm clock. The alarm was useful and the radio was always tuned to U100, the popular, local music station. Another year, Emmanuel gave Hannah and me a small, yellow, toy sewing machine. It had a wheel on the side that needed to be manually cranked in order to make the treadle go up and down. We used that machine for everything;

clothes for our dolls, curtains for our room, pillows and, eventually, our own clothes. Gideon gave me the most beautiful set of pajamas—the nicest I had. They were made of soft white cotton and had tiny purple flowers on them. If I had been allowed to spend a night at a friend's house, they would have been just right for eating late-night pizza or watching a television movie with a group of teenage girls. Deborah gave us a bag filled with a huge variety of fabric remnants.

It never embarrassed or shamed my parents that the overwhelming number of presents under the tree were addressed to Joram or Mama. While we were taught that the meaning of Christmas was not about materialism, that philosophy never translated into action. Our tradition was to watch as each present was opened, so the unwrapping of presents usually took many hours. Over and over again, we watched as Joram or Mama opened present after present. For Joram, all his Christmas wishes came to life; toy guns, GI Joes, games, cowboy hats, clothes, and books. Mama made out like a bandit; Papaji always hid some of the gifts he had brought from his trips and we watched as she unwrapped expensive silk sari after silk sari, French perfume and jewelry. Papaji had become somewhat of an expert on precious gems and delighted in presenting Mama with two or three lovely pieces of expensive jewelry.

Sometimes, I did wish for a pair of the newest style of shoes or fashionable clothing, but what I wanted most for Christmas was a pair of skates. The park next to our yard had been developed and had three skating rinks; a hockey rink, a practice rink, and a pleasure rink. The skating areas surrounded a small, heated warming house, which was always supervised by one of the more popular high school boys. A few winters Emmanuel and David had the job and made some extra pocket money. At dusk, the rinks were lit up and hockey players skated effortlessly, making loud gunshot sounds as their hard, black pucks hit the wooden walls. Hannah and I begged for ice skates, but year after year we were disappointed. To join in on the skating, we slipped around the ice on our boots. Sometimes we got lucky and joined a game of broomball which was meant to be played on the ice in boots. For Christmas of 1970, Deborah and Emmanuel combined the little money they had and bought us our own skates. They were white with red trim, had red and white polka-dot laces and, best of all, they were brand-new. We could hardly contain our happiness. Before long, we both were able to skate with ease, gliding along with the other skaters. The following Christmas all four of the Biggers pooled their resources and bought a wooden, six-foot toboggan. It was wrapped in paper and bore the tag, *"To the Three Stooges. With love, from the Biggers."* When I was older, I realized how unusual it was for teenagers to sacrifice so much for their younger siblings. I have never forgotten it.

The love and attention from the Biggers also lessened the sting of the lesson I was beginning to learn: Joram was special and more loved that I was. Papaji, Mama, and Joram went on vacations without the rest of us. When Joram was two, Mama wanted to introduce him to her family in India, and they accompanied Papaji on one of his trips in February. On that trip, like the others, the Biggers were left in charge and they made the days fun. I hardly felt left behind. Our pastor checked in occasionally, bringing casseroles or hot dishes, but for the most part the Biggers made our meals. Lunches were filling and delicious and we never walked back and forth to school during those bitter cold winters, but were driven, just like all the other kids. Miriam cooked dinner and Deborah made desserts—her famous and fantastic cream puffs. Even though he had moved out into his own apartment, Gideon came over to visit us. He made sumptuous meals, presenting the dishes with great panache and style. Table manners were relaxed. The Three Stooges bit our chapatis into little rounds and then added chicken curry on top and added another round chapati topper to make our version of hamburgers. When the regular chores were completed, we gave the floor an extra cleaning by throwing buckets of warm soapy suds on the floor and attaching scrub brushes to our feet and skating around, laughing and screaming with delight.

In the evenings, Emmanuel, true to his eventual calling of being a pastor, led our family Bible reading. This was different from Papaji's strict version, so the Three Stooges took this opportunity to goof off, laughing and passing notes. Emmanuel thundered when he saw we weren't paying attention and pounded his fist down on Hannah's blue hounds-tooth doll box, breaking it and causing Hannah to wail. Other days, we played games like Pass the Shoe, Prince of the Palace, or sometimes Miriam kept order by playfully whacking us on the head with a rolled-up newspaper. My older brothers and sisters never misused the family car, held a wild party, or stayed out late with their friends while my parents were gone. Instead, they took care of us and essentially, gave up opportunities to behave as teenagers.

We wrote letters to the three vacationing in India, enclosing a picture from Miriam's Kodak. Hannah still has the photo we sent. In it we are smiling and holding a sign that says, "We miss you Abbar!" our nickname for Joram which meant "strong" in Urdu. They went to India a few other times too. They also travelled to the Ozarks, Fuji, Europe, and Hawaii. But all the love and attention from the Biggers could not lessen the hurt I felt when I was left out of going to Florida. I tried hard not to cry and show my disappointment at being left out of a trip to Disney World. When they returned, Mama was filled with stories of how Joram had enjoyed the grand amusement park. Many times I heard and reheard Mama's story of his ride on Space Mountain.

To show how cute he looked, she would pull her mouth down into a mournful frown, blink her eyes, and express in a small baby voice, that Joram, after just getting off the roller coaster, with tears pooling in his eyes said, "I was just about to cry!" That particular story always turned my stomach.

I quickly learned to turn to Miriam for comfort and solace. The Three Stooges obeyed Miriam as we would a mother, calling her Didi which meant "Big sister." She scolded and disciplined us, loved and cared for us, and sacrificed for our happiness as a mother would do. I sought refuge with Miriam. When Gideon tried to force Hannah and me to participate in a dare, she would protect us. When we wanted to watch Rogers and Hammerstein's *Cinderella* instead of watching Vern Gagne and The Mad Dog Vachon wrestle, she marched with us and led our picket, even helping us make signs: *Down with Wrestling! We want Cinderella! Girls are the Greatest!* While our devotion to Miriam never bothered Mama, the relationship Miriam had with Papaji made Mama extremely jealous. Miriam and Papaji had always been close and so she was Mama's greatest competitor. Early on, Mama had not allowed Miriam to kiss Papaji good morning or good night as she had always done. When Miriam teasingly pinched Papaji's cheeks, Mama had admonished her and told her to stop it.

When Miriam married, it was a triumph for Mama, because Miriam had served as a stopgap or a watchman over the household. Gideon had never been much of a problem because he was a man and, because by the time Mama arrived, he had moved out. Emmanuel could have been a rival for Joram. But he was incredibly good, much older, a straight-A student, and Mama respected his brains. Deborah was easy to deal with because she had many friends and was labeled as someone who, "always is influenced by her friends." The word "friends" was made to seem almost as dirty as another F word— "fun." Deborah had dared to break our unspoken immigrant family code of silence and vented to a high school counselor about not being allowed to socialize with her friends. Papaji was strict and didn't want his girls to participate in after-school activities, sports, parties, dances, shopping, or anywhere with a possibility of encountering boys. The counselor had called our home and spoken to Papaji about his inability to be flexible.

"After all, Dr. Haqq, you aren't living back home. This is America and your daughter Deborah needs to be able to have a normal life," said the counselor.

"Oh, thank you for telling me I am no longer living in India. I didn't know," Papaji became sarcastic when his intelligence was questioned. Besides his PhD in Theology and Religions, Papaji had two master's degrees, one in Philosophy and the other in Persian. But Psychology and the workings of the human mind were his hobby. He had read just about every book on the subject. In our basement there were no less than 3,000 books on every subject from art to pop culture to zoology. Papaji did not just read books—he digested them.

"In my professional opinion, Deborah is experiencing a great amount of stress because she is trying to please you and still enjoy a normal life," the counselor said. "She is experiencing Acute Stress Disorder combined with Adjustment Disorder."

"Is that so? What you believe is very questionable, sir. I am not at all sure what sort of professional degree you have, but she does not have any of the symptoms of either one of those disorders," said Papaji.

The school counselor, who was used to throwing terms at easily impressed, small-town Minnesotans, was no match for Papaji. In a flash, he made mental mincemeat out of the puny counselor and shamed him into silence. Deborah was often reminded of her mistake of confiding in someone who was deemed to be of lower intelligence, and so far as Mama was concerned, Miriam was always a much greater threat than Deborah at diverting Papaji's attention and love.

Mama also did not like Miriam because Miriam did not allow acts of injustice to pass. In order to feed our large family, Mama made heavy, filling foods like rice and dahl, chicken tharkari with plenty of gravy, chana, aloo saag and chapati. Often we were told to, "fill in the cracks" by supplementing the meal with bread and butter. There were never seconds on meat—and the meat we were served was only the giblets. But for Joram, Mama washed all the spices off a fat leg or thigh before serving it to him with heavily buttered rice and his favorite pumpkin bread. He never ate a meal without the bread and it was strictly off-limits to the rest of us. Even though we were required to use good manners, Joram had atrocious table habits—squeezing his pumpkin bread into big, doughy, rust-colored balls and shoveling his food in great mouthfuls. We came to know the sound of Mama scraping the bottom of the pan with her metal spoon. It signaled that the meal was over and there was nothing more to serve. Miriam would always bristle at this because the noise was only a decoy. Mama always had seconds reserved for Joram. Miriam would angrily shake her head and transfer her own serving onto the plate of whoever had been denied seconds. To this day, Miriam cannot bear to hear the noise of a spoon scraping a kettle and grimaces anytime she hears it.

Miriam was also our champion because she confronted Mama about her practice of keeping separate dishes. Mama began keeping our plates, glasses, and utensils separate from the ones used by herself, Papaji, and Joram. At first, this happened because one of us was ill, but then after we were all healthy, the division remained. Mama also instituted the use of a separate sponge when washing "their" dishes. Many years later when I went back to

India, I came to understand how much this must have bothered Miriam. In India, the culture of servant and master/mistress is very much alive. In private homes, servants or laborers are not allowed to sit on furniture, use the family bathrooms, sit at the table, or eat and drink from the family utensils. Miriam remembered life in India. She knew that Mama's act of separating our cups and plates indicated something much more significant.

I never saw Miriam get in trouble except for one time. She was defending me because I had chosen to invite her to my school concert instead of Mama. My attendance at school events was not optional; it was mandatory. Mama never attended no matter how many times I pleaded. On a concert night, Hannah and I walked to the school, sang in the performance, and returned. It was embarrassing to be the only child who had no parental representation and I began lying and making up stories to save face. I finally gave up and invited Miriam to be my mother at a concert. That particular evening, I was so happy because instead of walking, I rode in the Volkswagen with Miriam and Emmanuel. Miriam wore a sari and sat with Emmanuel in the audience. Our class sang the Fifth Dimension's "Age of Aquarius" and "Up, Up with People." Afterwards, Emmanuel sputtered about the humanistic lyrics of our songs while we mixed with the other families. I was proud of them because they were both good- looking and my classmates thought they were my parents. I lied and said they were.

After we came home, I stayed outside and kept Emmanuel company as he plugged in his car for the night to keep the engine warm against the frigid Minnesota night. Nothing was said about the concert right then, but when Papaji returned home after his trip, Mama told him that I had disrespected her. Papaji was furious. Miriam, who never spoke back, especially to Papaji, responded angrily and received a stinging slap—he had never even spoken crossly to her before. When I went to console her, she held me close and cried, mumbling something about Papaji not even knowing what was best for his own child.

Separate vacations, separate dishes, separate food, separate lives, and separate love—it was a running theme in the house by now. As I grew older, I began to fight my own battles when I saw something unfair. I was often the mouthpiece for the Three Stooges because of my willingness to say what we all thought and pay the price for it. We learned quickly not to involve Papaji in our conflicts with Mama. Sometimes, I would forget and tell him about an injustice and he would step in. But when he left for yet another faraway place, I would be faced with weeks of separation without his presence. Mama punished me with silence and isolation for informing Papaji. For someone as verbal as I was, this was the worst punishment in the world. When Papaji was around, I actually enjoyed it if Mama wasn't speaking to me. When he was gone, it was another matter. Once, I told Papaji about Mama's laundry practices.

"I'm tired of having my clothes look and smell dirty!" I was crying and shouting. Hannah was sitting next to me.

"What are you talking about?" Papaji asked.

"She never uses soap in our clothes!"

"What?" Papaji leaned forward in his chair, his left eyebrow cocked.

"She only uses bleach sometimes," said Hannah.

"No, I don't think she would do that."

"It's true! And she won't touch our clothes, she uses a stick to put them in and take them out," I said. As was the case with the vacuum cleaner and dishwasher, we were not allowed to touch or operate any appliances. Using an old branch, Mama put our clothes in the washer and the dryer. She never touched them.

When they were dry, it was our responsibility to remove them from the dryer and fold them.

"Why would she do that?" Papaji seemed genuinely puzzled. "Hannah, is this true?" Hannah couldn't answer because by now she was crying as hard as I was.

"Our clothes aren't good enough to be washed with Joram's or yours or hers! She always does them separately," I said. *Was Papaji that clueless about Mama's behavior? Or maybe he just didn't want to know.*

"Huh. Well, I'll just see about this," Papaji left the room and went upstairs.

After a few minutes, Hannah and I dried our tears and put our ears to the master bedroom door. Within moments an argument began. Even when fighting, Mama didn't raise her voice but spoke in her usual, well-modulated, controlled manner. Papaji shouted and asked her about the laundry but we couldn't hear her responses. For a while after the incident, she added soap and we enjoyed clean, sweet-smelling clothes. She never used the fabric softener as she did with her own clothing, but I was just so happy to have the soap. She still used a stick to handle our laundry, though. A few weeks later, she went back to her old ways but not until I had endured three weeks of cold, hard silence. As was usually the case, I didn't have the strength to bring the issue up to Papaji again.

Hannah rarely answered back, even when she knew she was being told something wrong. Once when Mama asked Hannah to remove the clothes from the dryer, Hannah put her hand in the dryer and cut her hand. The inner drum had cracked and a sharp metal piece sliced her finger almost to the bone. She was bleeding profusely. Hannah went upstairs and tended to her own cut. The next day when Mama was doing her own laundry, she asked Hannah to put her hand in the dryer and locate the sharp object which had cut her so deeply the day before. For Hannah, it was at that moment when she realized that this woman who called herself mother had absolutely no regard for her well-being. She was so hurt by Mama's request the only answer she could give was, "I don't know." She gave up trying to win Mama over.

David learned of Mama's contempt in his own way. Our neighborhood had an annual tradition. Every year, South River Hills Day was a day designated to celebrate our community with garage sales, church rummage sales, bake sales, and car washes. David was obsessed with soccer and, even at a young age, was a gifted player. Emmanuel played soccer on the university intramural team and David was skilled enough to play with the older boys on Saturday games. He had joined the junior high cross-country team but had not tried out for soccer, because he did not own cleats. At a garage sale, he found a used pair for 50 cents. He ran home excited and out of breath. But when he asked Mama for the two quarters, she responded that she didn't have any money. I had never heard David plead. He usually was too proud and never wanted to give Mama the satisfaction of denying him something. But this time he begged for the money. Mama was unyielding. Since Papaji was out of town, David was unable to buy the cleats. Later on that same day, Joram saw a small toy he wanted at one of the garage sales. He grinned in delight as Mama paid a dollar for the item. We were so angry that we three cried privately behind the house and wrote "I hate Mama #2" on the exposed cement blocks. David seemed to physically deflate after the soccer shoe incident. It was painful to watch my carefree, lighthearted brother become sad and defeated.

We Three Stooges had long pleaded for bikes. We were told that our parents could not afford bikes and we learned to ride by borrowing our friends' bikes. When Joram was old enough, he was given a brand-new bike. It was red and white with matching streamers and a banana seat. He was too scared to ride his bike on his own and never ventured out of the cul-de-sac. None of us were allowed to touch his bike. David rode it just once and Mama punished him. The bike was just another marker in the long line of things that were denied to us, but not Joram. Bikes and soccer cleats only reminded us of how little we were cared for and how different our lives would have been if Mamaji was still alive.

The Three Stooges presented the biggest problem for Mama because we were the youngest and our stay in her house was to be the longest. In my view, David had it the worst. He had always been the apple of Papaji's eye. Hannah and I knew that Papaji preferred the company of males, and for us it was easier to absorb the fact that he had quickly become inaccessible to us and that his love and affection was mostly showered on Joram. But for David no such excuse existed. He had a habit of sitting on Papaji's lap while he reclined in his favorite Lazy Boy. The two would hold long conversations, laughing and enjoying each other's company. Even when he was almost a teenager, David still climbed into the Lazy Boy and shared the chair with Papaji. On one occasion, Mama came downstairs while David was sitting on Papaji's lap. She furrowed her brow and put her hands on her hips.

"David? Why are you sitting on his lap?"

Both David and Papaji looked surprised. "Madam, we're just talking," said Papaji. "Madam" was Papaji's name for Mama. They never used each other's first names. She called him "Raja," which meant king.

"I think it's absolutely ridiculous for a boy your age to be still sitting on his father's lap," Mama said. David looked uncomfortable. "Get down from there and don't ever let me see you sitting on his lap again. You're much too old for that."

David's mouth dropped open and he looked at Papaji. But Papaji only patted David's back, stood up and left the room. I cannot forget the look on David's face. He was completely devastated and it was as though he had lost his best friend. He never sat on Papaji's lap again.

✳✳✳

One summer a man came to visit our home. He spoke English with a British-Indian accent. He had horn-rimmed glasses and a friendly smile. He sat on the couch and discussed medicine with Mama. Miriam sat next to him. She wore a sari with a shifting green, blue, and turquoise pattern. I loved that sari. It looked as if the impressionist Monet might have painted cool green and blue water on the material. Occasionally, she giggled in a way I had never heard. The man joined us for dinner and then, afterwards, as we gathered for our usual family Bible reading, he stayed. Papaji talked for a long time about Adam and Eve and then the man put a ring on Miriam's finger. Then Papaji did a strange thing—he cried. I had never seen him cry before. It was then that I realized that this man was not going anywhere. I was certain he had just married my sister!

"What a stupid wedding," I said to Hannah. We were hiding under the dining room table. Papaji, Mama, and Joram had gone upstairs, Deborah and the boys were downstairs watching television, and Miriam and the man were sitting on the living-room couch talking.

"I know," said Hannah.

"We didn't even get to wear a nice dress or anything."

"I know," said Hannah.

"No flowers, no music. Nothing. We get cheated out of everything."

"I know," said Hannah.

Miriam noticed us and smiled, "Hannah and Elisheba? Come here. I want you to meet someone." We slid out from under the table. The man held out his hand to us and we shook it. "This is Richard. He's going to be your brother-in-law."

Richard smiled. "So you're not married?" I asked him.

"Not yet, but I'm looking forward to it," Richard said.

Maybe this Richard person would be good for something. At least we would get a fun wedding out of it.

Miriam began to plan her wedding to take place the next year. In the meantime, Gideon surprised us by announcing that he was engaged and introduced us to a girl named Colleen. They arrived at our house together, holding hands. Gideon had allowed his hair to grow long since moving out—something Papaji had never allowed. He wore new aviator glasses, a suit jacket, and shirt. He had left the buttons of his shirt open and wore a gold chain. Colleen was beautiful. She wore frosted lipstick, a big hairdo, and a dress that was well above her knees. They were to be married in a few months at our church. Colleen was a Catholic but had promised to become a good Methodist.

Gideon was the cool brother, Somehow even with all his financial and immigrant restrictions he managed to dress cool, drive cool, talk cool, and date cool. He dated American girls, grew his hair over his ears to his collar, planned to live in California, bought and played a guitar, and wore sunglasses. He had narrowly escaped being drafted and sent to Vietnam by enrolling in seminary at Bethel College. He was definitely voted the least-likely-to-ever-be-a-minister, but it was either fake it at seminary or run away to Canada, and my parents were not American enough for that. He was also a neat freak and despite David and Emmanuel's habits, he had kept the boy's room neat.

I had always been scared of Gideon. His idea of play and fun frightened me. He would organize terrifying, haunted houses in the basement. He played chicken with a hot, bare light bulb which David lost and still has the scar from the game on his stomach. Once Gideon wrapped a sheet around me like a diaper and laughed. Even though his games filled me with fear, they were always the most compelling and daring. I desperately wished to be more like David who had the courage to be an active participant. Both Gideon and Emmanuel were amazing artists, painting beautiful works in oil. Emmanuel painted landscapes and once gave Mama a picture of a graceful oak tree. When the gift was ignored, he eventually took it back after he got married and framed it for his own house. Gideon's subjects were never tranquil. One painting of his had a bright red background. The main subject was a close-up of the dry, white bones of a hand and wrist. Encircled around the wrist was a black shackle attached to a gray stone wall with a black chain. It was a masterful piece of art and it hung his room. While Gideon fascinated me, he also frightened me.

Weeks before Gideon and Colleen were to marry, Hannah and I carefully picked out our best Sunday dresses. I chose my peach dress and Hannah selected her ruffled yellow one. We resolved to "save" them and not wear them again until the wedding. Mama never asked or thought about what we would wear for our brother's wedding. Colleen's parents hosted a reception in their yard. I was fascinated by the ice cream which came shaped like a wedding bell.

In the summer of 1970, Miriam and Richard were married. It was a simple wedding, but was different from any other held at our Minneapolis church, because instead of wearing a wedding gown, Miriam chose to wear a beautiful white sari with gold threadwork. She wore a fingertip veil, white gloves, and an armful of gold and white glass bracelets. She also added one single red bangle, as red was traditional for Punjabi brides. She was the most beautiful bride I had ever seen. Richard wore a white tuxedo jacket and black pants. Deborah and Mary, who was Miriam's friend from college, wore matching green saris. In order to make them, Miriam had purchased six yards of light chiffon from Minnesota Fabrics and hemmed each piece. Then she and Deborah made the cholis—the matching short blouses worn with the sari.

Hannah and I were the most excited about our clothes. For the first time, we would be getting new dresses, without waiting for our birthdays or Christmas! Miriam bought the material and Mary made both the junior bridesmaid dresses which were empire-waist style. The bodice was made of green lace with bell sleeves and had a satin skirt to match. She also made green bows for our hair. As if that was not enough, Miriam also bought us new shoes. Hannah and I both had new patent leather, shiny white shoes, with a square one-inch heel. We had never had heels before and marveled at the clack-e-ty sound they made. Instead of wearing socks, we were given beautiful, opaque white hose. The other bridesmaids thought we should wear anklets but Miriam saw the look in our eyes and bought the hose instead. We all carried a bouquet of multicolored flowers. Joram was the ring bearer and wore a dark blue jacket and white pants. He was an adorable three-year-old with large green eyes. The wedding was officiated by Papaji and our pastor, Joe. Standing at the altar, watching Miriam and Richard exchange vows, I saw Papaji cry once more. Mama sat in the pew with Joram, dry-eyed in a sophisticated blue and pale-green silk sari, with sparkling sapphire jewelry.

The excitement of the wedding never prepared me for what was to happen after the short church reception. Miriam was going away. It never occurred to me that my roommate would be gone forever. I was devastated. I did not know who I would turn to when I needed help or got into trouble. It was as though I had lost another mother. Right then I decided that I did not like my new brother-in-law. When they returned after their short honeymoon, I refused to speak to him, angry that he had taken my sister from me. And even worse, Miriam was moving to England.

Miriam told me years later, that after she married, she had asked Papaji if David, Hannah, and I could live with them. She had hoped to provide love and a sense of continuity for us. My older sister and her new husband had offered to put their needs of privacy aside because of what they believed would be best for us. But Papaji did not agree to this arrangement. At times, I imagined how wonderful my life could have been living with Miriam and Richard, two people who I knew loved and cared for me. This thought drove me mad when I allowed myself to contemplate all the, "if only..." situations that could have been possible.

I could not even keep in touch with Miriam. Communication was through letters as trunk calls were expensive and reserved for emergencies. My letters remained unmailed because I had no money for postage stamps and Mama would not give me any. I was not allowed to use the sky-blue Air Mail Aerograms Mama used to write to her family, so Hannah and I began to scrounge for stamps on incoming mail. We noticed the post office often forgot to cancel stamps, or sometimes the ink on the seal was quite faint and we reused them. We gathered a multitude of used stamps and tried many methods to remove the ink; pink school erasers, hard, gray typewriter-ink erasers, and green ballpoint-ink erasers. In the end, we found that plain old saliva worked the best. Extremely careful, precise licking removed the ink without defacing the stamp. Hannah even started a stamp collection so we could browse incoming envelopes without arousing suspicion. Once, while we were furiously licking stamps, Emmanuel stood and watched us for a few minutes and then commented, "You know that's against the federal law, don't you?" It was the first time we had heard it said out loud. But his warning didn't stop us and we continued to reuse stamps until we were grown and left the house.

Miriam and Richard lived in the UK for a few years while he

completed his surgical training and then decided to move permanently to India. There they worked together in a rural mission hospital, Richard using his surgical skills to provide care for Indians who had few options for health care. Although I was proud of my Didi, I felt abandoned and alone.

Miriam's wedding day, Minneapolis, August 21, 1971
(Left to right Elisheba, Hannah, Deborah, Papaji, Joram, Mama, Miriam,
Richard, Emmanuel and David)

CHAPTER
EIGHT

B Y THE TIME I completed first grade, I had lost my Indian
accent and the scarlet thread in my ears had been replaced by
shiny gold hoops. I was the only girl in first grade who wore earrings. I settled into the school routine and was an expert reader
but always struggled with math. I consistently received an "E" for
Excellent in Reading and Spelling, an "S" for Satisfactory in Math
and Science, and an "N" for Needs Improvement in Self-Control.
I longed to improve my grade in Self-Control, but wasn't sure
which of my behaviors generated it. I suspect it might have had
something to do with my observation of a chubby girl named
Robin, who not only wore a dress short enough to show her white
cotton underpants, but the garment always evidenced her problem in controlling her bowels. I cheerfully reported the incident,
"Robin pooped her pants!" But my teacher, Miss Anderson, did
not find this amusing. Or maybe it was the stories I told when I
stood to share at Show and Tell. I never brought anything to show
but told grand lies of our pretend family vacations.

"This weekend my family went to Disney World."

Miss Anderson furrowed her brow and leaned forward, "Really?"

"Yes, my father has a RV and we rode the teacups, saw the living Lincoln, visited the Small World, and saw Cinderella's castle."

"You did that this past weekend? Isn't that a long trip to make in just two days?"

"It wasn't too long. And then we stopped at Mt. Rushmore on our way back," I said.

Miss Anderson pursed her lips and shook her head, "That's enough. Sit down."

Later on, I made friends with a girl named Becky, and along with Laura, we three became fast friends. I told them stories during recess under the dark stairwell in the basement of our school. I was the master storyteller. At first my friends questioned me about Mamaji and, as always, I embellished.

"What was it like when she died?" Becky asked.

"It was a dark and stormy night."

Laura's eyes grew wide, "Oh my god, sounds scary."

"I was all alone when it happened," I said. "She needed my help and so I called the ambulance, but she died before anyone could come."

"Wow, that's so brave!"

I also exaggerated the accounts Papaji gave us after he returned from his trips to India or other countries. My classmate's fathers worked at Honeywell, Cargill, Land O'Lakes, and Northwest Bank. Papaji traveled all over the world preaching at churches, open mass meetings, and lecturing at universities. Most of my classmates had never even heard of India. The teachers and adults at school repeatedly said that my family had come from "Africa, or Pakistan, or one of those countries." I was given carte blanche to say just about anything and it was accepted as the gospel truth. When Papaji told us that he had been asked to pray for a woman who was acting out as a result of her illness, I combined Papaji's story both with a Bible passage about a man with an impure spirit from the gospel of Mark and also from what a classmate who had been allowed to see *The Exorcist* had described.

"And then my dad, (I always used "mom" and "dad" while in school) saw that she was foaming at the mouth. And then she started shouting. First in her own voice and then in the voice of a man."

"Why?" Laura started to cry with fright.

"Because she was...DEMON-POSSESSED!" I shouted and lunged.

Becky and Laura screamed and held each other, "What happened after that?"

I was impressed with them. What courage and tenacity they had! "Well, she screamed and ripped her clothes. Then my dad told the demon in her head to go into this bunch of chickens."

"Oh my god!"

"All of a sudden the lady started shaking, and then she just fell on the ground. And then the chickens started going crazy and they all ran around and finally fell over a cliff and died."

"Oh the poor chickens!" Laura said.

"What happened to the lady?" Becky asked.

"She was fine. She got up and made dinner."

As my fame as a storyteller grew, so did my audience. Sometimes there were five or six girls listening to my tales. I never lacked material, because I freely drew from the stories of the Bible and changed the names and identifying details—David cuts off Goliath's head, Moses and Aaron cast the bloody waters of the Nile, Herod eaten alive by maggots, the stoning of Stephen. I focused on the ones with the goriest or frightening details, changing names and places and adding to them generously. Almost all the kids in school were Catholic and they left school early every

Wednesday for religion classes, but their knowledge of the Bible was nothing compared to mine.

It was clear that I was different and unlike any of my classmates but there were days in which I tried to find ways to conform—such as the time I tried to get the nickname "Liz" to stick, but I still stood out just because I looked different. Students with everyday faces and names; Daphne, Vicky, and Chris, brought out the worst in me. I was on edge, defensive and angry. Daphne took great pleasure in pointing out my worn clothes and hand-me-down shoes and asking me if I was poor. Vicky was well-liked by my teacher and her favorite names for me were Nigger and Blackie. In return, I hit her, punching, kicking, and biting. For some reason, my side of the story was never important and I spent many hours sitting in the cloakroom or with my desk isolated from the rest of the class. Years later, Vicky happened to be working with Hannah at a nursing home, and she had the gall to inform Hannah that I had once beat her to a pulp, conveniently leaving out the fact that she had called me nigger. When I saw her at my twentieth high school reunion, she smiled at me and said, "Hi Elisheba! Do you remember me? I'm Vicky. I married our class president." I walked past without acknowledging her, suddenly warm, my temples pounding, not trusting myself to speak.

Chris was a boy who lived in a green ranch house on our way to school and was known to be the toughest boy in school. Chris took any opportunity to insult me and Hannah, calling us Squaws, Niggers, and Black Hawks—no one could pronounce our last name correctly and kids taunted us by calling us "hawk." Papaji taught us to out-philosophize him.

"How can he call you black? You're not black, you're brown," said Papaji.

"Yeah, but he still calls us black," Hannah replied.

"Why don't you show him a black and brown crayon?" asked Papaji.

"What?" I was puzzled. Obviously Papaji didn't have to deal with the level of ignorance we did.

"Then it will be simple for him to see the difference and know that you are not black but brown," Papaji said.

The next time Chris began his jeering, I tried Papaji's high-level argument.

"Look, idiot. I'm not black, I'm brown. Don't you know the difference between the two?" I grabbed Hannah's hand and we turned our backs and kept walking.

"Huh?" Chris was clearly too slow for this type of reasoning. "Whadya talking about? You and your sister are nothin' but Nigger Squaws!"

I was through trying to reason with Chris and I turned around, punched him and then proceeded to give him a good old Black Hawk beating.

"I'm gonna tell!" Chris promised as he ran away crying, bloodied and bruised.

I felt no remorse, only a deep satisfaction knowing that I was able to defend both myself and Hannah. That evening Papaji received a phone call from Chris' mother and he repeated the conversation to us.

"Your daughter is out of control. She beat up my son today. His nose was bleeding and he has bruises all over."

"You need to question your son, and find out why my daughter had the need to defend herself," Papaji was always exceedingly polite but his words cut to the core. "His comments were rude and ignorant."

"I'm not sure who you people think you are. But we don't teach children to hit in this country. Your daughter beat up my son!"

"Well, Madam, if I were you, I would be more embarrassed that my daughter was able to overpower your son. Perhaps you should tell him to stop talking to my daughters. I will tell my children the same." He affectionately rubbed my head after he finished narrating the conversation, "*Beti*, we have to try and get along. Try to talk first, if you can."

I promised to do my best, but fighting Chris seemed to have had a positive effect. I had developed a reputation for being a hothead and, for the most part, Hannah and I were not bothered after that. But using my fists wasn't a long term defense and, eventually, I learned that sarcasm and humor were a much more acceptable response to ignorance and blatant racism. Laughing and jokes provided a way to cope with and make light of situations that could have been traumatic. I was grateful I had brothers and sisters at home who helped me develop my sense of humor and repartee to cope with the outside world and also the changes inside my house.

Even so, I was at a loss when it came to dealing with unjust adults. We had been taught to respect and submit to authority, so when teachers treated me unfairly, I did not know how to respond. When I defended myself from another classmate during class, Mr. Swanson picked me up off the ground and repeatedly banged my back and head against the classroom wall. He received the Teacher of the Year award, after I graduated high school. Miss Braun reminded me, "I don't know about where you came from, but in this country we behave civilly to each other, not like savages." She promptly removed all but one of my poems from the class creative writing booklet. Mr. Canna, who was a cool teacher with long hair, bell-bottoms and teardrop glasses, became enraged when he saw that Hannah had amended his name to "Mr. Canna-Banana" on my math workbook. Hannah had the affectionate nickname of "Hannah-Banana." He shouted at me in class, "Do you think this is funny? You people have strange ideas for a joke." Then he isolated my desk. My old friend Shirley turned on me when she caught me running in the hallways and made me crawl to my classes on my hands and knees for the rest of the school day. I was so angered by this betrayal; I slipped into her office and stole fifty cents from her purse, and for once enjoyed a delicious hot lunch. On Fish Wednesday, Laura gave me her Fish-Wish sandwich from the cafeteria to which she was allergic. Trading and sharing food was common and all the kids did it. I was mortified when the lunch lady appeared from behind the counter and snatched it out of my hand. She was a typical lunch lady, fat, dark horn-rimmed glasses with a hairy mole. I grew hot from embarrassment and loathing.

I was also different because my parents spoke English with a foreign accent. Mama wore saris and in my house Hindi was spoken. I was often asked to say certain words "In India." It was not until I was in junior high and high school that I grew weary of this microscopic-science-experiment conversation and responded with sarcastic remarks instead of the good manners I had been taught. The two most common translation questions were how to say their own name—which never made any sense to me, and how to say hello.

"How do you say 'Hello' in India?" a boy asked me. I had given up trying to explain I didn't speak India, because India was a country, not a language.

"*Salaam*," I said. Actually, the correct word was Namaste, but I had grown tired of trying to teach the correct pronunciation of that word. I tried a different tact. Instead of teaching him the traditional hello, I thought perhaps the word for "Peace" would be cooler and maybe easier to pronounce.

"Whaaa? Sarong?" the boy asked.

I thought of another approach, "It's sorta like salami. Just don't say 'ee' at the end. Just say, *Salaam*."

"Huh? You guys say Salami for hello? I don't get it."

"No, no. It just *sounds* like salami. Not really just salami—*Salaam, Salaam!*" Clearly, I was dealing with an idiot.

"Oh, okay, so I'd say, 'Slama, right?" the boy said.

I gave up, "Naw, not Slama. You know what? Instead of saying *Salaam*, you can just say Bologna. Most people just say Bologna anyway."

That answer seemed to make sense to him and thereafter whenever he saw Hannah or me, he waved happily and said, "Hey, Bologna, you guys!"

My sense of humor and storytelling skills earned me a number of friends, but I could not maintain normal social relationships. Friendship meant social outings, sleepovers, home-cooked dinners, and welcoming mothers. All of these were either forbidden, nonexistent, or taboo in my house. Close friendships caused anxiety because it would mean I had to work around my great constraints or I had to mask them. Emmanuel had a friend he invited over now and then. He was tall, thin, and had a pockmarked face which prompted the Three Stooges to nickname him Liverwurst. There were others as well; some from Youth Group and others from the University. But for the most part Emmanuel's friends were not encouraged to spend time at our house and he met them elsewhere. Deborah had a high school friend named Jean who stayed a close friend well into her adult life. Jean was willing to put up with all the ins and outs of Deborah's social life.

I made friendships with great angst. Mama did not allow any friends inside the house and I could only entertain them in the yard. I could not go over to their homes and offering them any kind of food or drink was strictly off-limits. David was able to have a few friendships because he spent time with Emmanuel or completely on his own. Hannah and I carefully carved out time with our friends at school. My friendships were largely one-on-one as it was easier to manage just one person at a time. I dreamed of being comfortable enough to have a group of friends who could come over and eat and laugh and talk *inside* my house. When Papaji and Mama went out we sometimes snuck our friends over. Once I had Laura over to the house to watch *The Wonderful World of Disney*. I was so embarrassed because the only food available was Shoppers City white bread and Indian food. How I longed for a bag of all-American barbeque chips or a soda to magically appear! Deborah saved the day and shared a can of Tab she had bought with her own money. Basic socialization was a complication that would become even more complicated as we grew older.

I remember a day when Joram had a friend come by for a visit. With our friends, Mama's absence, open disdain or even an outright removal was embarrassing and we avoided introducing them at any cost. With Joram's solitary friend, Mama was all smiles. She came downstairs not in her usual housecoat but dressed in normal clothes and wearing lipstick. She baked cookies and made pizza from a box kit. She spoke to Joram and his short-lived friend in a tone completely unfamiliar to me—oozing with charm. She fretted and fussed over the friend so much she must spooked the boy, because we never saw him again.

Papaji was not a huge advocate of friendships outside the family. The people he considered closest were limited to a brother and one work relationship. While Mama socialized superficially now and then with the neighborhood ladies, Papaji's closest adult relationship was with his brother, my Peter Chacha, who lived about forty minutes away.

We lived next door to the nicest all-American neighbors in the world, the Lenertz, for over 20 years. Their house and yard looked like the cover of *Better Homes and Gardens*. I often wondered what they must have thought about the comings and goings in our house. One terrible summer day, Mr. Lenertz had a terrible accident while waterskiing and broke his hip. Mama, who still filled in for vacationing surgeons now and then, was able to offer helpful advice during the recovery process. The incident brought our families together, but the adults still never became close friends. Though they invited us for cookouts or other social gatherings, we never shared one meal together as families.

When we first moved to Burnsville, Papaji and Mama occasionally had visitors to the house. Sometimes they held Bible studies, had friends over for dinner, or hosted visitors from India. Mama usually made a boring American company dinner—roast chicken or meat, boiled peas or corn, and mashed potatoes. The guests ate on the formal dining table which had been set with one of Mamaji's fine bone-china sets which she had brought over from our Chandigarh house. We never were allowed to touch any of this china. Since Mamaji had enjoyed entertaining, she had acquired some exquisite china. As with all of Mamaji's belongings, the china was now in Mama's possession and she only used it for company.

When guests came, the only interaction the Three Stooges had with them, was when we politely went up to say hello and goodbye. Other than that, we were not allowed to venture one toe into the upper sanctum and for the remainder of the visit; we were banished to the basement. Mama rarely came downstairs because the basement was cold and dark. Since we preferred Indian cuisine, the bland, colorless company menu was difficult to swallow. To amuse ourselves, we disposed of the meal by waging huge food fights. We loved our time alone in the basement.

But soon the visitors coming to the house dwindled as did my parent's relationships with others outside the family. We still had family visits as Peter Chacha and Maureen Chachi visited regularly. One summer, Papaji's father, my Dadha, came to visit from India. He was an amazing man and I could not take my eyes off his pure white hair, beard, and mustache. He had strong, classic features and best of all he always wore a long black Nehru-styled achkan over cotton, white salwar bottoms. Papaji and Dadha spent hours in deep discussion. They argued and compared notes on the Bible, Islam, politics, science, and theology. Dadha told us stories of his incredible and often dangerous life in India. He told us of the time he had been beaten and left for dead and how he survived being poisoned with strychnine when his former friends learned he had converted from Islam to Christianity. It was better than any movie, and he used beautiful poetic Urdu words. Every day he walked around the neighborhood for two or three miles. He was already 88 years old but he walked like a young man, his pace quick and his steps sure. His presence was so big that I couldn't help but be a little frightened of him. I was in constant awe of my remarkable Dadha. He lived in our Chandigarh house for many years and died there in 1980 of a sudden heart attack. He was 92 years old. I always regretted that I had not been old enough to know my grandfather better and spend more time with him. Papaji was heartsick over the loss of Dadha. While he had always loved his eldest son, Dadha had never quite approved of Papaji. All his life Papaji wanted his father to be proud of him and show him he loved him. While Dadha always spoke proudly about Papaji's life and accomplishments to others, he never directly expressed his feelings to his son.

By the time I was in my teens, my parents entertained no one. My socialization was limited mostly to our immediate family gatherings and outings. Papaji loved going on picnics. He packed the fishing rods and we all crammed into the light-blue station wagon. It was a great memory, because we Three Stooges always sat in the rear-facing, third seat of our station wagon. We waved and smiled at the drivers of other cars and we all sang Punjabi songs or Gospel songs together. Papaji always enjoyed this and he always sang along with us and became his long-ago self, jolly and just so happy to be with his huge family. On picnic days, Mama made her special spicy picnic chicken, egg salad sandwiches and shikanjvi—a mixture of ice water, lime juice, sugar, and salt. It was refreshingly cool and I loved squeezing the plump pulp between my roof and mouth, enjoying the quick burst of tart lime. For dessert there was a huge whole watermelon cut with a giant butcher knife. My favorite part of the day was eating huge chunks of watermelon, spitting seeds into the lake with juice dripping down my mouth and wrists.

I remember one particular picnic. Mama looked especially nice that day, sitting gracefully, her dark hair swept up and the folds of her sari spread around her. She wore a light-pink silk sari. We never sat in the sun like the other families but always in the shade of one of the huge trees. Papaji and the boys fished nearby and since he did not allow the girls to wear shorts, we rolled up our pants to mid-calf and cooled our feet as the small waves slapped against the sandy shoreline with their lazy *plup*, *plup*, *plup*. The algae-green waters sparkled jade in the sun-lit areas and pine green in the shady ones.

Around the lake, families were littered all over the thick emerald sod. Couples giggled as they made out on blankets or girls in bikinis and shirtless boys with their gleaming, slick torsos passed by. Since Papaji and Mama were with us, we tried not to stare at all the skin on display and blushed at the debauchery. As much as we were fascinated by such open displays, we knew it was respectful to turn away, as we did when we accidently witnessed "deep kissing" on television. A family was picnicking nearby, and the mother and father were busy snapping pictures of their sturdy blond-haired children. They looked up and noticed our family.

"Oh look, some people from...oh, they look nice," said the woman.

"That lady is wearing one of those sah-rah-pee things," said the man, pointing at Mama. "Maybe they wouldn't mind just one picture."

"Should we ask them? Would they understand English?" asked the woman.

The conversation was loud and carried easily across the grass. It was as if we were invisible. Their open discussion of my family made me feel as though I was being viewed under a microscope.

"Excuse me, I don't mean to bother you, but are you from Pakistan?" the man asked.

"Yes," Papaji replied courteously. "Well, actually we are from India, not Pakistan."

"Yeah, well, same thing. I just love your sarong, it's so beautiful," the woman fingered the light material.

"Thank you," Mama replied, without correcting her.

"Actually it's called a SARI," I added loudly.

"Elisheba, mind your manners."

"Wow! You speak English so good!"

"*But you don't,*" David said under his breath.

"My wife and I were wondering, well ah, could we please get a picture of you and your family? We've never seen a family that is, um, that is not...well, a family that is foreign."

"We've also never seen a sah-rah-pee before," added the woman.

"Certainly, certainly. Children? Come, stand close and smile for the picture," Papaji motioned and directed us into place in the bright sunshine.

The man pointed at Mama, "Could you take that cloth away from your head? I can't see your face."

I scowled as I reluctantly rose to my feet and walked slowly next to Mama, grumbling under my breath. I imagined how that picture would turn out; my parents standing tall, smiling so proudly, Joram playing next to them, perhaps Hannah smiling a weak, pleading smile alongside my dark scowl. When we got home that day, I noticed there was a tan line where the edge of Mama's blouse met her neck. She was always so careful not to let her skin tan but the incident at the lake had left a mark.

Dadha
Chandigarh, India, 1980

CHAPTER
NINE

U NTIL I LEFT the house as an adult, watching television was a treat and something I did only with permission. With each departing Bigger, the household rules became increasingly stricter for the Three Stooges but not for Joram. He was allowed free reign over the television. I envied the way he nonchalantly walked over to the TV set and snapped it on. On Sundays, we still asked, "May we turn on Walt Disney?" before watching our one-hour weekly allotment. Most of the time Joram watched television in the master bedroom which he shared with Papaji and Mama. But sometimes he turned on *Sesame Street* or *The Electric Company* in the basement and we were allowed to watch it with him. Even when David, Hannah, and I were all in our teens, the only television we watched "legally" was of Joram's choosing. I was most angered, not because TV was restricted but because it showcased and openly displayed such frank injustice.

But the strict rules for television didn't stop us from keeping up with our friends' conversations about television shows at school. On many weekends, Papaji, Mama, and Joram went out for the whole day. After their departure, the Three Stooges finished our assigned chores and then settled in to watch television. Hannah took her place at the kitchen window and watched television from the open basement door. If David and I heard the basement door slam, we knew that was Hannah's signal that the car was coming up the road. In a flash, the TV was turned off; David ran to his room in the basement and Hannah and I climbed two sets of stairs two at a time and were lounging and innocently reading before the station wagon even pulled into the garage.

Other times, when the three left the house for one of their marathon all-day-long shopping excursions, we would pick the lock on the master bedroom door. Like a well-oiled team, David or I expertly picked the lock and began to scrounge in their room, eating forbidden fruits, cashews, sweets, and taking swigs from open cans of 7Up and Tab. We went through Mama's drawers, pocketing quarters and dimes from the huge piles of coins she stashed. I tried on lipstick and eye shadow while David stretched out and watched television. Mama had a huge problem with David's feet—he was a casual washer and he often didn't bother to spend time cleaning his feet. I remember once watching with great satisfaction as David tromped barefooted over a pile of Mama's expensive silk saris, giggling and grinding his feet into the soft material. Hannah was always the responsible one and kept watch in case of an unexpected return, so we shared our treasures with her.

Most of the time we used the stolen money to buy frozen pizza from the nearby Tom Thumb convenience store. Mama only made pizza for Joram, so we always craved it. The ladies behind the counter knew us and jokingly called us "The Pizza Girls" because Hannah and I bought frozen pizza so often. We stored the pizza under piles of frozen meat and vegetables in the freezer and heated it up when we were on our own.

One Sunday, I noticed an extra-large pizza in our church freezer. I was elated and stuck the vacuum-packed pizza under my coat. Later on that day, Mama found out I had stolen the pizza. "How could you steal from church?" She had real tears in her eyes. It was the only time I ever saw her cry. I was with her when she received news that her beloved father had died and also when her mother died—she never shed a tear. But for the pizza I saw huge tears in her eyes.

"I don't know," I mumbled. I was more embarrassed at being caught. Stealing from the church freezer didn't bother me.

"How could you do that? I'm so ashamed. You have to return it."

"I'm sorry. I'll put it back," I put on my saddest and most contrite face, then I went outside and put the pizza on top of the garbage can. When I came back in, Mama shook her head mournfully, wiped her tears and went upstairs.

"Are you really going to throw it away?" Hannah asked.

"Naw! You crazy? Let's eat!" I grabbed the pizza, unwrapped it, and threw it in the hot oven. Hannah and I grinned while gorging on the cheesy goodness. It was an extra deluxe pizza and was absolutely delicious.

Because we were restricted from participating in what were normal everyday activities—watching TV, listening to records, going out with friends; we found other ways to pass our free time. I fondly remember so many games and jokes that took imagination and summoning of all available resources to execute. As grown adults, we laugh at our old antics and take delight in the many ways we entertained ourselves. Most of the time, we didn't know what we were missing because we took pleasure in the challenge of making do with what we had while enjoying our jokes until our stomachs hurt.

For years I had longed for a Barbie and when I finally got

a real Barbie, Hannah and I constructed our own houses using Kleenex boxes for beds, plumbing washers for jewelry boxes, and cardboard cartons for rooms. We made "triangle" dresses for our dolls, using a method Rashida Chachi had taught us—folding a cloth over, cutting a hole for the neck and sewing the seams on the side. Hannah was so creative that she even found a live pet for our penthouse. She caught a fat, overfed fly and removed its wings. Then the fly was allowed to freely roam around our Barbie house. Hannah declared proudly, "Look! My Barbie has a cat!" I was amazed at her ingenuity, and every time we played Barbie, we obtained a fresh cat. Eventually, David presented Barbie with her very own Rottweiler which was a large gray moth with amputated wings.

We played Tasters Choice, a game whose title came from Mama's jar of instant coffee. The Taster closed his eyes, grabbed a random ingredient, combined it with a few other blindly selected ones and was compelled to create an interesting snack. The other two players were required to eat whatever was created. David always created horrible concoctions combining hot, sour Indian mango pickle with hard raisins, syrup, and tuna. Hannah was deemed the worst player because she somehow managed to find all the stale ingredients.

Sometimes the game was Rich Man, Poor Man. It drew generously from the story of the Rich Man and Lazarus from the Bible. We acted out all the gory details—eating crumbs from a table, boils and dogs licking sores, the fire of Hades, the torment of eternal thirst, and the booming voice of Abraham from the sky. The rich man ate a diet which consisted of leftover chapatis. Eventually, the game ended when David as the rich man, acquired all our possessions. Then David whooped, pounding his chest and Hannah became exasperated at the dark, defeated Nietzsche-like nature of the game, and shouted, "I'm not playing!" There was

Tuti Man, a game that blended the Hindi noun for excrement with English, and we avoided the imaginary filth as we jumped from couch to couch avoiding touching the floor. David had the best ideas and as the leader of the Three Stooges he played the mad scientist in a game called Licked-a Formula. Different jars and bottles were filled with oil, milk, tea, or any other liquid he could find and then mixed together to formulate a new drink, which of course was forced down the gullet of a reluctant Hannah or Elisheba.

Sometimes we laughed and examined the juxtaposition of two cultures; poking fun of the stupid questions we were asked over and over, "Did you used to have a tiger as a pet? Do you guys have hookahs filled with weed?" or, "Are those people part of your culture?" and, "Did you guys used to live in a hut?" Once, a classmate unfamiliar with non-Midwestern accents called my house. After Mama called me to the phone, my friend asked, "Wow, was that your British maid?" At times our entertainment arose from Papaji as he contended with a culture he was convinced was determined to ruin us. Our teachers at school were uneducated on strategies that respected differences in global cultures and Papaji found their attempts to westernize us objectionable.

In the mid 70s, the flower-child culture was everywhere and it had an effect on my academics as well. The arrival of brand-new, hippie college graduates as teachers resulted in some drastic changes. They wore jeans or bell-bottoms to school and used phrases like, "Far Out!" or, "Hey, Peace Man." This absolutely enraged Papaji, as he took education seriously and did not allow us to even wear jeans to school. The rigid, three A's curriculum was replaced with a much more free, learn-at-your-own-pace and learn-what-you-feel type of program. Every Friday was deemed as "Friday Activities." Instead of traditional learning, the entire day was devoted to unstructured, open learning of our own choosing designed to develop our creative sides such as wood carving, tie-dye, macramé, weaving, guitar lessons, or pottery. Friday Activities was not lost on Papaji who already thought our school's academic standards were compromised and had a dreadfully low opinion of our teachers. Often, we took advantage of his views and begged Papaji to let us stay home with him. He barely needed persuading and said, "No problem, stay home. What could you possibly learn from those third-rate teachers?"

One of the teachers, Ms. Kamoff, decided to offer Social Dancing not as a Friday Activity but in place of our usual gym class. Papaji did not allow dancing and most certainly did not want me to dance with a boy. When he read the notice she had sent home, he refused to permit me to participate.

"What is this *bakwaas*? This crazy *besharam* hippie woman wants to dance socially."

"It's Social Dancing, Papaji," I corrected.

"Social-Pocial, she has no right to mix her own values with ours. No daughter of mine is going to learn to dance with boys. Is this a school or is this a pick-up bar?"

"It's nothing," I protested.

"Be quiet, what do you know? Soon you will be like those other American girls, running after boys, all that hugging-shmugging, taking your mind off studies," Papaji turned to address Mama. "You know? That woman has these children addressing her using her good name? And she uses that *paagal* 'Miz' in front of her name to show she is oh, so liberated. They try and teach us about liberation, while we Indians have already elected a woman as prime minister! What is this duffer trying to teach us about women's rights? What nonsense! All this *bewakoof* dance business."

Instead of dancing with boys, while the rest of the class was in the gym, Ms. Kamoff decided that I should write an in-school essay on the evolution of dance in America.

✳✳✳

A typical weekend for me comprised of homework, Saturday cleaning, chores, and church. Every Saturday, we cleaned the house from top to bottom. Emmanuel scrubbed the downstairs half bathroom, and he and David tidied their room. But the rest of the house was left for the girls to clean. Mama straightened only her room since it was off-limits to us. I hated Saturdays and grew to hate them even more when Miriam and Deborah left the house.

The Saturday cleanings I remember the most was during the time when Hannah and I had become the sole domestics. In all the time I lived in the house, Joram was never required to do chores. And the weekend cleaning was in addition to the daily chores that we were responsible for—washing and drying stacks of dishes, scouring pots and pans, wiping tables and countertops, and sweeping at the end of the day. For Saturday cleaning we rose early in the morning and took turns each week with either the upstairs or downstairs. The upstairs included our rooms, the long hallway filled with rows and rows of Papaji's and Mama's chappals and Joram's shoes, the upstairs bathroom, the stairs, the living room and dining room. The downstairs consisted of the half bathroom, the enormous kitchen and eat-in kitchen area, the stairs to the basement, and the basement. We were not allowed to use the vacuum cleaner because Mama was afraid we would break it, so the carpets had to be swept with a broom. Saturday cleaning also included other chores—gardening, mowing the grass, shoveling snow, organizing the garage, and the ever-present, forever-chore of preparing for cooking and then cleaning up after eating.

Hannah and I called the preamble to Mama's cooking, "Prepare Ye the Way." Mama cooked simply, and our job was to prepare the entire mise en place for each dish, so she could easily combine the ingredients into the pot, just like a TV chef. We cut mounds of onions and vegetables, finely diced large piles of fresh garlic and ginger root. Our knife skills, even at a young age were stellar. Mama would warn us, "*Acche bārīkī se katnā!*" She wanted nothing but the finest dice possible, forcing us to chop and chop the garlic and ginger until it was almost a paste. On a good day, Prepare Ye the Way could take anywhere from two to three hours. On a day when the Chachas were expected, three to five hours in the kitchen was common. When I had my own home and made Indian food, I learned how ridiculous this practice had been. I was able to chop the onions in seconds using a food processor, a gadget Mama had but never bothered to use. I could make the garlic and ginger into a paste in moments using a blender, which was another appliance Mama hoarded but never used. She made it harder for us on purpose.

Saturday Cleaning would end with the weekly allotted shower and hair wash. My hair was so long and thick that it took an entire day to dry. It was the one day in the week I was allowed to wear my hair loose in a low ponytail without any braids.

For about four or five summers, every Saturday Cleaning and Prepare Ye the Way took on an added dimension because Papaji took up fishing. At five on Saturday mornings, Papaji, Emmanuel and David, would join Papaji's assistant and friend Walter for a day of fishing. Walter and his wife were one of the few family friends we had. They had children the same age as Emmanuel, Deborah, and David. Walter was an expert fisherman and handyman, two things at which Papaji longed to become adept. Fish Saturday would end at dusk. With the extended summer light, this could be as late as eight or eight-thirty. By the time they reached home it was close to ten.

When the dark-blue Mercury pulled into the driveway, Papaji would triumphantly open the trunk which would be filled with no less than 20 to 30 huge walleye, lake trout, and northern pike. As each fish looked at us girls with its bleary eyes, we sighed—it would be a long night. The freshly cleaned house was no match for the mess those fish would make. In the first phase of Fish Saturdays, Papaji would begin cleaning the fish in the kitchen. Guts, blood, and scales would splatter the freshly cleaned walls and countertops. We tried to contain the mess, but before long the kitchen was filled with the smells and waste from the fish.

After gutting the fish, Papaji and the boys left to shower and the second phase began. Walter, who hated Indian food, took his thin fillets and headed home. We thoroughly cleaned the kitchen for the second time that day. Then the third phase began with Prepare Ye the Way as we readied for an elaborate Indian meal featuring what else but fish curry and chapatis. After the heavy meal was over, Mama went upstairs. The final phase of Fish Saturdays commenced—the cleaning up after eating. To cook Indian food lots of pots and pans had to be used. Huge kettles had to be scoured. Soiled plates, glasses, side plates, and cooking utensils filled the sink. We were not allowed to use the dishwasher. Mama used it as a storage compartment so each dish had to be washed and dried by hand. Then the table and countertop had to be cleaned. Rolling chapatis left hardened bits of dough all over the countertops and the stuck pieces had to be scraped off. By the time the last dish was put away, and the dish towels were hung to dry, it was usually 2 or 3 AM. The last chore on Fish Saturdays was our trip outside in the dark, carrying the guts and bones from the raw fish. Initially, we had left the remains to decompose in the garbage cans and this had produced a putrid smell and clouds of flies. So, Hannah and I were sent to dig holes in the dirt and bury the smelly mess. In less than ten hours, the whole cooking and cleaning process would begin again. I learned to hate chapatis and fishing.

Hannah and I also had to clean up after Joram's messes and hobbies on Saturdays. Joram read everything he could about nature and watched every National Geographic program that was aired. I always believed that when he married, he could only marry a grizzly bear, because his idea of a romantic trip was camping and living off the trail. For as long as I could remember, we had longed for a pet but had never been able to convince Mama of this. Long ago, in Chandigarh, our family had a black German shepherd named Jet, but the only pet I got was left over from science class—a dusty meal worm burrowing in an old jelly jar filled with oatmeal. Joram was scared silly of even medium sized dogs, so when he asked for a pet, he was granted a huge fish tank filled with horrible, sour-smelling orange and blue fish, Siamese fighting fish, and a white bird cage that contained an ugly yellow-green parakeet. It was part of our responsibilities to clean up after his pets.

While I was used to cleaning, it was so much more than just dealing with the fish excrement, bird droppings, or scouring toilets that bothered me; it was the way the chores made me feel. Hannah and I were nothing more than servants. It was not enough that we literally were being worked like hired hands but, in addition, we were given jobs that were demeaning and were created to conquer and subjugate us. Not only did we clean up after human waste and filth but now it also included Joram's animals. It was no wonder that his pets didn't bring any kind of pleasure into my life. That bird became the apple of their eyes. The harmonious tone Mama used when she spoke to that stupid bird was one I had never heard before. In the morning, she gently uncovered the cage and then dripping with honey, sweetly wished it, "Good morning! How did you sleep last night?" The nicest greeting I ever got from her was a curt, "good morning" without even meeting my eyes. She allowed the bird to fly inside the kitchen and even let it sit on her shoulder. I knew it was wrong to compare myself to a bird but I couldn't help wonder how something as insignificant as a parakeet could garner so much affection when I could barely muster a quick nod now and then.

"Let's call her Joy," Mama said.

"How about Snotnose?" I asked.

Mama glared at me while Joram smoothed Snotnose's ruffled feathers as they both cooed to the bird and then put it in the cage.

Papaji also had many messy hobbies. The problem was that while he thought he was a great handyman, his projects usually never worked out the way he intended. I learned all the Don'ts of painting from Papaji. His idea of choosing a paint color was limited to the cans of "Oops" paint sold at a huge discount at Menards or Plywood Minnesota. The only requirement was that he had to find enough of one color to paint whatever room he was looking to destroy. One Saturday he decided that our huge kitchen needed a paint job. Without telling anyone Papaji slipped out early to Menards and came back with rollers, brushes, paint, and masking tape. We could never reuse any painting supplies because after each paint job, they forever vanished into the Bermuda Triangle of the garage.

Hannah and I woke to a loud call of, "*Oye, Kurie!* Come down!" from Papaji. By the time we reached downstairs, just minutes later, Papaji, clad in a wifebeater and cotton boxers, had already begun rolling paint randomly in the middle of the kitchen wall.

Hannah and I looked at him in dismay and our cries of, "Wait!" and "Just let us cover the floor!" or, "Give us five minutes to tape first!" fell on deaf ears.

He painted madly, spattering paint all over, covering moldings, and dripping on the floor. When he came to the light switches, the phone, or even our doors, as we quickly tried to tape the woodwork, he just simply painted right over and moved on. Hannah and I frantically followed behind, still in our pj's, trying to wipe off as much of the paint as we could. While I was bending to clean the floor, he rolled paint high on the wall and gobs of paint dripped on my head. "Oh!" was all he said without breaking his stride. Even worse was that the paint was the ugliest shade of pale mint-green and clashed horribly with everything. After covering the walls, he dropped the roller and brushes, looked around satisfactorily, and walked up to shower and dress. It took the remainder of that day to clean all the painting splotches and splashes and then finally complete the regular Saturday Cleaning.

I never really minded cleaning up after Papaji. While he was messy and disorganized, he never intentionally made more work for us. There were days when he even helped me out, in particular when it came to outside chores. I never minded the extra work when he was close by. When he dropped paint, he was like an absent-minded professor, bumbling through a chore that required a skillset he did not have. His messes were annoying and required hours of work but usually brought me amusement rather than angry tears. I couldn't help laughing when he brought home an electric vegetable chopper and diced his way through mounds of carrots and onions. Then, without waiting for that mess to be cleared away, he went outside and grunting and pulling, David and he carried the entire lawn mower into the kitchen. Papaji turned it over and grabbed the butcher knife that was being used to cut chicken. Then he lay down on the kitchen floor and began chipping off years of caked-on grass and dirt which clung to the mower's blades. The mess was fantastic. Hannah and I looked at the disaster and shook our heads—annoyed but not crushed.

Working in the kitchen was a dream job compared to yard

work. Our acre lot was almost all grass. Mowing the lawn was a task that took David three hours. Once, during the Fourth of July holiday, the garbage man skipped the usual pickup. Instead of the normal ten bags of grass clippings, there were twenty. It had been a wet and soggy two weeks and the mulch inside the bags had already begun to decompose. When it came time to move them to the end of the driveway for pick up, each bag moist with noxious gases split open, spilling its contents. David, Hannah, and I gagged at the foul, black ooze and then began to laugh. Joram came out, turned green and vomited all over the gooey mess. We leaned on the house for support, holding our stomachs, our eyes tearing from the stench, all the while gasping for air through our hysteria. Papaji came out to see what the commotion was, pointed and sternly told us, "Bag that smelly!" This caused us to dissolve even further into breathless, boneless laughter. When David moved out, only Hannah and I were left to contend with the yard work. We continued all the inside chores and the heavy outside work on our own, including the mowing and snow shoveling, until we left the house.

After the Saturday chores, going to church the next day was always something to which I looked forward. Soon after our move to Burnsville, our family decided to attend Emmanuel Methodist church in Minneapolis. We teased Emmanuel about having the church named after him, we all pointed at him while singing, "O Come, O Come, Emmanuel! Rejoice, Rejoice Emmanuel!" Despite being an ordained Methodist minister, Papaji did not have his own church as he was employed full time as an itinerant evangelist. Mostly, we went to church on our own either because Papaji was traveling, Joram was sleeping, or Mama had a migraine. In Emmanuel's green Volkswagen, Miriam sat in the front, Deborah and David in the back, with Hannah and I perched on their laps. All six of us squeezed into the tiny VW bug. Occasionally, even Deborah's friend Jean squeezed in. When we reached, it was as though a clown car had stopped in front of the church.

Our church was a warm, inviting place. I learned all about Swedish traditions. Many Sundays we had a potluck and we tasted regional specialties. Christmas was magical and our church hosted the crowning of the new St. Lucia ceremony. In the spring, the Lenten services were moving and cumulated in a triumphant Easter morning; we all stood as the choir sang Handel's "Hallelujah" chorus from *Messiah*. During summer, we participated in Vacation Bible School and all-church picnic and we attended camp at Red Rock when Papaji was the featured speaker for the week. We made many lifelong friends—all of them mistakenly thought our family was from a storybook. Pastor Joe was so enthralled with Papaji that after he retired as pastor, he wrote a biography on Papaji's life.

A typical day at Emmanuel Methodist started with Sunday school. We gathered for our singing time and then split into classes. All the girls, myself included, had a crush on David's friend, Bruce Johnson. I never knew how to talk to him like the other girls did. Once, when he pointed at the leather mini pocketbook, Papaji had given me from India and said, "Do you call that a purse?" I swung it, hit him in the stomach and said, "Does it feel like a purse?" David laughed and told me I should have kicked him as well. I was shy and awkward with boys because I was afraid Papaji would find out and thunder at me for flirting. We were given points for memorizing Bible verses. We were always far ahead of any of the children since Bible memorization was a part of family devotions. Mamaji had begun this practice long ago in India.

Hannah and I devised all sorts of ways to entertain ourselves during the long church service which followed Sunday school.

Since were known as PKs (Preacher's Kids), the pressure to behave and present a perfect family picture was intense. Every Sunday we were given a comic-style Sunday school paper called *Pix*, which illustrated a Bible story and a modern-day Christian story. We saved *Pix* and read it during the sermon. Sometimes, we snuck out to the Little General Store behind the church and bought a nickel package of apple Now & Later or a Jolly Rancher Fire Stix. We cut the candy into small squares to make it last longer. When there was no nickel, Hannah and I rubbed our fingers in a cut lemon before leaving the house and waved them to dry. Then, during the sermon, we slowly licked each finger, enjoying the sour taste.

One Sunday, after eating mutton curry the evening before, we saved a four-inch bone in the fridge. When it came time for the sermon, Hannah took out our miniature toy table from her pocketbook and placed it on the pew next to her. I opened mine and daintily placed the dry bone on top of it. Together we began to enjoy the delicious bone, properly placing the bone back on the small table after each taste. Unfortunately, it was one of the Sundays that Mama had decided to attend. When she saw our little doll table and bone treat, her eyes widened in horror. She leaned over and pinched our ears and narrowed her eyes. In a flash, we fished the table and treat into our purses. After that day, Miriam was in charge of checking our pocketbooks for contraband.

Hannah and Elisheba
Burnsville, Minnesota, 1969

CHAPTER
TEN

I WAS ALMOST 14, and like most girls I craved mother-love. I was still young and, in many ways, stupid enough to believe that I could have what others took for granted. I wanted Mama to love me, but I had a big mouth and often challenged and irritated her by vocalizing what I found unjust. Hannah and David knew to just shut up, but for some reason, I could not learn this. Mama and Hannah seemed to get along much better and due to Hannah's ability to internalize, they had come to a truce of sorts. David had withdrawn almost completely, leaving his bedroom only to eat, and almost never interacted with Mama.

As she had done from the early days of our relationship, Mama rejected me. I tried not to notice when she wiped my compulsory good night or good morning kiss from her cheek. I shrugged it off when she stiffened and pushed me away from the hugs I was required to give her. Until I left the house, there was barely a day when she wholeheartedly hugged me. There may have been a hug or two when she was in a rare good mood on her birthday or anniversary, or if I had given her something or done something that pleased her, but for the most part she avoided touching me.

When I was good to Joram, she smiled and spoke to me with her version of kindness and care. When I upset him, she stopped speaking to me for weeks or even months and answered my pleading questions about her headache or her blood pressure in monosyllables. I can honestly say there was not one single day in all my life when I asked Mama, "How do you feel today?" to which she responded, "Great! I feel wonderful!" or, "Today is a good day!" Every time, each time, and all the times I asked how she felt that day (that is, on days when she was speaking to me) she would respond with, "My head hurts" or, "My blood pressure is terrible today" or, "My feet are swollen." Most days she was much more detailed with the extreme and colorful symptoms. She didn't just have high blood pressure. Oh no, she had to have high blood pressure accompanied with migraines, black spots, light-headedness, and swooning. If she had a migraine, it came with bouts of facial flushing and profuse sweating. Many times she even swatted at gnats flying around during her episodes. As I grew older, this became almost a game for me—I asked her, "How are you feeling?" every single day just to prove that she never responded to that question with a positive answer.

Being around sickness and death made me hate being sick. Even when I was ill, I pretended I wasn't. As an adult, I rarely let on when I don't feel well or am in pain. When I gave birth to my first son, I was in 27 hours of labor without even a Tylenol. For three weeks I overlooked the pain of severe tendonitis in my right shoulder due to overuse. When I finally saw a doctor, he admonished me for letting it go so long. Even a simple sickness like a cold or cough I disregard because I don't ever want to have to admit that, "I don't feel well." Having two mothers who were sick made me almost allergic to being weak or vulnerable.

Most of the time, Mama was displeased with me and completely ignored me; holding long, chatty, and warm discussions with Hannah. This proved to be the most effective and devastating punishment. Her silence, along with keeping Hannah away from me, was always more than I could handle. Even if I had resolved not to apologize, I broke and begged her to forgive me, pleaded my case and cried out my love for her. After I endured the prescribed time of isolation and followed by what I felt was a great deal of excrement ingestion, she conceded to speak to me. Then I had to endure a lesser level of the silent treatment for a few more days before things returned to our accepted version of normal.

Mama had the ability to turn something I didn't want to do into something I begged to do. We girls all took turns massaging her feet with lotion. She taught us all the pressure points that needed to be pressed in order to remove the migraine of which she always complained. Rubbing her feet was hard work—it took strength and endurance since each session lasted a minimum of two hours. As always she was clever and somehow convinced me that it was a kind of privilege to be allowed to massage her feet. While I worked, she talked and gossiped or turned on an old movie. Once, on a rare good day, when we were watching Gregory Peck and Audrey Hepburn in *Roman Holiday*, she told me about her trip to Italy and the occasion she had met Gregory Peck. Before her marriage, she had lived a life I could only dream of; horseback riding and camping in Kashmir, a high-class medical education in Scotland, trips to Europe with her friends, movies and socializing with classmates, and a father and mother who worshipped her. I admired her and wanted so much for her to at least like me. When she was angry with me, which was for about 90% of my life, she would reject my offer to massage her feet and choose Hannah instead. The door to her room would remain closed and I would be left outside, while Hannah joined Joram in their room. Since I had no ability to control my mouth, this was usually the case. Of course, Hannah could not refuse this privilege and I understood her quandary. Very rarely, Hannah and I would both be allowed to rub her feet, like two servant girls, in tandem. This was the time with Mama I enjoyed the most. No rejection, no divisions, no isolation, and no anger.

Mama was an expert on rejection. A few times, while wiping my kiss from her cheek, she had been caught by Papaji and he had asked her about it. From then on, she was smart enough to only do it when Papaji was not in the room, but she found other ways to send her message to me. Most of the time it was in small ways like refusing to pose in a picture with me or refusing my pleading offer to make tea for her. On one occasion, when Mama and Papaji were putting their coats on to go out, she was looking for a scarf. I ran upstairs and brought mine for her to wear. Although she did not seem angry with me, she refused to use my old, worn scarf. I blinked back my tears at her refusal and went upstairs. I could hear Papaji scold her and then he called to me. When I came down, Mama was wearing her coat with a pale-blue pashmina wrap. Papaji held his coat open and smiled at me, "I don't have a scarf. Can I use yours?" I was so hurt by Mama's rejection that I couldn't make myself bring it to him. To this day it brings me to tears when I remember his face. I play that scene over and when he opens his coat to me, I run to him, hug him, and place my threadbare scarf around his neck.

I hated myself every day for allowing Mama to twist my emotions and play with me. I wasn't sophisticated enough to know how to stop wanting her love, like Hannah and David had done. I wanted more than anything to be cold and stop feeling anything instead of begging for love from someone who I had put into a unique position to spurn and hurt me. Each time Mama rejected me, I was even more ashamed and angry. Sometimes I even shouted at Mamaji for leaving me and putting me in such a hopeless situation with someone who hated me so much. My diary was filled with pages and pages imploring to God to work a miracle and bring Mamaji back. I vowed to kill myself but I was too scared of God to do it and, instead, cried out to Him to please let me die.

The year I turned 12, a month before Mother's Day, the local paper, *The Burnsville Current* announced an essay contest. The subject was "Why My Mother Deserves Roses on Mother's Day." The mother of the winner of the contest was to receive a dozen long-stemmed roses. For the contest, I submitted the following essay:

I think my mother deserves roses for Mother's Day because she is not only a mother to me but also a very thoughtful friend. There are many reasons for why I think this, but one of the main reasons is that she is an understanding person and very easy to talk to. She shows her love for me in many different ways.

The other big reason why I think my mother deserves roses, is that years ago, she made a very big sacrifice for me and my brothers and sisters. When I was three years old, my first mother passed away. I was young and when my father remarried it took me awhile to adjust.

I didn't realize it then, but now I realize the career that my mother left behind, because she wanted to be a good mother to me and my seven brothers and sisters. She had a very good career as a successful surgeon. She left the medical field to become a mother.

Never has she once said what a big sacrifice she made to be a mother. My mother works once in a while at Abbott Hospital and I know that when she operates she enjoys her work very much. But she considers our family life too important to go back to work permanently and places it above everything.

These are a few of the reasons why I think that I am truly blessed with the best mother in the whole world.

The essay won second prize and it was my first published piece. I even received a fan letter from a lady who read the essay and was moved by it. Second prize was a gift certificate of $25 for a local florist's shop. I wanted to make the trip with just Mama and make an occasion out of it, picking her gift together. But no matter how many times I asked, Mama never made the time to come with me. Finally, a day before the gift certificate was due to expire, I went with Emmanuel and picked out a large ivy plant climbing up a tall trellis. For Mother's day that year, I gave Mama a card with a note, the newspaper clipping of my essay, and the plant.

Dear Mama,

Well, this is what you've wanted! I wrote it because Mama, you are very special to me. I found it so special the way you came into my life just when I needed you. When God brought you into my life, He did the best thing. I can't put into words everything you mean to me. I just hope sometime you will understand how much you really mean to me.

This essay is one of the few pages and pages and pages I could write about you. I wish I were poetic and could say something really lovely but I'm not very good at that kind of stuff so I'll just say I LOVE YOU! Please believe me. I know I'm an awful person and I don't show you that very well, but I'll try more and more. I love you forever. Thank you for everything. Love, Elisheba

Many years later, I found the card with a copy of my essay tucked inside, in the middle of a pile of old, dusty correspondence. As I read it again, my emotions took hold of me and I could not bear to leave the card with her and took it home. The essay, card, and plant did not have the magic effect that I had hoped for. Mama stayed removed and distant from me. She never once commented on the essay or the letter but she kept the plant in the foyer for many years. I understood that was all I would get, and for the younger me that was good enough.

It was clear that I would never have a real mother. But I hoped Mama and I could at least be friends. The key to her heart was Joram. Even though he was the cause of much of my anguish, I still loved him. I had to find a way to make Joram not only love me but also tell Mama that he loved me. But playing with Joram was a double-edged sword. It had to be carefully edited to make certain he would not tattle. The Three Stooges were used to playing with teasing, name-calling, pushing, and even fighting. But Joram was not. At any small infraction on our part, he would run and tell Mama. Either we would be lectured or punished or both. The final verdict was always that we were jealous of Joram and our behavior was vengeful because of our resentment. This accusation followed me for many years after I left the house. The fact was: I *was* jealous of Joram. I so wanted just a small piece of what he had. But admitting jealousy was almost as bad as hating Joram—and I was much too scared to allow myself to feel that.

Mama had also reoriented our entire life calendar. Instead of using B.C. and A.D. like the rest of the world, our house was synched to B.J and A.J—Before Joram and After Joram. He became a new jesus. Whenever there was a doubt about when a particular event happened, Mama would furrow her brow and say, "Oh yes, well that was two years before Joram was born so it must have been in 1966," or "Well, Joram was two, so it was

1970." As I grew older, it became so tiresome that I gave up and threw myself completely into the Great Joramian Calendar, "Well, Joram fell and scraped his knee in 1974, so that means I was 12," or, "Joram pooped his pants in 1967 so that was when I was in first grade." Even when Joram grew to be a man, all events were measured according to this calendar.

I was often put in charge of Joram's entertainment and he and I played many games together. We made food from modeling clay—the gray clay martini complete with green clay olive being our favorite. We acted out one of Joram's favorite shows *Wild Wild West*; he was James West and I was the sidekick Artemis Gordon. We played Big Boss and Worker with a similar theme of Rich Man Poor Man. This game featured Joram in the power position as the Big Boss coming to dinner and stealing all the food from me the Worker, because currently his wife was only, "big as ONE barn! She needs to be as big as FOUR barns!" Sometimes we played outside with the other neighborhood children. Statue Maker was a game that he liked. Joram was always the Statue Maker and guessed what kind of statue each player was. Joey Freder always chose something unsavory—crouching and making noises, claiming to be a fanny. His brother Paul was Joram's age and aspired to be the Pope someday. We also played Karate, GI Joe, Action Jackson, and whatever else Joram's little heart desired.

Once, when we Three Stooges and Joram were acting out scenes from *The Boxcar Children* book series, we decided to build a fire. Up to that point, our game had been harmless. We used dirt and stones for stew, flat stones for plates, and large leaves rolled into tubes for glasses. For some reason, we decided we needed a real fire. We found kindling and branches and began cooking our muddy stew. The fire burned in a controlled manner for a short while and then began to spread to the dry grass under the huge willow tree where we were playing. David frantically kicked the dry dust to smother the flames and, after a few chaotic minutes, the fire was extinguished. We breathed heavily, spooked with our near-miss at disaster. Joram sensed our fear and ran in and told Mama what we had done. We three were sent to the basement to await punishment from Papaji.

While Mama used silence as her punishment, Papaji was a talker. He did not like tension and an apology would immediately break him. We were required to sit for a long lecture afterwards, but I much preferred this to the endless weeks of cold silence and isolation that Mama used. After the fire incident, Papaji told us he would come and discipline us in an hour or two, after watching Walter Cronkite deliver the news. A usual spanking consisted of a chappal on our backside. Sometimes we hid all the shoes and chappals in sight and Papaji would resort to using his hand—this never hurt as much as the leather slipper. If he couldn't find a shoe, he would call for someone who was not being punished, to find one for him. Instead of responding, we made ourselves scarce. If we could help it, we never remained in the same room while others were being punished. But when Joram was asked for a chappal, he would obediently fetch a few pairs, hand them to Papaji and then gleefully watch while the spanking ensued.

As we waited in the basement, we contemplated how we could thwart the impending punishment. We discussed removing any shoes in sight but we knew Joram could be counted on to find plenty. We thought about hiding but knew that, eventually, we would have to reveal ourselves. Finally, we decided upon a fool-proof plan—we would wear all our underwear, an extra pair of pants and add a few *Time* magazines under the seat of our pants to cushion the spanking. Dressed appropriately for the occasion, we waited.

When Papaji finally descended the stairs, we were ready. First he lectured us and we listened, growing warmer by the minute. Then he stood up and took off his chappal, "David? Come here." Instead of his usual desperate dodging tactic, David stepped right up. Papaji laid on a few whacks and then stopped, "What's this? What are you wearing?" He looked at all of us, our faces flushed, our usually round, skinny bottoms sharp with right-angle edges stuffed tight like sausages and he began to chuckle. Then he laughed and laughed until he held his stomach and bent over. Finally, he tossed the slipper on the floor, "Don't do anything so foolish next time—you could have burned the whole place to the ground."

His face was filled with humor and I loved him so much I thought my heart would burst. We tried the too-many-underwear trick a few more times after that, but it never worked again.

Joram had all that I did not have. I had always envied that he not only had a mother who was living and was able to shower him with love and affection but he had his father as well. All the "normal" milestones in life seemed to be so Norman Rockwell-ish when it came to Joram. New clothes for school, freshly sharpened pencils, a shiny bike, thick meaty sandwiches, Twinkies in an appropriate lunchbox, his mom as room mother, and Disney World vacations. I tried hard but in my younger years I could not understand why he was given such preferential treatment. He didn't seem to be any smarter or braver or stronger. In fact, he was always much more fearful than me—to a phobic degree.

As a five-year-old, Joram was tall and stood head and shoulders above the other kids, but any mention of leaving Mama to attend school brought him to tears. During my last year at elementary school, I was given the task of escorting the leviathan to kindergarten. Hannah was in her first year at Metcalf junior high school and I was starting sixth grade. Joram was to begin half-day kindergarten and had developed an extreme phobia associated with school. No amount of talking or persuasion could dispel his fears. It was no small feat to send out Joram into the big bad world. He was the only one of us that was treated to a back-to-school shopping excursion. His school bag was filled with brand-new school supplies, while the rest of us salvaged old stubby pencils and half-used notebooks from years past.

On Joram's first day of school, he went with both Mama and Papaji. After that, the task was left to me—it was a cross I was prepared to bear for an entire year. Every night I would receive special instructions on how to handle my flat-footed lug of a brother, how to talk to him, handle his anxiety, dry his huge tears. In the evenings our Bible reading and prayer time would be filled with emotional incantations to; Please Protect Big Joram, Keep Him from Harm, Protect Him from the Effects of the Evil One, Help Him not to Be Scared and Sustain Him so He May Do Well in School. His teacher was Miss Bliss. She was sexy, blond, had a huge bosom and looked like a Playboy bunny. She was the stuff of any boy's dreams. But Joram only sniffed and wailed and couldn't appreciate the natural beauty available to him. I must not have performed to my parents' expectations or perhaps he had reported my shortcoming and his suffering but, nonetheless, the situation became too much for Mama who decided to handle the delicate-as-a-flower Joram herself.

I was promptly fired from the job and, thereafter, I walked to school on my own. About ten minutes behind me, Mama would bring along a whimpering Joram. It was at this time that Mama, who up to now had refused to learn how to drive, decided to take lessons from Emmanuel—who had taught Deborah and some of our fresh-off-the-boat uncles. As was the case with most upper-middle-class Indians, Mama had been raised with servants and drivers and never had bothered to drive herself anywhere. But that was before the great and powerful Joram.

Mama signed up for, *The Emmanuel Haqq School of Immigrant Drivers Education* and she became what is most likely the worst driver on the face of the earth. While I do not like to perpetuate generalizations, in Mama's case I must agree that this particular Indian Woman Driver was just about the scariest motorist ever to shakily make an overly wide turn, or with great trepidation ever so slowly, slowly, change lanes in 55mph traffic, her indicator blinking for miles before and after the lane change. Mama began to drive on short trips to the corner Tom Thumb convenience store or the nearby grocery store. When the weather turned cold and I began my walk toward school alone, Mama would tell me, "We'll be coming right along." A short while later, when I was about halfway to school, I would see the family car inch slowly past me, with Mama hunched nervously over the wheel and a sniveling Joram tucked inside. Of course, I was not included on the ride to school and I had to pretend that I did not notice Mama purposefully driving only Joram back and forth to school.

My job—taking Joram to school, didn't help garner affection from Mama as I had hoped. She and I remained separated, and I learned to retreat to my corner and lick my wounds privately when she rejected me. Now and then, I would still extend an olive branch. In the hope that she would spend some time with me, I asked her to teach me to knit, as knitting was in vogue at school. Many girls made colorful scarves and hats. Mama was a lightning-fast knitter, making sweaters and scarves for Joram and all her nieces and nephews in India. She never made even a pair of mittens for me or my other siblings. Mama refused to teach me and it was finally a family friend, Janeva, who sat Hannah and me down and showed us how to cast on, knit and purl stiches, and how to bind off. She gave us thin, metal-blue knitting needles and endless amounts of fine, 100% cotton, white yarn. She showed us the stitches required to make long, narrow strips of knitting. After we had many long strips, Janeva took them to her church and the church ladies wound the strips into rolls and sent them to missionaries to be used as leper bandages. Hannah and I made miles and miles of the dressings that were eventually wrapped around the wounds and sores of needy, limbless, digit-less lepers. When some of the girls in school saw us industrially working away on a long, white, thin section they asked, "WHAT is that?" We found a perverse pleasure in watching their horrified reaction when we exclaimed, "Leper Bandages!"

My trip to the fabric store for my seventh grade sewing project was one of the nicest moments I spent with Mama. The project was to make a knee-length apron that tied at the neck and waist. The instructions sent by Mrs. Farber, my Home Economics teacher, were specific. We could make an apron or a caftan. We were to buy the pattern, fabric, four packages of bias tape, and two spools of matching thread. For weeks I avoided asking for the required supplies. Just thinking about how I would go about asking Mama gave me a stomach ache and made me sweat. One Saturday, just as Mama and Papaji were heading out for one of their marathon shopping trips, I took a chance and mentioned the Monday deadline for materials. To my astonishment, Mama agreed to take me right then. She and I drove to the nearby Minnesota Fabrics. Together, we went inside the store, chose the fabric and other materials. She allowed me to choose a material I really liked. I saw a classmate in the store shopping with her mother. I watched happily as the two mothers chatted and exchanged pleasantries. For once, I felt just like any other girl out on a Saturday shopping trip with her mother.

"I really like that material, it's so pretty," my classmate said.

"Thanks," I carefully folded the navy material scattered with tiny pink roses.

"Do you like Mrs. Farber?"

"She's okay, but if I hear you know, 'People, people check your bobbins!' one more time, I'm gonna puke."

My classmate laughed, "Hey, my mom and I are going to Farrell's for ice cream. Do you and your mom wanna come too?"

I swallowed. I had always wanted to go to Farrell's. It was an old-fashioned ice cream parlor that was famous for the crowd-sized treat called "The Zoo." I had been invited to many birthday parties which had been held at Farrell's. The huge concoction of ice cream was decorated with tiny plastic toys and flags. All the party-goers dug in and enjoyed a huge variety of ice cream flavors. I had never been allowed to attend any party.

At my classmate's casual invitation, I broke out in a sweat. "Uh, thanks, but we can't. My mom and I are going to a movie this afternoon."

"Oh, too bad!" At the cashier counter, she nudged her mother, "Hey, Mom? I invited Elisheba and her mom to Farrell's but they're going to a movie. Can we go too, after ice cream?"

Mama's eyes ever so faintly showed surprise, but she gave no other reaction. She paid the bill and said a polite goodbye. She never mentioned my lie to me.

Hannah remembers her project a bit differently. Her plea for supplies was ignored for weeks on end. Mrs. Hopper, who was Hannah's Home Economics teacher, wrote a stern note to Mama explaining that Hannah would flunk the course if she did not bring in the materials for class. Finally, Mama complied and sent Hannah to school with material and a dress pattern. At the conclusion of the sewing class, a fashion show was held during school hours and the mothers were invited to watch their child model and take pictures of what had been made. Predictably, Mama never showed up for my show.

Sometimes Mama would take Hannah and me shopping to the new Burnsville Center. Even though she only bought things for herself, Papaji, or Joram—she told jokes, gossiped, narrated amazing stories, and we all had fun together. Unlike my friend's mothers, she carried herself with a sort of elegant confidence that could not be ignored. One summer day, Mama, Hannah, and I were driving on Highway 13 with the windows open. A car full of men drove up alongside us. The men in the car looked over and catcalled and leered at us. Mama disdainfully scowled at them and asked, "What are we? Ripe Fruit?" We three laughed at the shocked look on their faces. It was on such days that I wanted so much for her just to be my friend. My admiration for her was boundless and I wanted nothing more than for her to accept me.

Once I asked Mama a carefully edited version of the one question that had been swirling around in my mind repeatedly for many years. What was it that made her—an intelligent, accomplished woman, do something so ludicrous, so stupid as to marry a man with seven children, *without ever meeting even one of those children first?* It was one of her rare good days, and she laughed at my assessment and paused before answering me. Then she said that when she had heard that Mamaji had died, she prayed God would help us in our time of need. She had recently seen *The Sound of Music*, and was struck by the similarity between the Von Trapp and Haqq children, and she had felt sorry for us.

But I was not content with that answer and I wanted to know more. I needed to know *why?* Mama's answer just didn't make sense to me. No one takes on seven, unknown children out of sheer pity! The idea was absolutely outrageous. I knew it had something to do with the fact that since she had solely focused on her career, she believed she had lost her chance to marry. When she met Papaji at age 37, an opportunity she thought was gone presented itself.

On one occasion, I was browsing through Papaji's piles of books and I found a book that had been published by a small, unknown press in India. It was a biography of Papaji's life and was written by his old friend Joe Grostephen who had a great admiration for him and our family. Even though Joe had been our pastor for many years and had officiated both Miriam and Gideon's weddings, he still had no clue about the reality of our family life. I knew of this book as I had seen both Papaji and Mama carefully go through it, fastidiously editing and correcting the facts and details before it went to print. It was a rather unremarkable book and I thumbed through it carelessly. But I sat up straight when I came to the following passage. It finally gave me the answer I had been searching for. The author had written:

> "I once asked Dr. Delora Haqq this question: 'It must have been a terrific transition, from a busy surgeon's life to that of a mother of seven children, wasn't it? She replied, It certainly was! I think if I knew—the doubt in my mind before I married was—seven children!'
>
> She went on to explain that she would have certainly remained single rather than marry the wrong man—implying of course that becoming an instant mother of seven children was a small price to pay. 'Well,' she replied simply, 'I loved them all.'"

What Mama revealed in her interview to our unassuming pastor confirmed what I had known all along. Even she had felt hesitant at the thought of taking on seven children. Instead of thinking of how those children would be influenced by her actions, she pushed her own doubt aside because she wanted to *marry the right man*. She had wanted Papaji so fervently that we seven children were "the price" she had to pay. We were the levy or the punishment due in exchange for the life she wanted. No one has enjoyable or pleasant feelings toward a penalty. Saying she "loved us all" meant nothing. It is a phrase used by Miss America contestants, politicians, or rock stars when speaking to their fans—"I Love You All!" Real love is personal and intimate. Love was only a word she used to complete the picture she wanted the world to see.

Whenever *The Sound of Music* is on television, I never miss it because I rather enjoy the pleasure and the torture it gives me to watch my life served up in two ways—movie fantasy and reality. It was the first movie I had ever seen, right after Mamaji died. It also was the movie Mama watched when she took pity on us. Both the Haqq and VonTrapp families had an older girl who was 17 and a younger one who was three at the time of their mother's death. In the Hollywood version of my life, the children are raised by Maria who genuinely loves them, closes up her womb forever, and never has more children. The selfish Baroness who wants to put them in a, "delightful little thing called boarding school" is banished, and the Captain gallantly puts the needs of his children first. They gleefully sing their way through the snowy mountains into safety and lifelong fame. But in real life, the Baroness didn't say, "Auf Wiedersehen, darling." She stayed. And even though the Captain didn't send us to boarding school (how I wish he had!), he began to hoard his love, and then doled out just a little, and finally nothing at all. Instead, he lavished it on the Baroness and the beautiful new family. To this day, when I see Maria, dressed in white, preparing to walk down the aisle, I have such conflicted emotions. A part of me longs for my own Maria, to give my life the Hollywood, fairytale ending. The other part shouts at Maria, "Don't do it! Turn around! It's not going to work!" No man is worth the strain of stepping in and trying to raise his seven children. I would have never done such a stupid thing, and I wish with all my being Mama never had.

But as much as I tried to garner Mama's affection, my anger

was just as fierce when she treated me unfairly. As much as I admired her, I could also despise and detest her with the same fervor. During our yearly viewing of *The Sound of Music*, the connection between Mama and the Baroness became clear. I am not sure which one of the Three Stooges first said it, or if we all agreed at the same time, but during the movie we all decided the most appropriate name for Mama was the Baroness. From that moment on we referred to her as the Baroness—only in private. When we spoke to her directly, we still addressed her with a respectful term she had not earned.

My verbal communication with Mama was limited to her pointing out something I had or had not done. I avoided having a conversation with her because I generally ended up losing my temper and rattling off a long litany of what I thought was wrong or unfair. None of this sat well with her. I found myself apologizing over and over and over. I desperately tried to find ways to suppress my feelings and contain my boiling anger. To get back at her I mocked her and became an expert at mimicking her. Sometimes while she stirred a pot, I wiggled my hips and twisted my mouth to the side just like she did. When she drove, she always gave a great sniff of accomplishment after successfully completing a turn without ramming into an oncoming car. This always drove me bonkers and I sniffed right along with her. Anytime I apologized, her stock answer was the sarcastic, "I'm sorry too." I always knew this was coming, so when her back was turned, I would open the cupboard, lean inside and, like a ventriloquist, silently mouth the words, "I'm sorry too" just as she uttered them.

Mama had been brought up in a strict church and had been taught to cover her head during prayer or Bible reading. When she was at church, she gracefully brought the long pallu from her sari around and used that to cover her head, but at home she had begun wearing pants and had to resort to a scarf. Sometimes when a scarf was not handy—usually for grace at the dinner table—she would clamp a paper towel on her head. This was hilarious because the paper towel remained curled up on the ends and when she placed it on her head, she looked like the flying nun. Sometimes the fan would blow the napkin off her head and she would hold it down with two fingers on either side, or tuck the ends behind each ear, which did nothing to improve the look of a rolled paper towel on her head. At family devotional time, I hid the scarf she kept by her chair in the living room just so she would have to use a paper towel. Then I spent the entire time laughing privately. Hannah and David usually collapsed in laughter whenever I made fun of Mama and that gave me even more impetus to put on a show. But Mama was smart and she caught me about 50 percent of the time, which did nothing to improve our already tenuous relationship.

I tried other ways to get back at Mama. I ate her strawberry yogurt and lied when she asked about it. I emptied most of the jar of her precious English marmalade which had been sent by her sister. She had a bad habit of keeping four or five mugs of tea or coffee all over the house—sipping from the beverage as she passed. Papaji found these mugs and emptied them in the sink over her loud protests of, "Raja, Raja, no, no, no!" He scornfully said, "Madam, this is filled with tannic acid!" as he dumped the liquid. When I saw this, I happily emptied all the secret mugs I found, knowing full well that it would be blamed on Papaji's fight against tannic acid.

I also stole money from Mama's purse on a fairly regular basis. I was only able to steal an occasional dollar when she wasn't watching her purse. But David had become enormously adept at getting into the locked master bedroom. He climbed onto the garage roof and snuck in through the window in the master bedroom. He regularly took twenties and tens and he was never without pocket money. Even though Hannah and I babysat regularly, we were not allowed to keep our earnings and to get some of it back, I began to steal.

Hannah and I took turns with our babysitting jobs. Between the two of us, we had pretty much sewed up all the babysitting business in our area. Unlike the other babysitters, we not only took care of the children but cooked dinners and cleaned the house. Usually our customers paid us well above the expected 50¢ an hour, because they would arrive back to a sparkling house and children who had been well fed and cared for. I enjoyed getting a chance to get out of the house. But when I returned from a job, I handed over my paltry babysitting earnings to Mama. Most of the time it wasn't much more than $5 to $10, but she always knew exactly how many hours I had worked and expected the entire amount. She even demanded that Hannah and I turn over the occasional birthday money sent to us. Except for what I stole, I never saw a penny from my earnings. David worked part-time at the movie theatre and his check was endorsed and handed over. We loved David's job because he brought home huge plastic bags filled with popcorn at the end of his shift. Even though he was allowed free movie passes, we were never allowed to use them, because Papaji did not allow us to go into "movie houses." Emmanuel and Deborah were also earning, and their checks were turned over to Mama with only a small amount given back for pocket money. In order to keep track of our paychecks, Mama started marking each paycheck on her Bible verses calendar. It was a practice she was to keep until the day I left the house and I could never glance at a calendar again without feeling rage boil inside me.

Some of my best memories of Mama were also the ones that happened the fewest times. These occurred when Mama went to the hospital to fill in for a vacationing surgeon and we were home alone with Papaji. The day was a rare treat. Papaji left very early to drop Mama off at the hospital. After he returned, he talked to us while he drank his tea, and had breakfast with us. Then he waited until we got ready and drove us to school just like the other kids. Sometimes, we would beg Papaji to let us stay home with him to which he often agreed. Sometimes we shopped for groceries, but he was always fun and full of laughter. In the afternoons, if we had gone to school, we would rush home and find him busily cooking up one of his famous curries. He was an experimental cook, dropping in new and inventive ingredients. Anything could be tossed in; cashews, peanuts, cardamom pods, raisins, coconut, radishes, spinach. He used whatever he found. It was always interesting. After putting the pot on the stove to simmer, he sat and played the piano as only he could do. He only had two or three songs in his repertoire but he knew them well. They were old Punjabi songs, and he stylized them by pounding them out with both hands, using the same keys on different octaves. Sometimes he sang in his beautiful, rich voice old Indian love songs and even "Khushi Khushi Mano," which we sang along with him. He was happy, jolly, handsome, strong, and smelled wonderful. Hannah and I hugged his broad back as he played. David sat next to him on the piano bench. Joram played nearby and even the Biggers took a break from studying. At dinnertime, we ate Papaji's delicious curry together. He told silly jokes and never once scraped the bottom of the pan. We all got real pieces of chicken not just giblets. My stomach was always full and comfortable. I loved it when Mama was gone. It was a glimmer of what our lives could have been if Papaji had never married and had taken care of us on his own. After dinner, he left to pick Mama up and I braced myself for her arrival. She was always tired, had a headache and swollen feet. When she got home, the party was over.

Papaji
Mussoorie, India 1957

CHAPTER
ELEVEN

T HE YEAR BEFORE the miniseries *Roots* was aired on television was the year I first met Keisha. It just so happened that most of us had been given a homework assignment to watch the miniseries, and it was the first time that many of my classmates realized that I had *not* come from Africa. Other than Hannah, I was still the only brown person at our school.

One day in November as I was walking down the hallway during my high school freshman year, my eyes fixated on a particular girl. She had black hair with bangs that were curled under, a huge smile and, wonder of wonders, her skin was actually brown. I walked closer and found myself face to face with her. Her expression was as surprised as mine and within a few seconds we began chatting and laughing together as if we had been friends forever. I felt an instant connection with her. Even her name, Keisha Dobbins, was unlike the usual Chrissy Johnsons, Joe Eriksons, and Lisa Andersons I had grown used to hearing. She and I both expressed our relief at finally finding someone else who had brown skin. Finding Keisha was a saving grace. Her family could not have been more different than mine. Her father was a retired

Air Force officer, her mother worked in a bank, and she had two older brothers and a sister. But, at the same time, Keisha knew what it felt like to live in an all-white neighborhood and attend an all-white school. We instantly became best friends and for the rest of my school career our names were never mentioned alone but always as "Elisheba and Keisha."

As a friend, Keisha was loyal and accommodating of my seriously complicated social life. Many times, instead of going out on a Friday night, she chose to remain at home so we could talk on the phone. If she did attend a party or a game, she always played it down, stating it was no fun, or that it would have been much better if I had been there. Whether it was true or not, in her own way, she did what she could to make me feel like I wasn't missing out on a normal teenage life. Unlike other acquaintances and classmates, she never labeled my family as "weird" but simply accepted the limitations of my life. Keisha was cool and popular. She was athletic, smart, always had plenty of spending money, and wore stylish clothes. But she wore her hair the same way every single day, just like I did. Keisha pinned her hair back into a ponytail and curled her bangs under. She changed the color of the ribbon in her hair to match her extensive wardrobe, but other than that her hair remained the same. I had always worn my hair in two braids and then in high school I wore just a single one. I was always met with cries and demands from other girls to, "take your hair down!" but they never said any such thing to Keisha.

Keisha was the only friend I allowed my parents to meet. After a few months, I nervously mentioned that I had made a new friend and asked if she could visit. The visit was short; Keisha came inside my house for a few minutes, met my parents and then we talked outside. When Mrs. Dobbins came to pick her daughter up, she came in and met my parents. After a short exchange, I said goodbye to Keisha and went inside.

Mama asked, "Why didn't you tell me she was black?"

I was puzzled at her question and replied, "I didn't know it was important."

I tried hard for Keisha's parents and mine to connect and become friends. I hoped that this way it would be easier to be friends with her, but as it was with other adults, my parents did not become friends with the Dobbins'.

Keisha's car was the coolest car in the student parking lot. It was a chocolate Mustang Cobra. I was not allowed to learn how to drive and it went without saying that being in a car with a boy was absolutely forbidden. Indeed, it was a joke that Papaji referred to a car as a "Moving Bedroom." But during our lunch hour, Keisha and I drove to Dairy Queen or just rode back and forth on Highway 13 with the radio turned all the way up, singing loudly and laughing. Once when Keisha and I were speeding along the highway, we were stopped by a police car. After the policeman took Keisha's license and registration, he came back to the car and leaned inside to get a good look at her.

"You're Keisha Dobbins? The sprinter at the high school?" he asked. After Keisha nodded, he pushed back his cap and continued, "I oughta arrest you right now. You made my wife cry for a week when you quit the track team. She said that during her entire career as a coach she had never seen someone with as much promise as you. With your times, she said you were headed for the Olympics. It broke her heart when you decided to quit."

Keisha just laughed. I was astounded at this piece of news. Since I had never been allowed to go to any of Keisha's track meets, I had no clue about her talent as a sprinter, "Keisha! Did you hear that? You could go to college on a scholarship! And to the Olympics!"

"Yeah, the coach called my parents too. But I wanted to be a Bravette and I couldn't do both."

"Wait. You would rather be on a *danceline* than go to the Olympics? Why? Are you kidding? What did your parents say?"

"They just told me to do what made me happy."

I was speechless. I had never heard of such a thing. Keisha's parents actually allowed her to choose what she wanted to do and, furthermore, even when another adult intervened, *they still wanted her to do what made her happy!* The whole idea was completely foreign to me. Her parents were supportive of her talents and encouraged her to join whatever group she liked. Even more amazing was that they left the entire decision up to her! I had made absolutely no life decisions for myself. Even something as simple as choosing one of two electives for my high school curriculum was done for me. Most kids took a fun course like Film Study or History of Rock and Roll. But Papaji never allowed me to waste a course and I took think-tank courses for my electives such as Fun with Experimental Probability or Astronomy. The food I ate, what I thought, what I read, what I saw, my opinions, my beliefs, my value system, none of it was left for me to decide. Every single thing was preprogrammed and I regurgitated it as needed.

Papaji had strict standards for how females should behave in the outside world that I could not easily cast off. Our school gym class required that we wear a uniform that was navy and white. Mama refused to give me the funds to purchase the gym suit so instead, I wore a white top and blue shorts. Eventually, I found a cast-off gym suit and wore it just like the other girls. The only way Papaji allowed me to wear shorts was when he learned that gym class was not co-ed. I had never worn shorts before and this immediately became a problem. Both Hannah and I had dark hair and our legs and underarms grew plenty of it. If we had lived in Europe perhaps this would not have been a problem, but in Minnesota girls didn't keep the hair under their arms long enough to braid. Papaji resisted any markers which announced the onset of puberty and did not allow us to shave. So, I borrowed a disposable razor from one my classmates in order to shave. I kept it in my gym locker and practiced the sensual ritual of soaping and shaving my legs and underarms and then applying baby oil or lotion. My legs felt tingly and smooth without any hair. Even while wearing pants, the material brushed against my silky legs almost erotically. It was a distinctly sexual feeling, something I had never experienced before.

The lost and found became a great source of other clothing as well. Worn jeans, tops, shorts, T-shirts, and sweatshirts that had been abandoned by our classmates, all found their way to my locker. I used the clothing in school and changed into my "home" clothes after school. A friend gave Hannah a collection of fashionable clothing that she had outgrown. Hannah mistakenly brought it home, and when Mama found them she threw the clothing away. I wore my lost and found clothing, but constantly lived in fear that someone would recognize the clothes. Hannah and I would remake something the night before or modify it by adding a ribbon and other embellishment. When my Lost and Found flare-legged jeans went out of style, I simply sewed up the sides to make them into the fashionable straight-legged variety. Sometimes we pulled out the yellow, toy sewing machine that Emmanuel had given and used it to modify and update our clothing. Because we were used to managing with little, we learned how to be extremely creative with almost nothing. Our friends mistakenly believed we had a vast wardrobe because we constantly changed or altered our clothes.

The habit of creating something rather than purchasing it followed me into my adult years. I rarely bought an item if I could figure out how to make it or do it myself. As an adult, in my own house, I did my own painting and faux finishes, refinished old furniture, made curtains, duvet covers, and pillows, reupholstered furniture, made invitations and flower arrangements for parties, found inventive substitute ingredients for cooking, made my children's Halloween costumes, and helped them produce wildly creative projects for school and home. As a teenager, I resented my parents for the angst I felt when I had to figure out how to make do without something, but as an adult I was grateful for the skill.

Papaji's uptight views about sex and normal attractions between boys and girls caused him to be tight-lipped and tyrannically conservative, placing us girls under a purdah-like seclusion. No one had ever explained to me any part of human sexuality, but I understood that boys were off limits. Dating was out of the question, and we were not allowed to speak to boys on the phone or anywhere else.

If a boy called me to ask for a homework assignment, Papaji would become enraged, "Why is that boy calling you? Did you give him your number?" I often wondered what he could possibly be thinking. *Oh sure, I'd love to get one of your two-hour lectures, so why wouldn't I willingly give my phone number to a boy?* Finding my number in the phone book was simple as our last name was the only one with Arabic roots sitting amongst a sea of American last names.

First, Papaji would listen on the extension, breathing heavily the entire time. Then, as soon as I hung up, I would be treated to a discourse on the evils of "mixing with boys" and the harm it would do to my reputation. Any books or television shows with salacious details were banned. Papaji could not even say the word "sex." He stumbled over it if he was forced to use it and said "saas" instead.

Once when we were in the car with Papaji, he began humming and reading aloud the road signs as we drove past, "Lucky Twin Drive-In, Ben Franklin, Burnsville Bowl, Dairy Queen Brassiere.

Oh! I think it's, Brazier... *ahem*, that's it. Ah, Dairy Queen *Brazier*." His acute embarrassment at accidentally mentioning a woman's undergarment was so intense that he was silent the rest of the ride home. But both Hannah and I tried to muffle our giggles. My stomach and ribs ached with suppressed laughter as we shook silently in the back seat.

Normal changes that came with puberty caused abnormal complications. Even though Hannah and I had both begun developing breasts, we had never been given a bra. It became more and more embarrassing during our gym class to hide the fact that we didn't have bras. To rectify the situation, Hannah and I each found a bra in the lost and found. We had to hide them from Mama because we were not allowed to wear them and she did not intervene on our behalf with Papaji.

There was intense concern for female virginity, but I had no idea what constituted a virgin. Riding a bike or a using a tampon was forbidden and was somehow related to a hymen which was extraordinarily valuable. But I was clueless as to what the relationship was. I was furious at my someday husband and vowed that he should be properly grateful for all the mess I had to go through every month, just so he could have a stupid hymen. Even worse was the fact that every month we had to go through the ordeal of asking Mama for feminine supplies. Just as we always were forced to ask for toilet paper, she kept these hidden away in the huge great caverns of her closet or "storage rooms" and doled them out one at a time. I never understood why we couldn't have these necessary feminine and paper products stored in the bathroom vanity like other normal people. It was clear that this was a form of control. My anxiety grew greater and greater the thinner the toilet paper roll grew. I found ways to make it last longer—using just two or three squares at a time or using napkins I had taken from the school lunchroom. I tried to avoid asking for another roll as long as possible; we all did. Rarely did we get the roll the first time we asked. Generally, Mama made some excuse, "Oh, I have to go find some," or, "I'll get it when I go upstairs," while the elusive keys jangled on the metal ring, just out of reach. Why a roll of toilet paper had to be kept under lock and key, I never understood. But I knew I would never get a fresh roll without a struggle.

A significant event such as getting my period was filled with angst. When I started mine, Mama said nothing and gave me the allotted five pads. This was not enough, and when I asked for more, she asked me why I needed extra, ignored my request, or simply pretended to not have any in the house. I finally gave up and began stealing pads from school vending machines. I asked Miriam what the experience had been like for her. She smiled and recalled that Mamaji had told her with tears in her eyes, "*Meri beti bari ban gayi*" commenting on how her daughter was now a woman. For Miriam, it was a moment to bond with Mamaji. For me, it was just another way that Mama could exhibit domination and vindictiveness.

One summer, Hannah lost her period entirely because she had grown so thin and Mama only realized this because she had not asked for her monthly allotment of five sanitary napkins.

"Is there something growing in there?" she asked, poking Hannah's stomach.

Hannah was aghast, "No! Of course not!"

"There better not be," Mama said.

I marveled at the idiocy of the question. *As if we could even get pregnant! We can't step out of our yard, we have to be home right after school, a phone call from a boy causes Papaji to blow a gasket, and all males are off-limits—including classmates, uncles, a lone male cousin or two, and the fathers who we babysit for. And let's not forget: We're probably the two ugliest girls in the state of Minnesota!*

For some reason, Hannah felt particularly testy that day, "What would happen if I got pregnant?"

Without any hesitation Mama said, "I've talked to your father about that. We would put you out if that ever happened."

Well! This is valuable information: getting pregnant might be a good way to escape, once I finish high school. I tucked the episode away for future reference.

Our high school had over 3,000 students and roughly half of them were boys, making it almost impossible to avoid speaking to a boy now and then. I had to maintain a delicate balance—trying to enjoy myself while I was at school (since it was the only real social activity I was allowed), while still maintaining some sort of aloofness toward the opposite sex, so I would not be asked out. My constant refusals to socialize with boys or girls gave the mistaken impression that I was a snob or standoffish. Most of the kids just labeled me "weird" and I had a hard time arguing with that. While most kids looked forward to the big social events, I dreaded and avoided them.

There were a few boys that became friendly, in particular a boy named Dave. He sat next to me in one of our classes. He was tall and thin with blue eyes and a slow, easy smile. We enjoyed conversations about books, politics, and music. He asked me intelligent questions and made some interesting observations about my background. He planned to attend a college in Wisconsin. I felt comfortable with Dave, even to the point that I felt safe explaining some of my social restrictions. One day he asked me to go out with him.

"Have you seen *Kramer vs. Kramer* yet?"

"No, actually I don't go to movies."

"Really? I don't go to very many movies either, most of them are pretty bad. But that was a pretty good movie. We should hang out sometime," said Dave.

"I don't know. I think I see enough of you in school." I was teasing him but also trying to avoid the question of a date.

"No, I mean it. I need to hear more about why you don't go to movies."

"It's nothing, really. It's just that my dad doesn't really like me to go to movies."

"Oh. Okay. Well, how about prom? Do you think your dad would let you go to the prom with me?" Dave asked.

"No, I don't think so. I don't really date."

Dave smiled, "You don't date? So I guess we'll just be friends then. You know, friends can still go out together."

"Not if the friend is a boy," I smiled back.

The truth was I couldn't go out even if the friend was a girl. The idea of going to a school dance, much less prom, was so out of my realm of possibility, that I didn't even want to imagine what would happen if I tried to ask for a formal gown. That same evening when the phone rang an inner sense told me it was Dave and I ran to answer it. When boys called my house, my stomach churned and the need to vomit was immediate. After Dave identified himself and began talking, I was aware of Papaji's heavy breathing on the upstairs extension.

"I think you should change your mind and come to the prom," Dave said.

"Thanks, but I really can't."

"Why? Nothing bad is going to happen. I promise I won't try anything."

It would infuriate Papaji to know that a boy had even mentioned *avoiding* physical contact with me! "Ah, no I can't go with you."

"Look, I'll have you home early. Would it be easier if I just asked your dad?"

"No! It's very nice of you, but I just can't."

"You have to give me one good reason why," said Dave.

Now this was tricky. Without ever saying so, Papaji had made it clear to me that I was not to list his "no dating" order as a reason for refusing dates. My rational for not dating should come from some noble inner reason, not because I was forbidden to do so.

"Well..."

Papaji's booming voice interrupted my response, "I think Elisheba has made it clear to you that she doesn't want to go with you."

I cringed.

To his credit, Dave didn't miss a beat, "Well sir, I think Elisheba is a really nice person and I would enjoy getting to know her better. I promise to have her home early."

Papaji softened a bit, "I appreciate that, but Elisheba is not going to a dance."

"I see. Well, I guess I'll see you in school tomorrow, Elisheba. Bye, Sir."

I waited.

"ELISHEBA!" Papaji's voice bellowed from upstairs. I knew what was forthcoming. He would want to know exactly why Dave had called. What had I done to prompt the call? Had I been too friendly? Had I touched him? Did I show my teeth to flirt with him? His scrutiny would be intense, and his concern for my reputation would supersede any logical explanation I could offer.

"Elisheba? What is all this prom nonsense, *bakwaas*? You will not be dressing up to please some boy so he can show you around."

Oh sure, I'm just the kind of girl a guy would want to show off—baggy clothes, skinny with ugly hair—I'm more of a charity project than a date!

"You don't have time for all this dating shmating," added Mama.

Ah yes! What was I thinking? I forgot that I led such a massively packed social life! "He's a nice boy. And we're just friends."

"Hmmph. These boys don't want to be 'just friends'. Before you know it, there'll be some kind of trouble," said Papaji.

Right. Straight from prom directly into the moving bedroom. "Papaji, that's not how it is. It's just supposed to be fun."

"Fun? Just like an American, always talking about this fun nonsense. You have more important things to think about than fun."

Sure, Sure. Like chopping onions, weeding the garden, shoveling six feet of snow, adding to your bank account, keeping my mouth shut, watching Joram shove more pumpkin bread into his mouth and taking all of the Baroness' crap.

For a while I entertained the idea of actually attending prom. I commiserated with Hannah and promised to sneak out of the house and borrow a dress from Keisha. But I was too well-trained to actually try it. The next day at school, I had to live through meeting Dave in the hallway between classes. I was highly embarrassed and could barely look up to apologize for what Papaji had done. He was an intelligent boy and, truthfully, I wouldn't have minded spending time with him. He respected my point of view and I was sorry I was not going to be allowed to get to know him outside of school. Unlike other boys, who I had not been allowed to date, Dave and I remained friends. He did not humiliate or demean me for obeying my parents.

Mamaji, circa 1943
Lahore, Undivided India

CHAPTER
TWELVE

WHILE IT WAS true that food had always been a method of showing favoritism, I did not feel the full impact of actually feeling pangs of hunger until I was much older. I had always been thin, but as I grew older the need for calories increased. The year I turned 17, instead of being hungry occasionally, I was hungry constantly. I was growing fast and the skimpy school sandwiches and the Mama-portion-controlled meals satisfied less and less. When I reached home from school, I would be ravenously hungry. Usually I filled up on cheap starch like toast, but sometimes I would try something more creative. Papaji had just bought Mama a microwave, so I could bake a potato in four minutes and add some butter, salt, and pepper for an easy snack. Sometimes I made a sandwich with achar—an Indian sour and spicy relish made from limes or mangos. Other times it was a bowl of Cheerios, a glass of milk, or dry packets of Kool-Aid or dry Jell-O licked a fingerful at a time. If it was summer, we could eat all the tomatoes and cucumbers we wanted. But the simple carbohydrates only curbed my hunger for a short while, and within an hour or two my stomach was growling again. I was stick-like skinny and didn't weigh more than 95 pounds, but because of the heavy work I did, it was mostly muscle. My clothes were big on me and I had a collection of safety pins that I used to tighten the waists. It was a source of constant irritation to Mama. She wanted me to take the time to adjust the waistbands with a needle and thread.

Being hungry became sort of normal. On an average day, I woke up in the morning and got ready for school. Hannah usually had a bowl of cereal but I was still not able to eat breakfast without throwing up. After outgrowing my lunchbox, being expected to reuse the brown bag and plastic sandwich bag annoyed me. By seventh grade, my anger at being given a paltry lunch in the face of Joram's sumptuous lunches was so great that in silent protest I stopped taking lunch all together. Instead, I went to the library or socialized during lunch hour. Hannah continued to take the skinny sandwiches and usually had a container of freezer-burn cauliflower or broccoli that she had salvaged from the nobody-wants-to-eat-this-crap pile, which had accumulated in the coffin basement freezer.

After school, we would scrounge and find a snack to tide us over until dinnertime. In the evening, we ate what was put before us and it was the only hot meal we got all day. Mama was making more American dishes like Hamburger Helper, hot dogs, and meatloaf which Joram much preferred to Indian food. But these meals were becoming distasteful to me more and more. Emmanuel and Deborah often ate elsewhere or worked in the evenings, so Mama offered seconds. On the one hand, I was hungry and wanted seconds and, on the other, I did not want to give Mama the satisfaction of knowing that she was able to give or deprive me of something I needed. My pride won most of the time and I turned the offer of more food down.

The one exception to my rule was when we had Bisquick pancakes for dinner. I was crazy for pancakes and, on that night, I gave up my lofty aspirations to teach Mama a lesson and ate until my stomach hurt from being so full. On an average day, I had an intake of no more than 700 to 800 calories. Many times Papaji, Mama, and Joram went out for dinner on their own. Ponderosa Steakhouse was one of Joram's favorites. I had become so accustomed to this that I barely batted an eye. Instead I focused on what I could eat while they were gone.

The constant, gnawing hunger in my belly eventually caused me to commit a petty theft. I started working in the shoe department at Sears in the Burnsville Center the summer before my senior year. Keisha worked at the jewelry department at Sears and she encouraged me to apply there as well. This way, I could get a ride back and forth with her. Sears hired me on the spot and I began working after school and on weekends. Hannah was working at Dutch Treat Donut Shoppe right next to Tom Thumb. She often brought day-old doughnuts home with her. It was mostly Joram and Hannah who enjoyed the sweet treats. I preferred savory to sweet, but it was still nice to have fresh doughnuts now and then. Later, Hannah worked at Wendy's and I often envied the free lunchtime burger she was allowed. Even though Mama demanded we hand over our paychecks, the joy of getting out of the house was so great it seemed a small price to pay. Every payday, we dutifully endorsed the back of each check and turned it over to Mama. My colleagues at Sears excitedly discussed what they would do with their pay, planning their weekends and shopping trips. I often forgot to collect mine because it meant nothing to me. Sometimes my manager, Gwen, would mistakenly comment, "Elisheba, you must be rich, you never pick up your checks!" When I missed a paycheck, Mama would sternly remind me to bring it home. I didn't think to ask why I should give it to her. It was something I was expected to do. In a way, I still hoped that perhaps my contribution would someday garner a speck of appreciation or fondness and to question the practice would upset that delicate, frail hope.

One of the nicest things about working was when Papaji would come and visit me at work. He watched me work and made erroneous statements about the great value of my contribution to my job. When he visited Hannah at Wendy's and ate a burger, he would comment on the juiciness of the meat or particular freshness of the lettuce and exclaim as if Hannah had made the burger particularly for him. When he saw me ringing up shoes or straightening a shelf, he always talked about my great skill in hitting the right keys or making the displays look so artistic. He complimented the quality of the merchandise as if I had personally selected or manufactured it. I knew he was exaggerating, and I would try to not let him see my tears at his words. I wanted so much for Papaji to love me again, and when he talked this way, I desperately hoped I could win his love back.

I worked as much as I possibly could. I enjoyed being treated like a responsible person. I never had weekend plans. Most of the evening staff were high-school kids and they clamored to get Friday and Saturdays off. I was always willing to work those shifts. The only time I did not work was on Sunday mornings because I attended church. I often worked six- and eight-hour shifts, and when I worked the longer shifts, I was given a half-hour break. I avoided the food court in the mall because the smells and sights of the food caused my already empty stomach to grumble. It became more and more difficult to bypass the food court. I longed for a slice of greasy pepperoni pizza or a loaded baked potato from One Potato Two Potato.

One late afternoon I was nearly famished with hunger. My last meal had been my dinner the evening before. My half-hour break was coming up and Keisha and I were going to take our break together. The day had been slow. My manager had gone home early, leaving only me and Jeff, another high schooler in the department. Jeff was on break. I was all alone and had just finished ringing up a sale. I told the customer, "Thank you for shopping at Sears," and handed her change in cash. But instead of slamming the cash drawer shut, I left it open a crack. When I was certain there was no one in sight, I slipped a $5 bill into my pocket and closed the drawer. My heart was thumping. After a few minutes, I began breathing easy—no one had seen me. During my break, I enjoyed two slices of pizza and a medium Coke. Nothing had ever tasted so good. I resolved to never steal again, but I did. I stole fives and singles and once I even stole a $10 bill. Somewhere inside me, I knew I would eventually get caught but feeling full felt so good, I couldn't stop myself.

About two or three months into my stealing spree, my manager approached me. She said that an employee had quit in the linen department and they wanted me to cover for the next few weeks. I was immediately suspicious. I transferred to the linen department and firmly promised myself not to steal anymore. I began eating a bowl of cereal before coming to work. My resolution didn't last, because my blood sugar started to drop in in the early afternoons. When I didn't eat breakfast, I didn't have any problem and could go an entire day without eating. But in an attempt to curb my hunger during the dinner hour at work, I ate breakfast. This ended up being counterproductive. I worked two days one week and on both days I began shaking and sweating around noon. I sat in the back and ate packets of sugar from the free coffee area in the break room to recover. The next week the symptoms grew worse. I ate my usual sugar and managed through the afternoon but at dinner the shaking returned. After the next cash transaction, I grabbed a $5 bill from the till, bought a burger and Coke and wolfed it down. The shaking and sweating stopped immediately and I was able to focus once more.

The next day at work, I was called in to see Jerry, the store manager, "Elisheba, tell me, how long have you been working at Sears?"

My mouth was dry, "Umm, about a year, sir."

"Do you like your job?"

"Very much," I said. Right then I knew I had been caught, but I decided to keep up the charade as long as I could.

"I'm wondering if you can help me with a problem I have in the shoe department and the linen department," he said.

"I'll try, sir."

"For about the last three months I have been coming up short. Not much, only about three to five dollars at a time, but still short. I was short five dollars yesterday. Do you have any idea why this is happening?"

I was silent.

Jerry continued, "Well, our Loss Prevention supervisor noticed that we were short in the shoe department only when you were working. So I moved you to the linen department and nothing happened for a week. And then all of a sudden yesterday, it happened again. The till was short five dollars."

"Yes sir," I said.

"Have you been taking money from the cash register, Elisheba?"

I knew there was no point in denying anything, "Yes sir." I couldn't look at him.

Jerry paused a moment and then asked, "Can I ask you something?"

I nodded.

Jerry came around from his desk and sat next to me, "What I can't understand is why you only took one and five dollar bills.

Why so little? Why didn't you take a twenty or a hundred dollar bill?"

"I just needed to eat dinner," I said quietly.

"But you make minimum wage, surely you can pay for dinner."

I shook my head, "No I can't." I started crying, "I was just really hungry. I'm very sorry."

Jerry patted my hand, "I don't understand. Your manager, Gwen, says you are an outstanding employee; you always work hard, are extremely respectful, get here on time, and are willing to work during the weekends. But she also told me that you often forget to pick up your paycheck. What are you doing with your money? I know troublemakers and you just don't fit the bill."

"I'm sorry, sir. I just wanted some pizza."

"So you just bought dinner with the money? That's all?"

I nodded.

Jerry was silent for a few minutes and then he stood up and went back to sitting behind his desk, "Well, Elisheba, I'm a businessman. I just want what's mine returned to me. Since you are a minor I have to call your parents. I won't press charges because you have never been in trouble before. Frankly, I am just baffled by all this. I just don't know." He shook his head.

I waited outside his office until Papaji came to pick me up. Jerry told them what had happened and Mama wrote out a check to cover my theft.

Jerry looked at Papaji, "Your daughter is an exemplary employee. I wish I had a hundred more like her. But something isn't right. She told me she stole money so she could eat dinner, and given the small amount of money she took, I believe her. This whole thing just doesn't seem right. I can't comment on what's going on in your home, but I suggest you find out what's happening in your daughter's life. She's obviously trying to tell you something."

It was the only time in my life when Papaji was unable to respond to a stranger. I was mortified that I had put him such a position. Papaji shook hands with Jerry and in a few minutes I was in the back seat of the car. I was sure I was going to get a lecture to end all lectures. I was miserable and ashamed and could barely even lift my head. But I was wrong. Neither Papaji nor Mama ever mentioned the incident to me—it was as though it never happened.

By the time it was just Hannah, Joram, and me living at home, it was common to not even see Mama for days at a time, which was just fine with me. When I left the house she was sleeping, and when I returned she was upstairs in the master bedroom. Most of the time Papaji was traveling and, since we were required to make our presence known, I went upstairs and cheerily announced, "I'm home!" outside the locked master bedroom door. Then Hannah and I would go back down and spend an evening all on our own. Most of the time there would be a dinner of sorts on two plates sitting on the counter. Mama was cooking less and less, and when I saw a haphazardly prepared dinner, I had no desire to eat it. I knew the real food that she had made with care was being served upstairs. A few of the evenings, Hannah and I just put our plates back in the refrigerator without eating. One morning when Papaji was home he asked us about it.

"You didn't eat dinner last night?"

"No, I wasn't hungry," I said.

"I wasn't hungry either," said Hannah.

"You're gone all day long and when you come home you don't want to eat?" Papaji asked.

"No, not hungry."

"Your mother spends all day long cooking and you girls don't even bother to eat her food?"

As if the Baroness slaves all day to make meals for us! "We're not hungry," I said.

But I had learned something valuable. The fact that Hannah and I had not eaten Mama's food had struck a raw nerve with her and I sensed that she had been hurt and had told Papaji. After that, I rarely ate at home. All the meals left out for us were put back into the refrigerator. Many evenings I *was* really hungry, but my need to hurt her and teach her a lesson was so great that I never touched her food. It gave me so much power and a feeling of triumph that I devised new ways to eat before coming home. When we started working in Minneapolis, Hannah found out that free meals were provided at the Minneapolis food bank for the homeless. Then we began visiting the Minneapolis blood bank regularly. They gave us $25 if we donated our plasma. This was a wonderful bit of news and we were allowed to donate twice in any seven-day period.

The most painful memory of hunger happened during a road trip from Colorado. While it would have been easier to leave Hannah and me at home, Papaji was obsessed with the thought that if we were left alone we would run wild in the streets, invite men over, and before long we would be "spoilt" as though we were pieces of rotting fruit. While Mama did not want to take us with them, there was no other choice, and so we were grudgingly told to get ready for a trip to Colorado where Papaji would be the featured speaker for a week-long conference. While traveling, Hannah, Joram, and I sat in the back while Papaji and Mama sat in the front seat.

On the 14-hour drive to Colorado we read books, talked, and slept. We dozed and ate sandwiches we had packed for a late lunch. Colorado was a pure vacation for Hannah and me. The conference was held on the campus of Colorado State University. For the first time in my life I spent a week away from my parents.

Hannah and I gleefully moved our few things into our room in the girls' dormitory which we shared with two other girls. I made the most of my freedom.

The girls in the dorm were pampered southern belles and spent all day long getting ready and loudly exclaiming, Don't ya'll worry, I got plenty more pantyhose" or, "Ya'll think my hair looks okay?" They were extremely ladylike and prissy, but I pretended I was as normal as they were. Our meals were served in the dining hall and Hannah and I ate all we wanted of whatever we wanted. It was the best week I had ever had.

Our ride back to Minneapolis started early in the morning while it was still dark. We dozed on and off. We drove for a long time without stopping. In the late afternoon, I woke with a start and dripping with sweat. Hannah and I were alone in the back seat, the car was locked, and the heat and stuffiness had woken me. I nudged Hannah and we looked around and got our bearings. We were alone in the parking lot of a roadside restaurant.

"Where are they?" I looked around for something to drink.

"I don't know. They couldn't have gone far."

"Are they inside?" The idea seemed feasible. It wouldn't be the first time they had eaten on their own. "Oh, wait, here they come." Papaji, Joram, and Mama came out of the restaurant talking and laughing. "I guess we get the doggy bag."

"What did you expect? A four-course dinner?" Hannah joked.

I laughed, "Oh sure, nothing but steak and lobster." I had never tasted either one. Most girls my age daydreamed about clothes or boys. I often recounted to Hannah my fantasy of eating my dream meal—steak, baked potato with sour cream and butter, lobster, and for dessert a huge helping of strawberry shortcake.

The three of them settled inside the car without a word to us. The smell of food clung to their clothes and Joram mentioned a dessert he had enjoyed. Papaji started the car and we got back on the highway. I waited and waited but there was no mention of food or even something to drink. As Papaji drove on and on, my feelings went from hunger and thirst to hurt and pain to a boiling, raging anger. I could not believe they had absolutely no regard for our needs. They had slipped out while we slept, gone into the restaurant, enjoyed a sumptuous early dinner, used the bathrooms, come back out, and calmly continued the trip. It was as though Hannah and I didn't even exist. Even dogs and cats were given the opportunity to drink water and to be toileted.

My fury was so great I began to cry indignant tears and mumbled, "I can't believe they're doing this!" I wanted Papaji to hear so I could confront him, but he said nothing. Joram had slipped into a food coma and was sleeping soundly.

Hannah nudged me to shut up, "What are you so upset about? You don't possibly think they *care* about us, do you?"

I wiped my tears. It was still hard to believe that we were denied even basic needs like food and water.

On the veranda at the Chandigarh house, 1963
Hannah, David, Deborah and Elisheba

CHAPTER
THIRTEEN

T HE SEPARATION THAT had been created between Papaji, Mama, and Joram and the rest of us had grown to such a great extent that Hannah and I finally named this phenomenon. During one of the many times the master bedroom door was locked with the three of them inside, after Hannah made a remark about always feeling like an outsider, I said, "Oh who cares? I'm so sick of them always up there in that stupid room, just the three of them, with that stupid cabin fever!" Hannah and I started laughing, "That's good. That's exactly what it is—Cabin Fever!"

Getting into the "cabin" was no longer as easy as it had once been. While Mama never openly accused us of traipsing through her room, she must have suspected something because the easy-to-pick lock was replaced with a new doorknob. This one required a key and my amateur burglaries came to a halt for the time being. Other doors in the house that were off limits—the guest room and the basement storage room, also had new door-knobs installed. Mama wore a huge key chain and we could hear her approaching from the other side of the house, the huge jumble of keys jangling as she walked. Sometimes I would scornfully call her, "The Maintenance Man" when I felt particularly peevish.

Mama was a great collector of things. She enjoyed beautiful items like jewelry, perfume, and expensive clothing, but she was also a compulsive hoarder. Both she and Papaji threw nothing out. The room that formerly had belonged to Rashida Chachi was filled to the brim with thousands of costly items, many that had never been removed from their box or wrapper. The door was locked but every so often when Mama went on a forage to "find" something, I would get a glimpse of the sheer volume of excess items filling the entire room from floor to ceiling. The room was called "The Guest Room," although it was clear that no guest could ever use the room. Her collections and hoardings took on a life of their own. Eventually, not only was the guest room crammed to the ceiling with brand-new and used items but it spread to other parts of the house as well. The garage was almost impassable and the one family car could barely fit into the huge space. In order to get into the car, it had to be backed into the driveway because the garage was too full to allow the doors to open. In addition, the entire basement, except for a small space carved out for the washing machine and television, was packed to the gills with suits, saris, appliances, photos, dishware, linens, kitchen gadgets, gifts, thousands of Papaji's books, magazines, coats, clothes, shoes, furniture, lamps. They could have opened a department store! A small space was walled off as a small recreation area for us and the majority of the large basement was placed under lock and key behind which the mass of items grew and grew like a fungus.

While the house was full to bursting with things, I had just a few possessions. Indeed, when I left the house, all my belongings fit into five boxes. All the saris, jewelry, china, and other items that had once belonged to Mamaji had been appropriated by

Mama and she never offered them to Miriam or Deborah as they grew older. When my sister-in-law, Colleen, became the manager at the Estee Lauder counter at Dayton's department store at the Burnsville Center she brought an assortment of Estee Lauder cosmetics for me and Hannah—lip gloss, perfume, eye shadow, liners and mascara. It was our first time using such expensive products. We happily tried out the new shades. But after Colleen and Gideon left, Mama quietly went into our room and took all the products and stashed them in her room. Her own makeup drawer was already chock-full of expensive cosmetics. The drawer was so full, she couldn't even close it, but she still needed the few meager items we had been given to add to her collection.

One summer, Miriam and Richard came to visit us and brought a present for me—it was a beautiful pair of gold hoops. The gold was pure 22 karats and had a twisted rope design. It was the only valuable piece of jewelry I owned. I wore them for the entire summer and, at the end of the summer, after Miriam had left, Mama approached me.

"I don't think you should wear those to school. You might lose them," Mama said.

"I never take them off."

"Miriam would be really upset if you lost them. Why don't you let me keep them for you?"

I was unsure how to respond. If I gave the earrings to her, it was likely I would not see them again. But if I relinquished them, maybe she would be pleased with me. At the same time, I did not want to give away a gift from Miriam.

"I think she wanted me to wear them all the time and not take them off." I still held out some hope that I could please Mama, "You want to borrow them?" I asked.

She nodded and I handed over the precious earrings. She wore them that day and the day after that. Whenever I asked about them, she would agree that she had them, but never gave them to me. Then they disappeared for a while and the next time she wore them, she denied they were the same earrings that had once been mine. A few times I snuck into her bedroom in desperation and looked for my hoops, but I never found them in any of her three, huge overstuffed jewelry boxes or large jewelry drawers. When I got married, Miriam gave me a beautiful pair of garnet, pearl, and gold earrings. When Mama saw them, she again tried to "borrow" my earrings. But I was much wiser and held on to my wedding present.

I never coveted or begrudged Mama her expensive and varied collection of jewelry. However, there were a two pieces of jewelry that I wanted to snatch off her when she wore them. One was a gold and black enameled set which had belonged to Mamaji. The set was not expensive compared to what Papaji had given Mama, but she would not part with it. The second item was a ring that we had all given her one Mother's Day. Hannah and I had no money to contribute, but the rest of the family gave what they had and Papaji added in the lion's share to buy yet another new ring. It was a Mother's Ring. It had two rows of precious and semi-precious stones. There was an amethyst, aquamarine, ruby, yellow topaz, emerald, garnet, and sapphire to represent each month in which we children were born. The ring was presented to Mama by Papaji after he had read a scripture for her about the flawless wife from Proverbs 31. I have always hated that passage. "Who can find a virtuous woman? For her price is far above rubies." It went on to describe a perfect woman who worked hard in and out of the house, helped the poor, cared for the children and spoke wisely. The ending caused me to grind my teeth: "Her children arise up, and called her blessed; her husband also, and he praiseth her." Mama put the ring on her left-hand ring finger under her wedding set. Of all the expensive pieces of jewelry Papaji gave her, the

Mother's Ring is the only one I wanted to steal and keep for my own. It is a piece of jewelry that is meant to be earned through love, sacrifice, and care. The only person permitted to wear such a ring was Mamaji. To see it on Mama's finger caused the blood to rush to my face and my temples throb.

The intensity of Cabin Fever continued and contributed to what was Papaji and Mama's unrealistic and unhealthy attachment to Joram. At age 14, he was still living in the master bedroom. This strange arrangement only showcased the outlandish behavior between himself and his mother. For instance, Mama was fairly well-endowed and wore thin nightgowns. If my sisters or I knocked on the locked door, she would make us wait until she had put on a robe or at least held the robe over her breasts. Since Joram was inside the room, I couldn't understand how it was appropriate for a teenage boy to see her in a sheer nightgown, but when speaking to an 18-year-old female she felt compelled to cover up. Another bizarre example of their inappropriate attachment came each evening before bedtime. The usual quick hug and kiss was a different ritual for Joram and Mama; not just different, but downright disturbing. He would make a great performance of it. When he was younger, it was not a big deal, but as he grew older, the good night kiss became very creepy. First he kissed her on the cheeks. Then he squeezed and pulled her cheeks and then he kissed her again, biting and licking. This would go on for about three to four minutes, all the while she pleaded, "No, no, no Joram, no!" Her tone was one that made it clear that she really didn't want him to stop, but enjoyed each and every, wet, sloppy kiss. I could not stand to be in the same room when the good night ritual began. It physically turned my stomach and bile would rise to my throat. And, of course, she was the one who had forbidden Miriam and David from even an appropriate good night kiss for Papaji.

Papaji and Mama's love for Joram was not the same as other parents; an unconditional, sacrificial love. While it was true that they loved Joram, their love came with a price. He was compelled to love them back with as much fierceness and fervor as they did him. He was bonded to them forever because he learned quickly that not only were *they* the only two people *he* could trust, *he* was the only child *they* could trust. It was a disturbing alliance. I could not explain the three-way connection between Mama, Papaji, and Joram. It had become an unholy trinity

Joram's phobias were compounded because, instead of learning to face his fears, he was coddled and fussed over and this affirmed his apprehension. I always wondered why each of us had been quickly labeled as either neurotic or disturbed, and yet it had never crossed Papaji's radar that Joram had developed serious phobias. Hannah was Moody and Depressed, David was On Drugs and had Disruptive Disorders, I was in Spiritual Slumber and had a Bad Tongue. For Joram, his fear of the world was the beginning of a lifelong guilt trip. He was never allowed to experience or enjoy life like any other boy of his age. He was taught to depend on, rely on, and trust only two people in his life—Mom and Dad. The rest of the world, including his brothers and sisters, were not to be trusted because they were jealous, vicious, and only cared about their own interests. When he was forced to venture into what he viewed as an unsafe and unsavory world, a potentially wonderful experience became a terror-filled event. His inner anxieties manifested in physical tics. He cleared his throat, jerked his neck, and sniffed violently. It was a great responsibility to be a perfect creation. Joram not only had to be flawless but he had to be the third person in a tormented, co-dependent, guilt-ridden trinity. I felt sad for him—it was a great burden to bear.

My apprehension toward Joram turned to pity and at times,

understanding. In some ways, he was as helpless as I was. I couldn't blame him for being the chosen one. He had as little to do with his place of honor as I had to do with my place of disgrace. I had always fumed when Papaji read the story of Joseph and his brothers from the Bible. He held it as a great story of strength and the ability to persevere in a bad situation. I hated Jacob for favoring Joseph and causing a rift between him and his brothers. What sort of father would behave so unfairly? The lesson I learned from the account in Genesis was that parents can be unfair. Both Joseph and Joram had nothing to do with how their parents felt about them. The realization was a freeing one. Instead of feeling envy, I was eventually able to regard Joram as a brother.

In his older years, Joram refused to speak Hindi at all. He had never really used our mother tongue, and Papaji and Mama also began speaking mostly in English to accommodate him. Joram, for some time, had been calling Mama and Papaji, the relaxed American terms of "Mom" and "Dad." Instinctively, I knew that I was not allowed to use these titles, but we did eventually stop using the term "Papaji" and just began saying "Papa." Sometimes Papa stopped us and reminded us to use "Papaji." I am not sure what prompted the change. It may have been associated with the fact that we were speaking less Hindi and the "ji" at the end only seemed appropriate when speaking Hindi. It may have been that Joram's use of the word "Dad' was so much more casual. Or perhaps it had to do with a more subconscious reason—that more and more Papa was becoming as lost to me as Mamaji.

Mamaji and Papa Winter, 1963
Hopkins, Minnesota

CHAPTER
FOURTEEN

U NTIL MY SISTERS and I got married, we were kept on lock-down and not allowed out of the house. My brothers, while they still had to deal with Papa's questions and strictness, had a little bit more freedom. Even so, Papa mistrusted the entire practice of dating. His wish was that he would introduce us to some-one he found to be suitable, thus eliminating the need for any of us to date.

Months before Emmanuel told Papa of his decision to move out of the house, he experienced a series of fainting spells, stom-ach aches, and other stress-related symptoms. But when he finally worked up enough determination to announce his upcoming departure, it shattered Papa. At first he was angry and then his anger turned to hurt. He was attached to Emmanuel and could not understand why his son would want to leave home. When Papa was angry about something or someone, we would hear about it at dinner time or during devotions. But in this situation, Papa's hurt was so deep that he could not say anything about it. In all fairness, he was raised with old-school Indian values and children only left the family home at the time of their marriage.

When Emmanuel moved, he had no money for his first month's rent. Like all of us, he has been handing over his paychecks to Mama. He asked Papa for a loan of $125 to pay his first month rent on his apartment. When he moved in, he had a pillow and a blanket. Deborah visited him in the first few days and brought him a bag of groceries to tide him over until his first paycheck came.

As it turned out, Emmanuel's move from our house in Burnsville had more to do with a girl that he was dating than anything else. He had not been able to speak to Papa but he had confidentially told Mama about Jill Baker, a girl he had met in his class. He was teaching chemistry at North Central Bible College in Minneapolis while completing his dissertation entitled *The Dynamical Structure of the Pion*. Emmanuel had made his choice no matter what Papa thought, and soon was engaged to be married. One Saturday, Jill came to meet us. She wore a rust-colored dress and I was impressed with her ability to walk in four-inch heeled Candie's. She was sweet and spoke quietly. She had brown hair, pale skin and freckles, and I liked her immediately. During the questioning period, we learned she was from Michigan and she had been a gymnast in high school. The visit lasted a few hours, and after they left Papa began his breakdown and criticism of the afternoon. After any big event, he and Mama critically examined each and every facet of what had just occurred and added in their opinions. Hannah and I called this POBs—the Post-Occasion Blues. POBs occurred after a major event like meeting Jill or a family wedding, but also after other less important ones such as birthdays or dinners at Peter Chacha's house.

"*Humph.* Well, at least now I know why he wanted to move. She doesn't even have a college education."

"She's a very nice girl," Mama was more positive. It was to her benefit if Emmanuel left the house and married Jill.

"Nice, that's what people say when they can say nothing else. Did you see her feet? They were deformed."

"No, Papa," I said, "They're not deformed; she just keeps them pointed all the time because she used to be a gymnast." When Jill had removed her four-inch heels, she had kept her toes pointed when sitting. When she stood, she extended one foot in a modified frappé, lowering her leg up and down.

"Huh, what nonsense! They look deformed. And she also has spots on her face."

"Not spots, Raja, they're freckles."

"I liked her," Hannah said.

"Me too," I said.

"*Humphf.* What do you know?" Papa said. It would not have mattered if Jill had been of royal blood or the leader of a country—no one would have been good enough for Emmanuel.

After Emmanuel left the house, David also decided to move. For quite some time, David had been working at the mail center in Papa's office. Emmanuel had worked there before he got his job at North Central as had Gideon and Deborah. David went to classes at the University of Minnesota and then came home late after working the last shift at the mail center. He lived a separate life from Hannah and me and we saw little of him. Since the basement was a walkout, he didn't bother to use the front door anymore. Many nights he didn't come home at all. His long absences wore on Papa and he regularly asked David, "Are you on drugs?" To which David always responded in the negative, though his bleary, half-lidded eyes made me wonder. When I was older I asked David about it. His tiredness came from an inability to sleep. His allergies had been so severe he could barely function. In his classes he sneezed so much that he was asked to leave.

David's frustrations of living in the house became even more intolerable with the absence of Emmanuel. He didn't really want to go to college because Papa had chosen Chemistry as his major. David was a gifted musician and played the guitar, wrote music, and enjoyed philosophy. He longed to study theology or music. While he was considering his future plans, Miriam had written Papa from India and suggested that David could attend a prestigious medical school in Vellore, India. During his school breaks he would obtain hands-on experience at their mission hospital. David was excited about the possibility. While Papa thought it over, he bought some time and told David to pray about the idea. So David decided to put God to the test. As a teenager, his view of God was closer to that of a magician and he asked God to move the blades of a large, square, unplugged fan. He waited and waited for the them to rotate—after all, God had taken his mother, so why not show He cared by supernaturally turning the blades? But the fan remained still and Papa informed David the airfare to India was too expensive. The idea of studying in India was dropped.

David had always been nice-looking, but during his college years, he became an exceptionally handsome young man. He wore his hair longer and grew a beard. One night around 2 AM, I came downstairs for a drink of water and I heard some whispering and giggling in the living room. I turned the corner from the stairway and saw David embracing a girl. He seemed a little surprised but didn't skip a beat when he introduced her to me, "Hey Elisheba, this is Melissa." She was pretty girl with long blond hair. I was so impressed with David. He completely defied Papa and it seemed as though he was just begging to be caught. As always, I wished for David's courage. A few weeks later he moved out. When he talked to Papa about it, he was given a lecture about what a bad influence his friends were and told that he was going to the dogs. David simply packed a few of his belongings one Saturday and moved into an apartment with his friends. I was devastated when he left. I rarely saw him after that. I was glad he was out on his own living in freedom but I missed my crazy, fun brother.

With Emmanuel engaged and David out of the house, the attention now focused on Deborah. She had been working at Fairview Southdale Hospital for about two years as a registered nurse in Labor and Delivery. Deborah had desperately wanted to go to medical school but Papa had not wanted to invest that kind of money on a girl. Instead, he had encouraged her to become a nurse and told her she could return to school once she was married. Deborah was an overachiever. Once she set her mind to doing something, she would not only just complete it but she had to be the best at it. It was just the sort of mentality that would have served her well as a doctor.

For some reason, Papa had become weirdly fixated on the nursing profession. It had started with Miriam. She had started at Bethel College the year after Mamaji died. But the strain of taking care of the household and her siblings was too much for her and she was forced to drop out. Then she thought she might work as a stewardess for Northwest Airlines, which had their hub in the Minneapolis-St. Paul airport. Papa had initially agreed to this, but when he found out that stewardesses were required to serve alcohol, he forbade Miriam from pursuing a career in the airlines.

Instead, he found out that in a matter of ten months she could obtain her license for practical nursing. Incredibly, the Licensed Practical Nursing program was free and in return she could make $8,000 to 9,000 per year. She enrolled in the program and, in less than a year, was handing over her salary to Mama. When Miriam was working in 1972, the average American income was just over $11,000, so she was making good money. When Deborah expressed an interest in healthcare after her first year at the University of Minnesota, she too was put into the make-money-fast LPN program. Again, in less than a year, she was contributing

$9,000 to 10,000 to the household. But even with the fact that Deborah could bring in a nice tidy amount, she was single and that by itself was a red flag for Papa.

For Papa, a single girl past puberty was a constant source worry and he desperately needed his girls married off before they could get into trouble with men. He lived in constant fear that we would somehow break free from the rope he had lassoed tightly around us and find out that the world was actually a nice place to live in. So, he focused all his attention on convincing us to suppress our natural feelings, to control our desires, and to view anything remotely romantic as evil or dirty. Anything related to fun or freedom or an open discussion of feelings or emotions was immediately squashed or deemed to be wicked or mentally ill. Two of Papa's favorite threats were, "If you leave/ go out, I'll cut you off" and "If you date/ run around, I'll disown you." He had an unfounded distrust in all of us.

I had no one that could or would stand up to Papa. I had heard of stories from my friends about their fathers and how strict they were and sometimes they sounded similar to Papa. But they all had mothers that balanced their fathers. It was Mamaji who had rallied for Miriam, Gideon, and Emmanuel to be allowed to participate in normal American high-school activities like football games and parties. Indeed, she had dressed and helped Miriam get ready for her prom when she was a high-school senior. But I did not have Mamaji to counter Papa. I didn't have her to talk to him and help him see that his perspective was skewed. She would have made sure that each of us pursued our desires, not what was easiest or cheapest. She would have helped us find a partner who would help us grow and flourish, and would not have fought the inevitability of children growing up. She had known Papa from long ago, when he was a less confident young man, and she would have reminded him of his younger days and of his own passions that had brought them together. Only Joram had his mother who could temper and control Papa for him. Without Mamaji, I was left to contend with Papa alone.

I could never understand why Papa mistrusted me so much. I had done nothing to earn this and, in fact, I had done just the opposite. My classmates were drinking until the early morning hours, flunking classes, having sex, smoking pot, experimenting with drugs, and getting pregnant. My parents' biggest issues with seven teenagers had been our wish to become educated and a desire to express ourselves and to be heard. It was true that I also specialized in backtalk, but even then, my combined sins were relatively minor compared to that of the average teenager.

When Deborah's singleness became a greater liability than her potential to add to the household wealth, Papa began fielding offers from Indian fathers who would be happy to have their sons married to a beautiful, 23–year-old, living in America. Deborah had vocalized her wish for a man who was musically inclined and a non-doctor. She soon found herself engaged to a man she had never seen. Getting a visitor's visa was not easy, and Papa absolutely refused to allow Deborah to travel to India, even if she accompanied him on one of his many trips. Most likely, it was the cost of the ticket that was the prohibitive factor. Again, Mamaji, as any mother, would never have allowed her daughter to make such a decision without allowing the couple to meet and choose on their own, but in any case Deborah decided to marry, sight unseen. The couple began to write, send tapes, photos, and mementos back and forth. The idea that they could actually marry without ever meeting may have seemed strange to Deborah's friends, but her close friends accepted the unusual set of circumstances.

But before Deborah could be married, Emmanuel and Jill's wedding was to take place. The wedding was to take place about

700 miles from Burnsville in Flint, Michigan. Papa would be attending, but Hannah and I were to stay at home with Mama and Joram. One Saturday, early in June, Emmanuel drove up to the house. When he got out of his car, I was surprised that Jill was not with him. He said hello to me, but looked nervous and shaky. I followed him inside to where Papa was sitting in the living room. Emmanuel seemed preoccupied as though he had something on his mind. I left the room but stayed within earshot. The two talked about some of the wedding details and then Emmanuel took a deep breath.

"So, I'm wondering, I know you're coming, but what about everyone else?"

Papa sounded surprised, "Well, your mother will have to stay behind to take care of the children."

"I'm driving out to Michigan. You know Deborah is in the wedding and so is David."

"Well, Deborah is engaged, so she is free to go with you," said Papa, "And David? Well, I've written him off. I don't know about him."

"Yes. Well, you know Dan Larson and his sister Mary?" Emmanuel asked, "They're also driving from Minneapolis. They're going to take David with them. So I'll have room in my car."

"Room?"

"I'll have the extra space," Emmanuel said, "You know Gideon and Colleen and their boys are coming from Chicago."

"Huh. He's another one. He's gone to the dogs," Papa said.

Emmanuel began to stutter as he did when he was nervous, "Papa, I was hoping I could t-t-take Hannah and Elisheba along with me."

I was ecstatic. I had given up any hope of attending my own brother's wedding. But I never expected Emmanuel to make a special trip just to convince Papa to allow Hannah and me to attend. I felt awful that Emmanuel had been put in such a predicament. It was outrageous that he even had to make such a request.

"*Beta*, absolutely not. I won't allow it."

"But it's my wedding, Papa. I want my sisters there."

"You'll have most of us there. I don't want the girls roaming around," said Papa.

"I p-p-promise they'll only ride in my car and I'll make sure they stay with me all the time."

"No," said Papa.

"Please, I'll be in charge of them," Emmanuel said. "You'll be there yourself three days after we get there and you can see that nothing bad would have happened to them."

I was impressed with Emmanuel's tenacity and even more that this was all on our behalf.

"*Humphf*! Where will they stay? I don't want them in a hotel."

"No, no, of course not. David, Dan, and I are staying in a hotel. Deborah is staying with Jill at her parent's house and Hannah and Elisheba can stay with her. It will be safe. I'll be just a few miles away."

"No, I don't know. I don't want them running around, talking to boys."

After another half hour or so of questioning and balking, Papa finally gave in. I could hardly believe it. At age 17, I was to spend my first night in a different town, away from the watchful eyes of my parents. Papa decided that not only would we attend but he would purchase airline tickets for Joram and Mama as well. All of us, except for Miriam who was living in India, would be at Emmanuel's wedding.

It made me sad to think of how different Emmanuel's wedding would have been if Mamaji were alive. She would not only have been rejoicing at a family event, but she would have selected fine clothing for all of us to wear to my brother's wedding. Instead of Emmanuel begging for his younger sisters to attend, we would have all gone together as a family in a proper groom's baraat with great anticipation and enjoyment.

But, instead, on the morning of the great trip, Hannah and I packed a few things in a shared bag and readied the back of the avocado-colored Gremlin in which we would all be traveling. There had been no talk or discussion about what Hannah and I would wear to our brother's wedding. Again, as with Gideon's wedding, we were left to our own devices. David and Deborah were both to be in the wedding and so their clothing had already been decided. Mama decided on which one of her hundreds of costly saris she would choose and Papa had about the same number of suits to select from. Joram's wardrobe was almost as extensive as Mama's. My dresses were either ugly or grossly inappropriate and more suitable for a ten-year old. The least shabby one had been given to me for Christmas six years before. It was an A-line beige dress with a red rose appliqued on the chest. Along with this went a short beige jacket, which had puffed half sleeves and was tied loosely around the waist. It was horribly ugly and with it I wore knee socks and a pair of hideous beige, patent-leather Mary Janes. With this drab outfit, I was to wear my usual braid and glasses. Hannah had nothing to wear that could remotely be considered wedding wear and was told she should wear a sari. She only had one sari to wear; it was a sari that Miriam had left behind at our house. It was made of a cheap chiffon and had blue flowers painted on the material. The blouse was ill-fitting and the sari was made of flimsy material. I had no clue where Hannah had dug it up, but I had never seen it before. Along with an assortment of jeans and a few other pieces of clothing, we packed our wedding wear.

When we arrived in Michigan, Jill introduced us to her mother and father. Mrs. Baker was friendly and sweet, but Mr. Baker barely said two words the entire time we were at the house. Jill also had three brothers, aged 27, 21, and 19. I was shocked that not only were there boys in the picture, but as I was to find out, I would be *living* in the house with them for the week. I immediately began to feel nervous and sick to my stomach. Hannah and I were to occupy one of the bedrooms and Deborah shared Jill's room. The boys had moved their things into the basement and set up cots there. Jill's room was filled with wedding paraphernalia and her wedding dress and veil seemed to fill the entire room.

I felt strange; there was no one to tell me what I should or shouldn't do. I had no scowls or looks of disapproval to contend with. I was out, on my own, with no parents, at a real social event. Instead of the usual occasions which I had come to accept as social, such as going over to a family member's house, having Peter Chacha and Maureen Chachi come over, or attending choir practice at church; this was a real, honest-to-goodness, live social event with boys to whom I was not related. At first I was unsure of how I should behave, but then I began talking and laughing as if I had been doing this my whole life. Mrs. Baker was impressed with the help Hannah and I were able to provide. She exclaimed over our skills in the kitchen. I was so happy to have my work appreciated, I even offered to help cut and chop vegetables before dinner one night. As we chopped, Mrs. Baker realized that she did not have enough milk for dinner. Taking some money from her purse, she handed it to me and asked me to walk to the nearby grocery store for some milk. I agreed, and just as I was walking out the door, Jill's youngest brother, Mike came in.

"Where you going?" he asked.

"Your mom just needs some milk."

"Okay. Well, hold on. I'll go with you."

At this I began to sweat. I knew I was not allowed to go anywhere alone with a boy. Even a simple walk in broad daylight in the middle of the street was something that I knew was absolutely forbidden. "Uh no, that's okay. I don't mind going on my own," I said.

"Why? I wanna walk with you. Hey, I have a better idea. Why don't I just drive? It'll be faster. It's really hot today anyway."

Mrs. Baker nodded, "Yes, that's a good idea. Why didn't I think of that? It's much too hot. Mike will drive you." At this I almost threw up right on Mrs. Baker's sparkling kitchen floor. Walking with a boy was one thing, sitting in a car and driving somewhere with a boy was almost the same as getting into bed with him. I wished I had never heard of milk, Michigan, or Mike. All three of them were going to get me into more trouble than I could even imagine.

I panicked, "No, no, I like walking. And I have a lot to think about." I grabbed the money and started to walk out of the kitchen.

"Don't be ridiculous, Elisheba! Mike, take her to the store," Mrs. Baker commanded.

"Come on, Elisheba, let's go," said Mike.

"Okay," I could say no more. My head was pounding and I knew this short car ride would be responsible for ruining my reputation of being chaste, untouched, and virginal. For the first time in my life, I learned what it was like to have a man open a car door for me. I got in and sat as close as I could toward the car door, hugging the arm rest. Mike got into the driver's side and started the engine. When he backed out of the driveway, he put his right arm on the back of my seat so he could look through the rear window. The close proximity of his hand caused me to shrink even further into the corner.

"Everything okay?" Mike asked.

"Huh? Oh sure, fine, fine," I said.

On the way, Mike talked about something, but I remembered none of it, because I was certain that at any moment Papa would suddenly loom up in front of me, demanding to know what I was doing in the car with a boy. The entire trip lasted no more than 20 minutes, but it was the most agonizing 20 minutes of my life. When we returned with a gallon of milk and my purity intact, I excused myself and went to the room I was sharing with Hannah. It took me almost an hour to recover from the frightening episode.

The next day, The Cabin Fever crew arrived. Hannah and I stayed as far as we could from the Baker boys. At one point in the evening, Mike sat down next to Hannah and began joking with her. She laughed at something he said and accidentally hit his knee with her hand. I quickly looked up to see if Papa had seen this great transgression, but I wasn't sure. I tried to remain as non-interested in the events of the evening as possible—looking too enthusiastic or being too jovial could also prove to be dangerous.

On the day of his wedding, Emmanuel was dazzling in an all-white tux with white, shiny shoes. The bridesmaids wore light blue dresses and the groomsmen wore light blue tuxes with ruffled shirts. Jill walked down the aisle in a simple white gown. It was a beautiful ceremony—my brother and Jill were very much in love. Early the next morning, Hannah, Deborah, and I began the trip home, driven by some church friends who were also returning back to Minnesota.

When we reached Burnsville late in the evening, we were treated to a long list of POBs: the pastor had not been properly impressed with Papa and all his qualifications, the songs had been hippie-ish, the food was unsettling, the day had been scorching, Emmanuel's hair was too long and also hippie-ish, Mr. Baker had hardly spoken to Papa, the church was cramped—the list was endless. One thing that Papa was particularly upset about was that Hannah had worn such a horribly cheap and ugly sari. He scolded Mama for allowing this to happen and wanted to know why she had not given one of her saris to Hannah. Mama did not respond, but did what she always did when she was caught in a difficult situation. She sat in her chair, leaned forward, stared at the floor, crossed her left hand over her waist and covered her mouth with her right hand. I hated it when she did this. Whenever I asked her a question or confronted her with something that she did not like, she would assume this horribly annoying pose. My fantasy was to rip that hand off her face and command her to, "Speak! Say something, say anything! Just SPEAK!" But she was the Queen of Silence and she persisted in muzzling herself. Later on, Papa called Hannah and me into the living room. He was in his Lazy Boy and we sat on the carpet as we always did.

"Hannah? Elisheba? Why did you behave so shamefully with those boys?"

Hannah and I were caught completely off-guard, "What did we do?"

"Don't act so innocent. You know what you were doing."

"I don't," I said.

"Hannah, why did you rub that boy's legs?"

I almost started laughing. The image of Hannah sitting and rubbing Mike's legs popped into my head and I covered my mouth to suppress my laughter. *Why would she ever touch, much less massage a boy's legs? How dumb do you think we are?*

Hannah started getting weepy, "I didn't! I would never do that!"

"I saw you! You were laughing and rubbing his legs," Papa said.

At this, I burst out giggling. My mind was working overtime

and I saw Hannah cackling like an old witch, wickedly chuckling as she got her kicks by rubbing lotion into Mike's legs.

"What are you laughing for? You were even worse," Papa said.

"Oh really. What did I do?"

"Oh I heard about how you went with that boy in that moving bedroom."

I was disgusted, "It was his car and I had no choice, Papa. I tried to walk by myself, but Jill's mother insisted he give me a ride."

"Oh! So, now you listen to Jill's mother, instead of your own father. Why should she care if you go to the dogs! You couldn't wait to go around with boys. You girls are just panting after third-class boys. The first chance you get, you had to run to the car with that boy."

"I didn't run to the car. I walked."

"You know, Elisheba, you should control your mouth. You have a wicked tongue. Instead of making jokes and talking back, you should show some shame."

"I didn't do anything, so why do I have to be ashamed?"

"Oh, ho! So going with a boy is nothing. I see, now at least I know what kind of a girl you are," Papa said.

The lecture continued for a full two hours and was punctuated midway with Mama bringing in some tea for Papa to quench his thirst and give him energy for the second hour. We learned that we:

1. Had brought shame to the family.
2. Were akin to common streetwalkers.
3. Could be sure that no decent man would ever want us.

I had heard it all a million times, and as I had done during those million times before, I nodded my head now and then and visualized myself on a beach instead of listening to what Papa was saying. At the end of the lecture, we agreed that we:

1. Had behaved shamefully
2. Needed to apologize
3. Should give our solemn promise not to run like strumpets in the streets any longer.

Afterwards I asked Hannah, "Hey! Where did you imagine you were, while he was lecturing?"

"Oh, I was on a cruise. It was great—there was a huge buffet and the water was calm and beautiful. Where did you go?"

"I was on marooned on an island all by myself. Hey, you know what I do sometimes? When he's sermonizing like that, sometimes I imagine him in a pink tutu with ballet slippers and tights. So hilarious!" Hannah and I laughed.

The rest of the summer was filled with preparations for Deborah's wedding. But unlike an ordinary wedding, there were no mother-daughter trips to shops for flowers, cakes, or invitations. Instead of having her own mother help her plan for her big day, Deborah and Jean did the planning themselves. The only input Mama made was to keep harping on the expense. It was to be a extremely low budget, a bargain-basement-price sort of wedding. Poor Deborah had dreams of a beautiful, romantic day, filled with her favorite red roses, but it was not to be.

For her bridal shower, we were allowed the use of our living room and Deborah's maid of honor, Jean, paid for the day. Even though it was usual for a mother and sisters to host a shower, Hannah and I were not able to do so due to our lack of funds. Mama made no attempt to host one. Deborah's wedding was to be the only one in which each and every one of our family would be in attendance. Miriam and Richard, Gideon and Colleen,

Emmanuel and Jill all planned to make the trip—even David was to be there with his new girlfriend. There was a possibility for it to be a wonderful family event, but given the fact that Papa and Mama just wanted Deborah out of the house and there was no real concern for her happiness, this was not to be.

As usual Mama commenced to choose the most extravagant sari and jewels for the wedding and as always out-dressed the bride. But this time Papa stepped in and told her to allow Hannah to use one of her saris. She selected one and gave it to Hannah who thought the sari was pretty and was happy to wear it. The only problem was that after the wedding was over and Hannah returned it, Mama told her, "I can *never* wear that sari again!" Giving the sari to Hannah outright never occurred to Mama. I was told I had to wear a sari as well. But I was not given one of the hundreds from Mama's collection of expensive saris. Instead, I used the only one I had—a simple purple and blue sari that Miriam gave me. My parents' behavior was outrageous. Indian families place such a large emphasis on weddings. As sisters of the bride, we should have been dressed in appropriate wedding finery.

The wedding took place at River Hills Methodist church which was close to our house. Deborah wore a beautiful white and gold sari, elaborate gold jewelry given to her by her in-laws, and a long veil. The groom wore a black-and-white tux as did the groomsmen. In order to outfit her bridesmaids, Deborah visited Minnesota Fabrics to buy six yards of chiffon in light pink, just as Miriam had done. I often wondered why Papa didn't just buy real saris during one of his many trips to India. Deborah had wanted a bouquet lush with red roses but had to be content with a few roses and mostly filler flowers. The ceremony was an hour long with Papa giving a sermon. There had been a disagreement between Papa and Reverend Jean Lane who was filling in for the vacationing senior pastor. The fact that she was a woman pastor completely threw Papa off and he sputtered and balked at her directions during the entire wedding rehearsal. Reverend Lane was used to dealing with chauvinistic men and didn't back down. She enraged my parents so much that during the wedding POBs, I actually heard Mama indignantly stammer, "That Jean Lane! She is nothing but a, a, a...*Bitch!*" It was a magnificent moment and Hannah and I enjoyed a good laugh. After the ceremony, the reception was held in the church basement. There was no dinner and no lunch. There was punch, cake, chicken salad, rolls, fruit salad, and cheap melt-away pastel-colored mints. After Deborah was married, she went on a weekend honeymoon to Northern Minnesota where a friend of hers owned a cabin.

As with all my brother and sisters who had left the house, once Deborah was married, she became an outsider or a "they" or "them" during conversations inside the house. As in, "You know, *they* fill your head with lies" or, "*They* get together and *they* talk bad about us" and, "I don't want you to go over *there* and spend time with *them*." For about five summers, Miriam and Richard had stayed with us with their boys. They were the best summers because I actually had someone living in the house that loved and cared for me. But the visits ended suddenly because Mama complained that, "Miriam is a bad influence on the girls. They tell them bad things and then the girls have bad attitudes." It was not clear at that time, what it was that my parents were so desperately trying to hide, or did not want us to talk to our married siblings about. I could not be both friends or "pally" as Mama liked to say, with my married brothers and sisters and please my parents at the same time. For the time being, I only understood that I was being forced to pick a side.

On the one hand, I had grown to scorn the so-called affection or interest Papa and Mama took in my life. I knew Mama did not love me, but I was unable to untangle myself from at least hoping that they could tolerate me or, at the very least; not despise me. On the other hand, the only people I knew really loved me were my brothers and sisters, but as each one left the house, they joined a group that I was taught to view as the Betrayers, the Disloyal, or the Traitors. I could not show any kind of allegiance or love toward them, because then my life inside the house would be hell. I had to listen and even contribute to discussions and maligning comments about them. Sometimes, if Hannah and I kept quiet when this was going on, we would be egged on, "Huh, suddenly you are very quiet. You know Miriam is very *kanjoos*, very cheap, don't you?" If we didn't agree and add to the story, we would be branded as those who are siding with the enemy. I longed for the day I could also join the "They" group.

Deborah settled in an apartment that was walking distance from our house. Even with her close proximity, we were rarely allowed to visit our sister. Not only had she become the enemy, but an added issue was the problem of a new male to contend with. The couple was newlywed, but Papa still thought it was dangerous for Hannah and me to spend time at Deborah's house. I wondered if Papa ever really looked at us and saw just how undesirable we really were, but in any case he huffed and puffed and blew the house down, "What if Deborah is working and you are alone with *him*?" or, "I've heard of brothers-in-law who take an interest in their sisters-in-law." At the same time, while he was berating Deborah's new husband, he would also use him for his own purposes. If Papa needed a task completed or heavy work done, he would ask my brother-in-law to do it. When he wanted to hear a favorite Hindi song, he commanded his new son-in-law to sing as he was a gifted tenor. Throughout all his inane and nonsensical tirades, we could count on Mama to either leave the room or sit with her mouth covered as if a word of reassurance or compassion would fly out against her will.

***

I was now a senior in high school. And for me the worst thing about being a senior was that Hannah was not in school with me. She held a brief conversation with Papa about her wishes to pursue a career in Special Education or Psychology after high school, but Papa scoffed at the idea and put her into the Practical Nursing program, just like her two sisters before her. I had my own conversation with Papa about my post-high plans. Everyone at school assumed, because I had been taking math and science courses, I too would be pursuing a medical career like my mother. Little did they know that while Mama's father had supported her potential to become a surgeon, my own parents could barely dig deep enough into their pockets to pay the $1 per day training fee that Hannah's school required. But for some reason, all the resistance had not quelled my lofty dreams, and I girded up all my courage and fortitude to talk to Papa about my future plans.

"I've been thinking about what I want to do after high school," I said one day as he sat surrounded by books and yellow legal pads filled with his writing.

"Well?" Papa took his reading glasses off and looked up expectantly.

"I'm not very good at math and science."

"That's because you never study. You can't expect to get good grades without studying. Do you remember how much Emmanuel studied?" Papa asked.

No, it's because I hate math and science and the Baroness overwhelms me with so much work that I CAN'T study! "That's true," I said, "But anyway, I don't like the sciences."

"Science and Math are much better than other *faltu,* nonsense subjects."

"I like English and History."

"No, you can't do anything with English and History."

"I like to write. I was thinking that I could study Journalism at the university." There were no creative writing programs at that time and journalism was the only career I knew of that required writing skills.

"*Jāna dē!* What kind of nonsense is this? You haven't given this any thought. You don't know anything about writing," scoffed Papa.

"Well, I'd like to learn. Anyway, I've been thinking..."

"Huh! What do you know about what is good for you?" interrupted Papa, "You have no idea what is best. Just listen to me and I'll tell you what to do."

"But I don't want to be a nurse."

"Don't you want a stable job? With nursing you can always have a job."

"Yes, but I don't want to be a nurse. I want to write."

"You think you can run around and write and be a journalist? What happens if you have to travel or go somewhere on your own? You'll be a woman all by yourself. It's different with a man. He can protect himself. No decent man is going to want a woman who has been around on her own," Papa said.

"I can think about that later, I guess. I just want to write."

"Huh, just stop this *bakwaas*, this writing nonsense. You get your nursing degree and after you get married, you can do this writing shmiting or whatever you want."

"Oh, uh, I'm not getting married," I said.

"Oh, ho. You will be the first one to want to be married. You mark my words."

"I won't. Men are all so egotistical anyway."

"Huh, we'll see. For now, you listen to me. I know what's best for you."

Desperately, I tried an argument that was closer to his mindset, "But, Papa I really think writing is what God wants me to do."

At this he burst out in a cynical laugh, "*YOU* know what God wants? You know nothing. You will be a nurse."

I suppose I should have insisted. But at 18, I was impressionable and incredibly unsure of myself. While I knew writing was the only thing I wanted to do, I caved to his command and resigned myself to a career in nursing when, in reality, it was the last thing I wanted to do. I was devastated that I had not been able to stand up to Papa. I went to my room and wrote pages and pages in my journal, angry at myself for being weak, at Mamaji for not being around when I needed her most and at God for taking her from me. Years later, I reminded Papa about this conversation and he told me that if I had fought harder and been more insistent, he would have allowed me to pursue journalism.

While I grudgingly readied myself for a career as a nurse, Keisha, in her normal life, scouted colleges with her parents. I was heartbroken to think I would lose my faithful friend. While listening to my predicament, she expressed an interest in my post-high plans, so much so that she actually explored the Vo-Tech program with her parents. She decided that she too would attend nursing school with me. I was aghast and begged her to continue her education at a real college. I suspect her parents also felt disappointed and wanted her to experience college life as she should. But again, they were unbelievably supportive of their daughter's decision. Keisha and I decided go to Dakota County Vo-Tech which was relatively close to Burnsville, rather than attend the Vo-Tech in downtown Minneapolis like my sisters had done. She would pick me up in the mornings and drop me off in the afternoons.

When I graduated from high school, Papa was out of town. I went to the ceremony with Emmanuel, Jill, Hannah, Deborah, and her husband. Mama stayed home with Joram. Graduation day was bright and sunny. The bleachers were dotted with relatives and the football field was filled with a thousand black-gowned graduates. I missed having Papa at graduation because he could always be counted on for an entertaining blow by blow as each student received their diploma. Papa didn't think much of the fuss that was made for high school graduations. At other commencements, he had scoffed at students who enthusiastically high-fived each other shouting, "We made it!" or, "We did it!" as they crossed the podium.

"Well, this is probably the most they'll ever accomplish, so they deserve to be excited."

I had laughed and protested, "Oh, Papa. Not everyone can get a PhD."

"Humph, a PhD? You must be joking. Most of these duffers won't even complete a simple BS."

I was not allowed to attend the all-night graduation party sponsored by the high school or any of my classmates' open house celebrations. By this time, I didn't even bother to mention any social opportunities I was invited to, because I knew I would not be able to accept. Keisha gave me a small wrapped box after the ceremony and I cringed because I had no gift to give her. Mrs. Dobbins also pressed a small package into my hand after she hugged me. Many other classmates passed me cards and small gifts, and I had nothing to give in return. Later, at home, I unwrapped the box Keisha had given me. It was a silver link bracelet with a long clasp. On one side, the clasp was engraved with the words *Friends Forever*. On the other it said *Love, Keisha*. Mrs. Dobbins had given me a beautiful, 24-inch, silver chain.

When we got home, Mama had made a two-layer cake embellished with yellow icing and black licorice squares. I have one picture of me from that day. It's taken on Miriam's old Kodak camera that she gave to me. In the picture, Emmanuel, Jill, and Hannah surround me in my black cap and gown as we stand around the cake and yellow roses that Emmanuel and Jill gave me. Three years passed before I could gather enough money to get the film developed and see the picture.

Our high school graduation gifts had progressively diminished in quality over the years. Miriam was treated to a trip to London with Papa; Gideon had gone to Canada; Emmanuel had been given the VW bug; (as he was the only driver besides Papa at that time) and Deborah had been given an electric typewriter, which she was required to leave behind after her marriage. But David rode to his high school graduation with a friend and was forced to walk home because neither Papa nor Mama bothered to attend. Hannah and I missed his ceremony because we were still on Operation Lockdown.

When a deeply disappointed David arrived home after his commencement, he told Papa, "I graduated today."

Papa looked up from the book he was reading and said, "You're only a junior. You don't graduate until next year."

After Hannah graduated, she was treated to a dinner at the Embers restaurant in Burnsville. I got my present in September the week before I was to begin at Vo-Tech. I was given contact lenses for which I had been begging.

My school years had brought me both pain and joy. I lived a double life and outsiders believed that my family was a wonderful and close one. My formal education had been in Math, Reading, Science, and the Humanities. But as I stepped into the adult world, what I had learned outside of school had been my most valuable lessons. I learned to live without mother-love, and to live with someone who not only didn't love me but resented and despised my very presence. I learned to live with a father who had forgotten me. I learned to lie. I learned to steal. I learned to turn a tragic circumstance into something comical. I learned to make something from nothing. I learned that my siblings were strong

and to look to them as role models. I learned about real friendships. I learned to never, ever, trust anyone. I learned that injustice is almost as bad as not being loved. I learned that I feared God instead of loving Him. I learned to carry guilt. I learned to hate. And I learned that not having Mamaji in my life made my heart physically ache.

Mamaji graduation
Kinnaird College for Women
Lahore, Undivided India,
circa 1942

PART
TWO

CHAPTER
FIFTEEN

M Y UNIFORM FOR nursing school was an ill-fitting tunic-style top with white pants or skirt. It was required that we all buy the light-blue striped top with a built-in white faux pinafore but the white slacks and white shoes could be of any variety. We were to purchase at least two uniform tops. Keisha had three and I was given the money to purchase one. With this, I wore Miriam's old pair of white nursing pants and a pair of Deborah's white shoes, which, by that time, were not only used but more than ten years old. I also had to buy a stiff white nursing cap. Along with my new contacts, I was allowed to wear eye makeup and lipstick. My hair was braid-less and I actually felt almost presentable on my first day.

My new classmates were a surprise to me. Besides Keisha and me, there were two other girls fresh from high school. One of the greatest gifts I got from LPN school was meeting my dearest lifelong friend, Carol Christenson. We bonded instantly because she didn't bat an eye when I told her I was from a family of eight. She was a petite blue-eyed blond and the youngest child in her family of 11. The rest of my classmates were in their 40s and 50s. There were even two or three grandmothers in their 60s. Our entire nursing class numbered about 50, and I was enormously pleased that I had not been able to convince Keisha to go to college.

In addition to purchasing a large packet of printed material, which was to be used along with the lectures as a workbook, I was required to buy thick books on basic nursing, anatomy and physiology, nutrition, geriatrics, medical-surgical nursing, pediatrics, and obstetrics. Tuition for my course was $1 per day and it could not be avoided, but when I asked for extra money to pay for the required texts; Mama balked. Each time I questioned her, she said she couldn't find her checkbook, or that she would write a check the next day. I never got money for books and so I used the old textbooks that Miriam and Deborah had used. Hannah had just finished using them, so buying new ones for me seemed unnecessary. No matter that the books were of an entirely different title and edition, no matter that the books were nearly 15-years-old, no matter that the field of nursing had made advancements since the books had been printed—it only mattered that no extra money should be spent on my post-high education. I prepared to begin nursing school in my somewhat used uniform and my very used books. Keisha's parents purchased the needed textbooks for her and I was able to use them occasionally to fill in the blanks. I was an 18-year-old who was required to learn a skill I had not chosen and at the same time, I was denied the funds to buy the basic tools to study for it.

While I was happy to spend time out of the house, I was not happy to be stuck learning a vocation for which I had no interest and no support. In class I was antsy, doing the least amount of work possible. I counted down the months before my release from my training. Sometimes I paid attention and studied in the library, but most of the time I convinced Keisha or Carol to skip class with me.

In Keshia's Mustang, we three zoomed away from class, stopping for pizza and then going on to a movie or window shopping. I skipped so many classes that I was placed on attendance probation. My test scores were above average, so I could not be expelled for falling behind academically. My instructor was at a loss for an appropriate punishment and could only promise me, "Something would happen." For me, that was nothing—I was used to dealing with real consequences and I continued to skip class. By the time I actually completed the program, I had missed more than half the lectures.

What puzzled me was Papa's desire for all his daughters to become nurses. Since he was desperate to shield us from the world, Nursing was just about the most unlikely choice as a profession. In fact, it exposed me to more than he could have ever imagined. During the Human Sexuality course, I received my first sex education. Up until then, I had absolutely no clue about sex. I knew that a man and woman were built differently, but that was the extent of my knowledge. When I found out what intercourse actually was, I was horrified. It took me a few days to process the information, and when I realized that this was what Papa had accusing me of, all the times he mentioned, "Running around" or, "Getting into trouble." I was not only disgusted but mortified that he thought so lowly of me. I had never even seen a picture of a naked man and, all of a sudden, I was inundated with nakedness. Even after seeing so much flesh day after day, I was still extremely naïve.

I was incredibly unprepared to handle male patients and the first time I had to do so still stands out in my mind. As a nursing student most of my practical training was during Clinicals. This was on-the-job training which took place at hospitals or nursing homes. One morning, Keisha and I prepared to get Dante, an old, Italian man ready for his weekly tub bath. Keisha was as naïve as

I was. Dante was one of the easier patients because he was able to walk, feed himself, needed minimal assistance with dressing, and was still lucid. We wheeled him into the tub room, helped him to his feet and told him to get ready to get into the tub. We pulled the curtain and waited. After a few minutes, Dante called to us. Keisha pulled back the curtain. There was Dante—buck naked, smiling and fully aroused. I had never seen anything so horribly red in my life. Dante slapped his private parts, grinned and said, "Woo-hoo girlies! Come on! Let's get started!"

My eyes widened and Keisha and I ran out of the tub room and stood outside. We were light headed and woozy, and clung to the wall for support. I was sweating, in tears, and my head was spinning. Our clinical instructor came around the corner and asked us what had happened. We were still doubled over, trying not to cry. She had absolutely no sympathy for us. She scolded us and said, "Did you think this was a cocktail party? Quit your sniffling and get back out there!" and then proceeded to assign us the most difficult patients during Clinicals after learning of our inexperience.

The first job after LPN school was at Walker Methodist nursing home. It was the last place I wanted to work because I had my fill of cleaning and caring for oversized, diapered, and aging babies in nursing school. But when it came time to apply for a job, Papa made it extremely difficult to actually *get* one. He had a number of strict directives and from our perspective Hannah and I interpreted his rules as follows:

1. Get a full-time job—it must be on the city bus line.
2. If not on the bus line, then the job should be within the schedule of a friend who will drive and the friend should be extremely ingratiating to Papa.
3. If weekend work is required, make sure you find

someone stupid enough to take you back and forth without you ever helping with the driving.
4. The job should have little or no contact with males.
5. Even though you were not allowed to go to college, the job should pay the same as the CEO of Northwest Bank, and if not, FIND OUT WHY!
6. The job should be all daytime hours because everyone knows good girls aren't out past dark (even if they are full-fledged nurses).

With the rules in hand, I set out to find a job at a hospital. If I had to be a nurse, I wanted to work in pediatrics. I went on interview after interview, but as soon as I found out that every single hospital required all new nurses to pay their dues and work night shifts or rotate from days to nights, I was unable to accept any of the job offers. Since I could not fulfill Rules 2, 3, and 6, and still work at a hospital, I finally gave in and applied at Walker Methodist nursing home. I was offered a job before the interview was even over. I would work full-time on weekdays, every other weekend, and make the salary of a grown man. During the day, I took care of patients, administered medications, gave treatments, called doctors, assessed health issues, and gave direct patient care. When I returned home in the evenings, I was barely allowed to step out of my yard, could not go out on my own, was unable to speak to males, and still had to ask permission to watch television. In addition, I was not permitted to keep my paycheck.

An LPN working at a nursing home made about $13,000 annually. I was given $15 a month to spend however I wished. I was still expected to buy birthday, Christmas, Mother and Father's Day gifts with this money, so just a small amount was left over to spend on myself. I did not pay for room, board, food or for my monthly pass for the Minneapolis bus system which was about $30 a month. I had no control or input over what happened to my earnings. Even the tax-return checks issued to me by the state and federal government were endorsed and then handed over to Mama.

Around the same time, Gideon was promoted to regional manager at Tag & Tox, the leather company where he worked. Every winter before Christmas, Tag & Tox held a huge three-day, blowout sale, and Gideon asked Hannah and me if we wanted an extra job during the Christmas holidays. We happily accepted. We worked as cashiers and he allowed us to pull the leather goods we liked before the sale began. I found a beautiful, white, leather coat that had a side neck zip. Hannah found an ultra-soft, gray jacket that had a tight waist and a peplum. Gideon gave me a 70% reduction in the price and took this amount from my pay before my check was cut. In this way, I was able to pay for the merchandise before my check was turned over to Mama. I decided to buy both jackets, and gave Hannah the gray one as an early Christmas present. But there was a surprise awaiting Hannah and me. When we got home after our first long day at the sale, Mama told us, "I've decided that you can keep your checks from this job." *What? Are you being all benevolent with OUR money? Hey Baroness, what right do you have to tell us that we can keep money we earned with our great effort and sweat?*

But I was ecstatic; I had never had that much money together in all my life and when Gideon asked us to work overtime, we happily agreed. I still had to buy Christmas presents, but even then, I would have some left over to supplement my meager wardrobe. The money was a boon to us. Even though we were working full-time as nurses, we still worked at the sale for our own spending money.

Tag & Tox was also responsible for the second of my dearest and longest friendships. Once, when I had skipped class to spend the day at the mall, Carol, Keisha, and I stopped at the Tag & Tox store in the Burnsville Center. There, Carol introduced me to the assistant manager, Annette Saunders, who was her best friend from Rosemount High School. Annette was a red-haired Jamaican and I liked her immediately because she was as sarcastic as I was and also had to teach people the correct pronunciation of her name. She knew and feared Gideon. She told me how he had once come into her store and immediately fired an employee for sitting idly instead of working. Gideon had also banned all cigarette breaks because it wasted company time. He ran a tight ship and Annette's eyes opened wide when she realized I was Gideon's sister. I laughed, said something sarcastic about my brother, and this began our lifelong friendship.

Because I had extra cash that Christmas, Hannah and were able to purchase real presents, instead of making them at home. As usual The Cabin Fever members gave each other expensive and costly gifts, and doled out a few cheap items to us as a token. I always marveled at how Joram, at such a young age, was able to give expensive gifts such as a new lens for Mama's camera or yet another jewel-encrusted ring or necklace. Obviously, it was Papa buying the expensive presents for her on his behalf but our names were never included on those presents. We still purchased presents with whatever money we could scrape together. And no matter how much money we spent or how hard we tried to give a nice gift, these were always tossed aside and never used or appreciated. I always loved the post-Christmas visit from Peter Chacha and Maureen Chachi because I could always count on a real present. Maureen Chachi always asked Mama, "Now show me all the jewels you got for Christmas." I'm sure she didn't mean to be sarcastic, but it was always such a moment of justice for me as Mama proudly displayed her expensive gifts that were in contrast to the ones they had given us. I could see my uncle and aunt exchanging looks.

That year, there were two jewelry boxes for Hannah and me. We still got our presents in tandem—if she got something, I got the same, just in another color. We both received a gold cross necklace with matching cross earrings.

"Thanks," Hannah and I said together.

"Thanks? Is that all you can say? Those are real gold! Fourteen karat!" bellowed Papa.

"Uh, okay. Wow, it's great," I said unenthusiastically. Without showing anyone else, I showed Hannah and Deborah the tag that read *14-karat gold-plated*.

Papa was getting upset, "You know Madam? We get these girls these expensive necklaces and they don't even understand the value. I think we wasted our money."

Two can play this game! "Wow! Thanks so much, real gold. Oh my goodness! Look, Deborah, REAL gold," I put on my Academy Award–winning act.

"Wow REAL gold earrings too? Oh wow!" Hannah played along.

"You're going to have to be careful with those, you guys. I mean real gold!" Deborah chimed in as well.

The charade played well and we oohed and aahed over the jewelry, trying to cover our laughter. The real gold necklaces turned my neck green and I couldn't wear the earrings because the 14-karat gold infected my ears. A few Christmases later, I gave Hannah a silver ring with a tiny chip of a blue sapphire in it.

When Hannah opened it she said, "How pretty! Look, it's a sapphire."

Papa looked at it and scoffed, "Huh! What does Elisheba know about real sapphires?"

I appreciated the gifts I got from people who really cared

about me. Also, by that time, I was enjoying attention from young men my age who also gave me small gifts and cards, which I kept hidden. The joy of Christmas was no longer controlled by what Papa and Mama did or didn't give us. By the end of my first year as an LPN, I decided to go back to school and become an RN. It was not that I had decided on nursing as a career in particular, but I had a thirst for a college education and I figured I may as well pursue the path of least resistance with Papa. But when Papa realized he would have to pay for the university tuition which was over the $12-a-day tuition he was currently paying for Hannah at the community college, he told me he could not afford it. Papa and I had a huge argument and he told me I was selfish, bad-tempered, and ungrateful. I lost my temper and shouted—voicing all my frustrations over the unfair treatment regarding my paycheck, lack of funds for further education, and the general overall injustice.

I was puzzled by Papa's stingy, tightfisted behavior. I was never sure who was responsible for it, he or Mama. I had known Papa to be generous and giving when I was a younger girl, buying presents for no reason or bringing treats home for all of us to enjoy. He had brought expensive gifts from his trips for all of us and had bought a Volkswagen bug and a Gremlin for Emmanuel and a new orange Datsun for Deborah. When I complained that the meager $15 which Mama allotted once a month was not enough, he was surprised and immediately told her to give me much more. Although she never gave me the extra cash, at least Papa didn't hesitate when I asked. But, suddenly, the gifts stopped all together when he came home from his trips—except for Mama and Joram. He didn't want to spend money on a car for any of the Three Stooges. I wasn't sure what the reason was but it was clear that I would not have the funds to attend the university nursing program and I settled for a two-year program at Minneapolis Community College. It was the cheapest RN nursing school, about $650 a year.

Shortly after my conversation with Papa, Emmanuel and Jill invited Hannah, Deborah, and me for dinner at their house and then out to see *Star Wars*. First, Emmanuel had to beg Papa to allow Hannah and me to go out with them since Papa did not allow us to go to movie theaters. After dinner and the movie, I stood outside our house talking with Deborah and Emmanuel. I expressed my frustration at Papa's reluctance to spend money and my despair at ever getting more education.

"What did he tell you about your salary?" Emmanuel asked.

"He said he was saving it and would help out after I got married."

"Don't you think that's weird? Why not help you with school now?" asked Deborah.

"I don't know. I know you guys think they are being unfair, but I guess he's doing the best he can. He just can't afford school right now." Even as I said it the words sounded so hollow. But if I said what I *really* thought, deep down inside I was afraid it would actually be true. I knew something had changed with Papa. I suspected that I was being taken advantage of, but I didn't have any concrete evidence.

"Isn't Joram getting karate lessons? That's very expensive."

"Yeah, I know," I replied, "Everyone's so weird. Maybe they *will* help later."

"Huh, sure they will," Deborah replied sarcastically, "I thought the very same thing. I kept defending them and thinking the best of them, just like you are doing. And when I got married, wanna know what I got?"

"What?"

"Zero. Absolutely zero. Didn't even get my last check. I went into my marriage with exactly zero dollars. Plus, I had a husband who had just arrived to this country and didn't even have a job. Papa didn't even pay for a honeymoon. Thank goodness, Nancy let me use her cabin for free for the week. And by the time I got back, a pay period had gone by and I had one check to live on. Oh, I guess he paid the first month rent on our apartment, all of two hundred dollars; I guess I should be thankful for that. But I knew everything they told me was a huge lie."

"How could they do that? Are you sure? Maybe he just didn't have any more money."

"Elisheba, are you crazy? He's got more money than he knows what to do with."

"But he told me..."

"It doesn't matter what he told you. He's not going to help you. He didn't help any of us and, when the time comes, don't expect him to help you with anything," Deborah said.

"Listen, just do the math, he makes at least forty thousand," Emmanuel said, "You and Hannah make about thirteen thousand each. Right there that's over sixty-five thousand a year. And that's not even counting what all of us gave her."

I knew what Emmanuel was saying was true. Hannah had told me when she had applied for The Bean Scholarship, she was required to submit the income of her parents. After much hemming and hawing, Mama had finally told her and she had told me. My head was spinning. I knew the numbers were right. In 1981, an annual income of $65,000 was an astronomical amount. Suddenly everything became clear. I understood why Papa was on the phone three and four times a day with his broker, Mr. Graves. We all made fun of the number of times he spoke to him, but I hadn't understood the significance of it. Sometimes his broker even came over and sat in the living room and discussed investments for hours. I had never really listened but now, in retrospect, the conversations seemed quite significant. The reason Papa didn't have money was because he was investing all our money in the stock market. I felt as though I had been hit. I knew what Emmanuel and Deborah were telling me was true, but the waves of pain were so great, I could not even speak. At that moment I knew I was all alone without anyone to trust. For a long time, I had not had Mamaji to count on and now I could not trust my own father either.

The next morning when Papa saw me, he looked at me strangely. I thought I had hidden my feelings pretty well but then he asked me, "Why are you so different? Something has happened. Why are you upset?"

I shrugged my shoulders, "It's nothing. I'm fine." I denied everything, but Papa's instincts were right. I *was* different.

A year or so later, I asked him why Mama always took my checks from me. He admitted they were investing my money and said I would benefit later. He told me, "When you get married we'll help you." But even as he answered me, I knew I would never see my money again. There was no going back. I had reached a point of no return because I knew I was completely and utterly on my own.

Then one day, Papa let us know who mattered most. Hannah and I had just cleared dishes after dinner and suddenly Papa announced, "Well, you two girls are going to get married and leave. You'll never think of me again, so I'm going to make sure I make your mother happy." He finished speaking, got up, and left the room, leaving Hannah and me completely shocked that he would say such a thing—out loud.

Clear boundary lines had been drawn. I knew where I stood with Papa and I understood Mama did not want to be my mother or even my friend. In fact, what had become clear to me was that all along she had initiated and implemented a systematic plan to actually harm me. The plan was one that began long before Joram was born. For so long I had believed it was his birth that had changed my life, that it when she had her own son that she realized that she could not love me. But then I thought about her answers to Joe Grostephen when she was being interviewed about her deliberations before deciding to marry. She had only wanted Papa and had planned long before she ever met me to *not* love me. It had begun in India when she first heard Mamaji had died and she decided to marry Papa. She had felt pity for us, which was a poor substitute for love. And then, in her view, we were the price she had to pay in order to have Papa and the life she wanted. When she finally met all of us, she continued with her scheme through humiliation and cruelty to small children, and then progressed to removing my memories of Mamaji by eliminating my Nani and all of Mamaji's siblings from my life. Her plan was successfully completed when she finally convinced my own father to turn against me, and I lost him as well. Even though I knew what kind of woman Mama was, I held out some tiny fragment of hope that somehow she would cease her divisive and damaging ways. I should have known this was impossible. But the biggest revelation came when I learned how much advance planning she had done and her utter lack of care when it came to protecting my rights as a minor child.

When I was 18, I decided to become a naturalized citizen. The procedure to become a citizen was a relatively easy one—some paper work, two photos, and an interview with a judge. The judge asked me questions about my family background and my siblings, and was keenly interested in the timing of my decision.

"Why didn't you do this before? You could have become a citizen a long time ago."

"Well, your Honor," I said, "I thought I had to wait until I was an adult."

The judge looked surprised, "Aren't both your parents citizens?"

"No sir, I mean my mother is but not my father." Papa decided to remain an Indian citizen and a green card holder because it made his frequent travel back and forth to India easier.

"Well then, no problem! You don't have to go through all this. You can become a citizen under your mother's citizenship."

"I didn't know that. She never said anything to me."

"Well, maybe she didn't know. You were listed on your mother's passport when you came to this country, weren't you?"

"Yes I was, but my mother died when I was three. My father remarried."

"I see. So you have a stepmother?" The judge asked.

Papa hated that word and never allowed us to use it, "Well, yes," I said.

The judge picked up a pen, "Anyway, this is the same case because when your stepmother adopted you, all the minor children automatically became citizens."

"Ah, your Honor? I don't think she adopted us."

"What? No. Are you sure?" He looked incredulous. "Why not? What would have happened if something happened to your father? All you minor children would have become wards of the state. I'm sure you must be mistaken. Are you sure?"

I felt my temperature rise with shame and humiliation. I just wanted to get out of his chambers, "I'll double-check, your Honor. But just in case, can I still be naturalized?"

"That's no problem. You can come back here next week for the swearing-in ceremony. But you won't need it since your stepmother is a citizen."

I stood up, shook his hand and got out as fast as I could. On my bus ride back from Minneapolis, my anger grew. When I got home, I confronted Mama about what the judge had told me.

"Mama, did you know I could have become a citizen when you did? Back when I was in grade school?"

She was sitting in the usual muzzle position she assumed when she didn't want to talk about something. Her hand was just about ready to clamp over her mouth, "No, you couldn't have."

I was livid, "So you *knew*? You knew if you had adopted us back then, we could have also become citizens?"

"Yes."

"Then why? *Why* didn't you adopt us? I don't understand!"

"I didn't want to do that." And with that, her hand clamped over her mouth.

"But why? I don't get it! Mama! We're supposed to be your CHILDREN!" I shouted the last word.

But she would not say anything further. I stomped out of the room, ran to my bedroom, and slammed the door, crying tears of frustration and hatred. I thought about what the judge had told me. If something had happened to Papa, it would have been a dream come true for Mama. She would have finally been rid of us. She would have ridden off into the sunset as a rich, merry widow with Joram. Now I understood everything. Mama had never wanted to be my mother. But she had used the title like a badge of honor when she needed to prove a point to me.

She had looked at me with triumph one morning as in my best trying-to-be-nice voice, I gaily wished her, "Happy Anniversary, Mama!"

Instead of just her usual stoic response, she said, "Thank you," and then added, "Well, today I have been married to your father longer than your mother."

I was so aghast; I didn't know how to respond. But I grinned like an idiot and agreed with her, "Oh, that's right! Well, congratulations!" It was as though this was some sort of huge accomplishment or some statement of ownership that she had been with The-Pain-in-the-Neck Papa longer than Mamaji. *Yeah? But she was tougher than you and she stood up to him and would have never let him get away with all this crap. And don't forget he loved her first; you're nothing but sloppy seconds!* I waited until she went upstairs before I let the tears come.

More times than I can count, Mama had told me in her quiet, controlled voice, "If I wasn't a Christian; I would have had nothing to do with you." I had always wondered why she would say such a thing, but now I knew.

Her continued refusal to attend the church annual Mother-Daughter Banquet when I was younger should have been another clue. One year, during the church announcement of the upcoming banquet, Papa happened to be home and was sitting in the pew with us. When we got home, Papa, who still remained basically oblivious about what was really going on in the house, mentioned the banquet at lunch time.

"Well, Madam? Why don't you go with the girls?"

She visibly squirmed, "I don't think we are free that afternoon, Raja."

Sure, Hannah and I are on permanent lockdown. Yeah, let me check my packed calendar and see if I'm free. "What's he thinking? As if she wants to go with us. She's waiting for the church ladies to throw a Mother-Son banquet," I whispered to Hannah.

"Clueless. And who cares about what the Baroness wants. Why should *we* go with *her*?" she whispered back.

Papa looked over at us, "What are you girls whispering about? Don't you want to go to with your mother?"

Instantly, Hannah and I pasted on wide smiles and nodded, "Oh, sure, sure!"

"That sounds like fun, Mama! I'll bet no other mother can say that she has four daughters!" I exclaimed, enthusiastically holding up four fingers.

"Their food is always so salty. You know my blood pressure can't take all that salt, Raja. I'll be seeing black spots before the dinner's even over."

"Don't eat the food then, Madam. You are making excuses. Don't you want to go?" Papa asked.

No, actually, she doesn't want to go. Get a clue Papa!

She sighed, "We can go. I just hope I feel well enough."

Hannah and I nudged each other—*this oughta be good*.

On the day of the banquet, Hannah and I got dressed in one of our three faded and worn-out church dresses. It took us all of ten minutes to dress for the banquet, rebraid our hair and wash our faces. We waited downstairs in the kitchen for Mama to appear. As always, she was late. Finally, she appeared in an exquisite salmon-colored sari. She wore pearls on her ears and around her neck. Under her wedding band and diamond, her Mother's Ring sparkled. Her right hand flashed a ruby and diamond ring. Her makeup was flawless and the room was filled with her signature perfume—Nina Ricci's L'Air du Temps. She was impeccably dressed, and next to her we looked even shabbier.

In the car on the short five-block ride, Mama didn't say anything. When we arrived to the church basement, groups of mothers and daughters were gathered. The ladies were surprised to see her and fawned over her, "Delora! How nice to see you here! Are those pearls? What a beautiful ring! You look gorgeous!" We sat down to a lunch of iced tea, chicken salad, fruit, and a rice dish that unfortunately contained some hard, undercooked kernels of rice.

After the lunch, we had a short program. A church lady led us in a few songs and then there was a short Bible reading and someone sang a song. Then the MC asked all the mothers to stand and we politely applauded. After everyone sat down, the MC asked all the mothers who had at least two children to raise their hands.

Then she asked those who had three to keep their hands up, then those who had four, then five. At the number five all the hands dropped and only Diva Delora waved her sparkly bejeweled fingers in the air. She proudly sniffed after each number and looked around haughtily as the MC continued to count.

"Six?"

sniff.

"Seven?"

sniff, sniff.

"Eight?"

sniff, sniff, sniff.

At nine, she slowly lowered her hand, but not before smiling smugly at the women in the room, as if she had personally birthed, loved, and cherished all of us. I was so sickened by her display that I couldn't meet the eyes of the grinning church ladies. The pounding in my ears was so loud, I was sure everyone could hear it and I didn't trust myself to look up and smile. The MC then asked which mother had the most daughters and, once again, Diva Delora stole the show. The ladies all oohed and aahed as she took accolades when she deserved none of them. She was a close second to another lady who won for the most grandchildren, but it didn't seem to bother her that she barely knew the names of "her" grandchildren. Our first Mother-Daughter banquet was our last. I never wanted to sit through that charade and humiliation again. When the banquet was announced in subsequent years, Hannah and I refused to attend.

I also knew Mama had shared her aversion for me with her relatives. Her sister made it clear when she came to visit that she was only related to Joram. For years, Mama had required Hannah and me to write long, newsy letters to her mother and brother in India, reading each letter as we wrote it and making certain we signed it with "Love". It was the only time she freely gave us blue aerograms, cards, and stamps to write letters. I wrote to her relatives, hoping to please her by having a relationship with those she loved. I professed love, wished them well, implored them to come and visit us and told them how I missed them. I had never met them, but that little inaccuracy had never bothered anyone. I never got a single response. Not a birthday card, a postcard, or even a mention in one of the many letters that came to our house.

When our so-called uncle and grandmother arrived from India, they briefly acknowledged our presence with a curt nod and then proceeded to ignore us entirely. They brought presents and sweets for Joram but didn't even give us a postcard. During their visit, Hannah and I did the chores, served their food, cleaned their rooms and bathrooms. I moved into Hannah's bedroom so they could both have their own. We were commanded to call them "Nani" and "Mamu" but they never once inquired about me, asked me how I was, or even spoke to me, except to curtly command me to fetch something or clean something. For the entire month they spent at our house, they did not say hello, good morning, how are you, or offer any other human niceties to us.

When I finally understood that I basically had no standing as a daughter and was completely on my own, I did all I could to spend as little time at home as possible. It hurt me to look at Papa and Mama. I held Mama responsible for the outcome of my life, but I knew Papa had not been a vigilant father and had trusted her too much when it came to us. But I was still bound to both of them. I made plans to move out with Hannah and even bought some furniture, but at the last minute Hannah chickened out. Many times my friends asked me to move out and share an apartment but, for some reason, I wanted to sustain the relationship no matter how tortured it was and could never move out. I did not trust my parents, but I still wanted to please them and moving out would sever all my ties. While I was acutely aware that I did not have a loving parent-child relationship, it was all I had and I was not courageous enough to jeopardize it. And so, I persisted in living my life the best I could. I went to school during the day and then worked at the nursing home during the evening shift. Not only did Mama always make certain to get a check from me, but I was always treated like a servant and an outsider in what was supposed to be my home.

Emmanuel, David and Deborah-
University of Minnesota students
Burnsville, Minnesota, 1977

CHAPTER
SIXTEEN

S OON AFTER I had earned my RN, David got married. It was
a simple ceremony with only family in attendance. My
favorite memory of David from his wedding was right before the
ceremony was to begin. After Hannah and I hugged him, a grin
spread over his handsome face and, in true David style, he sheep-
ishly held up his tie to show us that the blue shirt he was wearing
with his good blue suit had only one button. Hannah and I cried
through the whole ceremony. It was the only sibling wedding
which brought both of us to tears. I was happy for David—he had
found someone whom he loved and who loved him. But at the
same time I was sad. It was the end of the Three Stooges and
adulthood had come crashing into my life.

Papa did not allow Hannah or me to date, and so we did not
tell him when we went on dates. Most of my dates were during the daytime as I was still not allowed to go out at night. On
weekends, Carol and Annette often went out to the clubs in Minneapolis along with a large group of friends. While they always
urged me to attend, I was never allowed and missed out on what
were some of the best club days in the history of Minneapolis.

At that time, a young Prince had come onto the scene and on Monday mornings; my friends would tell me stories of being at First Avenue: who they met, who they saw, and what happened. Annette even dated Brown Mark who was Prince's bass player. While I desperately wished to go along with them, I was still on lockdown and there was no way I could be out until two or three in the morning. My life was frustrating and infuriating, and I was quickly growing tired of being treated as if I was still a child.

One day while at work, I called the maintenance department for an issue with the medication room door. In response a tall, brown-haired, green-eyed, handsome young man responded. While fixing the door he introduced himself as Dan and we developed a rapport. After that he would find me and visit me on a regular basis. He had a serious girlfriend, so I was able to just relax and enjoy the friendship. We began to eat lunches together, see each other for breaks, and sometimes talked after work. But our relationship was strictly limited to work hours only. At the same time Hannah had become close friends with a young man she worked with named Angelo. Eventually, Dan and I began dating after he broke up with his live-in girlfriend. It was complicated for me, because even though he tried to understand all my limitations, he grew tired of constantly hiding our relationship. I rarely went anywhere alone with him. Our dates consisted of going out with our work colleagues, to movies or parties. Occasionally we went out with Hannah, Angelo, and my work friend Cindy, meeting other friends at Minneapolis dance clubs and restaurants. I even managed to find a way to attend the Prince Purple Rain Tour. But we always had to be back home by eleven o'clock. We often hid these fun outings under the cloak of a "Work Christmas Party" or "Hannah's Birthday Celebration."

It was much easier to go out when Papa was on a trip, because Mama was much more lenient when it came to socialization. Perhaps it was because she had enjoyed an active social life as a single woman or maybe it was because she was hoping we would meet someone, get married, and leave the house. She often looked the other way when it came to male company. One night, Dan called my house at midnight because we had somehow missed each other at the club, since I had to be home early. He was upset and I talked to him until 3 AM until Mama came out and told me to get off the phone, never asking anything further. Another time when Dan had shown up at my house late at night, she had caught me sneaking back in, but said nothing to me, except to make sure that the door was locked.

As time passed, my dating relationship with Dan became tense. His ex-girlfriend was jealous and called me a few times at work and threatened me. Another time she sent a package to my house—inside was a shirt I had given him. She had ripped it to shreds and soiled it with black motor oil. Dan wanted a committed, normal relationship between two adults. The problem was that I was not really allowed to function as an adult. I was constantly conflicted and anxious. I enjoyed his company but I did not want to marry anyone or even become serious. My dream was to travel and see the world. I wanted to live in India, buy a huge house, and fill it with orphaned children who needed a mother. Dan was born and bred in Minnesota. His idea of a vacation was going up north to the Boundary Waters or perhaps a visit to Florida. Even though I really cared about him, I could not see how our lives would ever complement each other. I wondered how he would ever fit into my family. I did not want to explain all the ins and outs of my house and it literally made me sweat and feel nauseated whenever he would mention the idea of coming over to meet Papa. Eventually, we decided to stop dating. Not being able to maintain a relationship reminded me of the strangely double life I lived. In the outside world, I was a grown woman with all the responsibilities and emotions that went along with it, but at home I was treated like a teenage juvenile delinquent, with absolutely no independence.

Months later, Hannah introduced me to her new friend, Sunil. He was an Indian man who worked with her. He wasn't short, fat or hiding behind thick spectacles, and didn't have the usual characteristics of the fresh-off-the-boat Indians I had met before. He was quiet, a little nervous, with lots of long, dark curly hair and deep-set, intense eyes. He was studying engineering at the University of Minnesota. We had an easy rapport and, even though he had only been in America for three years, he fit in with my other friends. We began an uneasy dating relationship. We were both scared—being Indian, he knew my father would not allow me to date, and I was dealing with feelings I had never had before. Sunil was a romantic; he enjoyed books, music and poetry. He sent roses to my nursing unit for my birthday and Valentine's Day. I took them home and lied when I was asked where I got them from. I claimed one of the elderly patients had died or a patient was allergic to flowers. Sunil and I met when we could. We watched *Scarface* but left before the end, I got sick on Mexican food at *Chi-chi's*, or sometimes we just walked around Cedar Lake.

My feelings for Sunil were more than just friendly, but I was afraid of them. I was too scared to allow myself to be honest about what I was experiencing. The hugeness of the emotions overcame me and I squelched them. I didn't want to talk to Papa because he would not be sympathetic, and trying to explain how I was feeling or that I was dating behind his back was more than I could take on just then. Once Sunil called me "his girlfriend" and I shouted at him and told him never to call me that again. I was afraid of what it would mean and what it would force me to contend with. Eventually, Papa did find out. Hannah, Cindy, Angelo,

Sunil, and I had decided to go to the Minnesota Zoo for the day. Since Joram was so enamored by animals, he also came along and met Sunil for the first time. For some reason, since Joram was 16, I thought he wouldn't tell Papa. I was wrong, and Papa sat me down for one of his talks.

"Who's this fellow you've been running around with?"

"He's just a friend. He works with Hannah at Willows."

"What's his name?" Papa asked.

"Sunil Matthew."

"He's from Kerala? A Christian?" Most Indians could easily be identified by their family name. It revealed not only their religious background, but also the state in India to which their family belonged. "What does he do? He's a doctor?"

"No, he's studying engineering at the U of M."

"Huh," Papa seemed unusually subdued. I was hopeful that perhaps he would allow me to continue seeing Sunil. "Well, you can't keep running around all over with this man. You have to decide what you want."

"We're just getting to know each other." I wasn't about to tell Papa the truth about what we really felt for each other, or how long I had been seeing him.

"If you want to spend time with him, he has to make a commitment. You can't just go here and there with him as if you are some kind of a loose girl."

"He's still in college so..."

Papa interrupted, "I met your mother when I was in college. I knew she was the one immediately and there was no nonsense. I told her right away we would be married. This fellow needs to do the same."

"You want me to tell him that he needs to make a commitment? I can't just tell him that, Papa. What do I say?"

"What do you say? It's very simple," Papa said. "Just tell him that he needs to decide whether he is going to marry you or not. Otherwise, I forbid you to see him anymore."

"Papa, please don't make me ask him that. I just can't," I wasn't interested in marriage and my relationship with Sunil suited me just fine.

"Is that so? You can't ask him to be honorable but you can run around at all hours of the night with him? Find out what his intentions are or just forget the whole thing."

I dreaded meeting Sunil after that. I avoided the conversation as long as I could, but eventually I called him and told him we needed to talk. He picked me up from work and we went to Lake Nokomis. I was so embarrassed that I couldn't tell him it was my father who wanted the promise of a commitment. I wasn't able to tell him the whole truth. He quietly listened to my ultimatum.

"I wish I could make a commitment, Elisheba. But I'm still in school," said Sunil. "I have two more years left. I want to at least be able to have a job before I make any promises. Right now I can only take care of myself."

"I know. I'm sorry. But I have to know. Otherwise, I don't think we can see each other anymore," I said.

"I understand. I wish I could tell you something different. I just can't right now," Sunil said.

It was a painful breakup because we both had strong feelings. We still spoke to each other now and then. Once I ran into him at a Lionel Richie concert. It was clear we still had strong feelings for each other and the meeting was tense and awkward. Once again, Papa had put his own needs above mine. What was even worse was that yet again, I had let him.

Soon after I stopped seeing Sunil, Hannah also stopped seeing Angelo. Papa focused his energies on finding a husband for both of us. He often remarked how finding two men and getting us married in a double wedding would be the most sensible plan. I was not anxious to marry, but if I was going to marry, I did not want a double wedding and neither did Hannah. It must have been a fond fantasy for Papa and Mama. One day, one expense, one headache, one occasion of pretending to be sad and then BAM! both Hannah and I would be nothing but a distant and unpleasant memory. What they had not taken into account was the amount of work that they would have to do when we left. Who would slave away around the house and still make all the monies for Mr. Graves' extensive investment portfolio? They would have to hire full-time servants who loved to work for free and who happened to hand over about $1000 every two weeks, otherwise the house and Graves' speculations would go to the dogs. Given their propensity to be tightfisted, I guessed they would take their chances.

In any case, Papa began showing us picture after picture of a huge assortment of Indian men. Papa's roster of men or "The Box of Chocolates," as we called it came in various shades of brown, ranging from a creamy vanilla, medium light brown to deep brown. He also had another method to "introduce" us to available men. Occasionally, he would throw black-and-white photos at us like a seasoned Vegas blackjack dealer, "How do you like this one? What do you think of this man? How about him?" Sometimes there would be a call made to work and Mama would say, "*Jaldi, jaldi se ghar aana.* There's somebody here you need to meet. Come home quickly and put on a sari."

At home, a strange man would be waiting—apparently Papa's idea of what our Shah Jahan should be. But the phone calls to the nursing home stopped working. It was so unusual to actually be wanted at home that we knew something was up and instead of going home, we would easily add on a late or extra shift and, thus, avoid meeting a would-be suitor. A number of times Papa showed me a photo of a man so downright unattractive that I was compelled to speak up.

"You want me to marry *that*? His part goes all the way from his forehead to the back of his neck. He's short and ugly and his pants go all the way up to his armpits. And besides, I hate that huge Zapata mustache."

"Why are you so worried about his looks? He's a brilliant doctor!"

I was incredulous, "Well, I have to live with him." *What I really mean is that eventually I'm going to have to at least let him kiss me once in a while.*

"Huh. Why are you so picky? Only the woman has to be beautiful. A man has to be smart, and he's the top in his field."

"Yes, but he's ugly. I'm not meeting him." Either all the better looking men had seen my picture and gone running, or Papa was so desperate that just about anyone who was willing to take me off his hands would suffice. There seemed to be no thought or concern put into who my husband should be. "I don't want to get married anyway," I said.

"What nonsense! *Dimaag kharab hai*? Of course you are getting married."

"I don't need a husband. I'm gonna manage on my own."

"On your own. Huh!" Papa said mockingly. "What kind of *bakwaas* is this? You have no idea what you want. What are you talking about?

"I want to live in India with Miriam and work there for a while. Then, someday, I'll buy a huge house and fill it with children."

"Well, you can't have children without a husband."

"Oh yes, I can. There are lots of children who need a mother. I don't need a man for that."

Papa was shocked, "*Besharam*! Have you no shame? A single

woman running around alone and then having children. *Khabar-dar*! Nonsense. What kind of girl are you?"

He had no clue what kind of girl I was. I was the kind of girl who knew her parents were not to be trusted. I was the kind of girl who thought it was natural and normal to actually enjoy the company of a man. I was the kind of girl that liked the dreaded *F* word and had *Fun* whenever I could sneak it in. I was the kind of girl that didn't think the greatest shame was in sleeping with someone, but in being dishonest, cruel, and spiteful. I was the kind of girl who often fantasized about what Papa's reaction would be if I suddenly told him I was a lesbian. I was the kind of girl who was sick and tired of constantly being accused of "running around" when I was barely limping around.

Despite my protests, Papa busily tried to make a match for Hannah and, at the same time, "select" a man for me. The method that Papa used was rather remarkable, but not in a positive way. One evening, Papa began a friendly conversation after dinner.

"Well, Hannah. What would you say about a man who had won the gold medal in Obstetrics and Gynecology at the University of Madras?"

"Pretty good, I guess," said Hannah.

"Well, this man, Stevens, is known all over India for his work in Obstetrics. He also studied in Texas."

"Okay."

"Yes, he's a very well-qualified obstetrician."

"Well, he sounds interesting," Hannah said.

"Well, actually, it is his *son* I'm thinking about for you. I have already spoken to them and explained to them that I have a daughter named Hannah who is of marriageable age."

"Oh," Hannah looked at me with confused look. We both burst out laughing.

Papa was so focused on the father, but he had no information on the would-be groom. Before Hannah could meet this son-of-an-obstetrician, he heard back from an old friend from the UK with whom he had already been discussing his daughters. Papa's friend was anxious to have his son, the cardiologist, meet Hannah as well. It all seemed providential to Papa. In a flash, he was overflowing with available, qualified men. Instead of allowing Hannah to meet both men and then decide which one she wanted to get to know further, he intervened and made a match for both of us. Without asking, he decided that I was to marry Dr. Stevens' son and Hannah would marry the UK cardiologist.

I was completely outraged. I did not want to marry at all, and I most certainly did not want to marry someone who had been selected for me in such a random and callous way. I was also not prepared to accept what I perceived to be Hannah's leftovers. I refused to be married and, without hesitation, told Papa to write to Dr. Stevens and tell him I was not agreeable. I had never seen Papa at such a disadvantage. He talked and talked, hoping to change my mind, but when I did not budge, he became enraged. It was the angriest he had ever been. When I still did not relent, he refused to speak to me. It was the first time Papa had ever used the silent treatment on me. I was used to Mama's long silences, but Papa had never done this to me. It was the worst imaginable punishment, but I resolved not to back down from my decision.

In the meantime, Hannah prepared to meet her dream cardiologist. When he arrived, he was surprisingly handsome and seemed to be a good fit for Hannah. The couple talked for a short while and decided to write to each other and get to know each other better. Papa finished one week of not speaking to me and began the second. While I was happy for Hannah, I was also miserable. I did not want to marry but my resolve was already weakening. I didn't know how long I could hold out.

I wished desperately Mamaji could be there with me. She

would have spoken up for me as any mother would. She would have wanted this time to be one of joy and eager anticipation instead of misery and isolation. When I spoke to Papa, he ignored me completely. The stress was unbearable. I couldn't eat or sleep. At the end of the third week of silence, I broke down crying, apologized to Papa and promised to do what he wanted. He was elated and told me I should look for a letter in the mail. I still had no clue about the name of this man to whom I was supposedly betrothed. I assumed he would make the trip from India to meet me, but this did not happen. Even though it was extremely wrong, no meeting was arranged between me and my suitor. Unlike other parents, Papa did not insist on this required introduction, so I could meet and decide for myself if I wanted to marry. Instead, he tried to quell my fears by telling me that he had given Mama a short video of the mysterious man. I would be allowed to view this once we started writing each other—as if that was supposed to make it any easier. It was the worst possible situation, but I had no resistance left. I meekly agreed to the circumstances. I received an engagement ring and began corresponding with my new fiancé.

I barely mentioned my engagement to my colleagues at work. Most of them were only concerned about the size of the diamond or asked, "What does he do?" I didn't love my fiancé, but through our letters I had begun to respect him and his motivation to succeed in his personal goals. I thought it was a good start. Trying to explain my rather unusual situation to small-minded people at work was never successful and so when I was asked, I usually told people he was either unemployed or a garbage man and they didn't ask any more questions. In a bold move, Hannah decided on her own that she no longer wanted to communicate with the UK doctor. When Papa turned the silent treatment on her, she paid no attention and didn't waiver in her decision. While I greatly admired her, I lacked the courage to do the same.

I planned to have Hannah as my maid of honor and Deborah as a matron of honor. In addition, I asked Carol to be a bridesmaid and then telephoned Annette.

"Hey. So I want to ask you something."

"Okay," Annette said.

"I'm getting married," I said flatly. "You can't ask any questions; I don't want to discuss details. So do you want to be my bridesmaid or not?"

Annette laughed a little and asked, "Wow! Okay, I didn't know you were seeing anyone, um. Am I allowed to ask his name?"

"I guess. His name's Mark. He's from India and I haven't met him."

"Okay. Sure, I'd love to be your bridesmaid."

I was matter of fact about the other details of the wedding. I begged Papa to have a simple ceremony and avoid inviting people by having the wedding at our house.

"No, we can't do that. People will think something is wrong or that something bad has happened."

I wasn't sure how something bad could possibly "happen" since an entire ocean and continent separated me from my fiancé but, by this time, I was functioning as a robot and allowing Papa to pretty much do as he liked. I was desperately hoping to avoid a regular wedding, because I knew Mama would not want to spend even a cent more than she had to. I would be married off in the cheapest way possible and I was embarrassed to invite people to a wedding with no dinner and no real reception.

Deborah offered to sew all the blouses for the bridesmaids' saris. I chose a bright turquoise-blue chiffon from the faithful Minnesota Fabrics for the saris and bought cheap costume jewelry for the bridesmaids' gifts. I had to pay for the bouquets and brass-candle aisle decorations. No plans were made for a photographer, so I found a man who was just starting a photography business and hired him at a reduced rate.

I quit my job at Walker and cashed out my accrued vacation hours, so I had some extra money for these expenses. I had been working at both Walker and Minneapolis Children's Hospital, so now I had only one job. Mark would bring my wedding sari with him. I requested an off-white and gold one. His parents would also give me gold jewelry to wear. For my veil, a colleague at work gave me her beautiful pearl headpiece. It had a pearl dangling in the center and I planned to wear it low so the pearl hung in the middle of my forehead. Annette's mother offered to sew the rest of the veil and paid for the yards of tulle and materials on her own. I bought a pair of $10 satin pumps and my wedding outfit was complete. I paid in advance for Mark's black tux rental. Emmanuel and the rest of the groomsmen rented theirs and Joram's was paid for by his loving father and mother.

The cake, invitations, altar floral arrangement, and refreshments were arranged and chosen by Mama and Papa. I was at work when these decisions were made, but I didn't really care anyway. The invitation was hilarious, because the term "Doctor" and various initials were so overused—*Dr. K. Haqq and Dr. D. Haqq request the honor of your presence at the marriage of their daughter Elisheba to Mark, son of Dr. D. Stevens*. It was a pretentious invitation to an extremely low country event. I attended the required premarital counseling alone. I sat in the chair and the pastor asked me questions like, "How many children do you want? What sorts of things do you value? How do you resolve conflict and show affection?" I answered for myself. I had no clue how Mark would respond. The pastor was accommodating and understanding of my unusual situation. No one had ever bothered to ask me what

I thought or believed or wanted, so I thoroughly enjoyed the sessions.

The Thursday before the wedding, which was to be the rehearsal day, I finally met the man I was to marry. His two friends from Chicago and his parents arrived at our house late morning on Thursday. I watched from my window as he got out of the car and then immediately ran to the bathroom and threw up. I had refused to wear a sari to meet him and wore a blouse and skirt instead. I practiced deep breathing in the bathroom, and soon I heard Hannah knocking at the door.

"Hey, are you coming down? They're here."

"No. I'm not coming."

"Come on, Elisheba. You can't stay up here forever."

"Oh, yes I can."

After my stomach stopped jumping, I brushed my teeth and slowly made my way downstairs. I avoided the living room completely and went into the kitchen. Mama was getting tea and orange juice ready on a tray.

"Elisheba? Take this tray into the living room and offer them something to drink."

"No," I felt like throwing up again.

She put the tray into my hands and gently pushed me toward the living room, "Go."

I took a deep breath and started my rounds. Papa was sitting and talking to Mark. I saw him, his parents, and his two friends. He was a complete stranger. Beginning with his mother, I offered them the tray and asked if they wanted something to drink. One by one I was refused, and I finally got to Mark. He reached over and took a large tumbler full of orange juice and smiled.

"I'll take it, only because you are offering it to me."

I nodded and smiled. *Yeah? Well, you better take it. That's more orange juice than I get in a whole year!*

After the horrible ordeal, we sat down to a traditional Indian meal. I was given my beautiful wedding sari, a gold necklace, and earrings. I had never owned such costly items. Then we all went to the church and walked through the rehearsal for the wedding. At the end of the evening, Mark asked me to go out for coffee. I couldn't eat a thing and drank water while he had coffee and French Silk Pie. We chatted easily, but I still had a horrible feeling in the pit of my stomach. When I got home, Hannah wanted to know how things had gone. "He's nice," was all I could say.

That evening I packed my bags. I was sick and constantly nauseated. I didn't want to see anyone. I stayed inside, packed my bags and talked to Hannah and Deborah. Then I sat on my bed and thought about all of the physical memories of Mamaji I was leaving behind—there was not much left that had not been taken by her successor, but making a mental list of such tangible items kept me from thinking of how much I wanted her with me that day. I was dejected and lonely and wanted to know what Mamaji would tell me to do. I thought about my life and what it had not been without her. Without Mamaji, I had not been loved, I had not reached my potential, I had not been protected, I had not been cherished, I had not been nurtured. I tried hard not to think how different it would all be if she was with me. I knew this was not how she would have wanted me to marry.

My sisters tried to reassure me that everything would be okay. Annette and Carol came over and also tried their best. There was nothing usual about my predicament. I felt trapped and terrified. I wanted to tear up my veil and run screaming far away from anyone who knew me. I never received any sort of discussion or talk regarding sex or the intimacies between a husband and wife. I finally asked Deborah a few specific questions. I felt bad for her, but I was desperate to find out what was to be expected of me. She blushed and said, "Wow, well, you really want to know those kinds of details? Um, how about this, if you don't figure that out after a week or so, let me know and I'll tell you what to do." That was my entire sex talk. If Mamaji was with me, she would not only properly teach me what I should do as a wife, but she would never have allowed me to feel pressured into doing something I wasn't ready to do.

On the morning of my wedding, I woke early and threw up. I took a shower, did my makeup, and then my sisters and bridesmaids helped me get dressed in the sari, veil, long white gloves, jewelry, and armfuls of white and gold bangles. Deborah slipped on the traditional red bangle that Punjabi brides wore. I was ready to be married.

We posed for family pictures. One picture in particular turned my stomach. It was one in which I stood in front of the mirror with Mama next to me. The photographer asked her to adjust my veil, as if she was helping me. She smiled at me—the nicest smile I had ever seen. She was wearing a lovely green sari, with her usual collection of gems. The photographer clicked away. I smiled and played along, as if she had really helped me get ready for the wedding. I hated my reflection.

All I could see was a dreadfully ugly, sad, scared, little girl all dressed up in a beautiful sari and veil, "I look horrible. I can't believe I have to go out there looking like this."

She patted my arm, "Don't be ridiculous. You look beautiful." Before going back out to the others, she leaned in and whispered, "Elisheba, I won't cry at the wedding today. I already cried last night."

Who cries preemptively? Her comment was completely ridiculous, but even then, I said nothing. Before I knew it, it was time for me to walk down the aisle. I was petrified. Mama prepared to swish down the aisle before the bridesmaids began.

I laughed shakily and asked her, "Any last-minute advice?"

Mama looked straight at me and said, "Don't ever expect a man to understand you." Then she took Joram's arm and sashayed her way to the pew.

I cried as watched Carol, Annette, Deborah and, finally, Hannah walk down the aisle.

Papa leaned over and said, "You don't have to do this."

Too late now! I knew he wanted to abdicate all responsibility, but going back was not an option. I took Papa's arm, and as I readied myself to begin my walk down the aisle, I thought about building a home that would be all that I wished mine had been. A home filled with fresh, sweet-smelling clothes, all the stamps I wanted, fresh fruit of every variety, delicious meat-filled sandwiches, and meals that actually filled my stomach. But more than that I dreamed of a home filled with love, affection, care, concern, nurturing, and passion. I thought about Mamaji. I knew she would want me to be strong and live an honest, truthful life. But most of all, I knew she would want me to build a home that would finally break the cycle of my past, and she would want me to be the kind of mother she had been. I took a deep breath, wiped my tears, and stepped into my future.

Hopkins, Minnesota December 1964 (left to right, Standing-Miriam, Emmanuel, Gideon and Deborah; Sitting-David, Papaji, Hannah, Elisheba and Mamaji)

PART
THREE

CHAPTER
SEVENTEEN

A	FTER MY MARRIAGE, I traveled back to India. The last time
	I had been there was when Mamaji was with me. I got my
first taste of life in India and I began the second half of my life.
Eight months later, I returned to Minneapolis and was the maid
of honor at Hannah's wedding. She had fallen in love with
Anand, a man whom she had met through Miriam and Richard.
He was a doctor and was just beginning his residency in Maryland. Her wedding was almost identical to mine; except this time
the saris were purchased from Minnesota Fabrics in a pale shade
of pink instead of turquoise blue. The newly married couple
moved to Maryland.

During my second year of marriage, Mark and I moved to
New York. Sadly, Mark also had to bear the brunt of Mama's contempt for me. Even though I was out of the house, she continued
to disrupt my life by finding ways to harm his. Since Mark did
not know of her true nature, he mistakenly used the Burnsville
address when applying for graduate schools. He scored well on his
GMAT exam and was offered a number of scholarships. At the
top of his list was the Kellogg School of Management at North-

western University in Chicago. When he didn't hear back from them, he accepted another offer. About 15 years later, when I was rummaging through some old papers that had been left out by Mama, I found some of my own correspondence, but the most alarming was a letter from the Kellogg School of Management. It had been opened and was addressed to Mark. It not only offered acceptance to the school but also a scholarship. I felt so much rage that her hatred for me had caused her to reach out her claw and attempt to ruin Mark's life, solely because she wanted to make sure *my* life was as difficult as possible.

When we left for New York, it was the first time we were completely on our own, away from our parents and any of our siblings. I found two new jobs, one with the state of New York and the other in a small community hospital, and we settled into our apartment. As my siblings had warned me, Papa and Mama did not help me financially in any way. Even though long-distance calls were outrageously expensive, I called them at least once a month. But they never called to see how I was getting along. Hannah and I visited each other as much as we could. To see each other, we took advantage of cheap flights that sold for $50 to $70, if they were purchased the day before. Emmanuel was living in Massachusetts and we often drove five hours to visit him. Gideon lived only two hours away in Connecticut. I began to build my own relationships with my siblings and made new friends all without the constraints I once had. I had a newly found freedom. Mark excelled at his studies and looked forward to finishing early.

But before Mark could complete graduate school, I found out I was expecting a baby. After getting over the shock, we both looked forward to being parents. Unfortunately, even with his new master's degree in hand, Mark was unable to find employment. Finally, we moved to Nashville, Tennessee, where Mark had secured a job at Meharry Medical College. He traveled ahead with the U-Haul and I arrived one week before my due date. We unpacked boxes and readied our apartment on our own. Then I saw the doctor who would be delivering our child. Almost as if my son knew, he waited until the last box was unpacked before he decided to make his entrance. After 27 hours of labor, I gave birth to my son, Philip. After two days in the hospital, I came home.

Even though I was a nurse, I was overwhelmed by my job as a new mother. I knew how to bathe and care for Philip, but I was less sure of what was happening to me. I wasn't sure if I was nursing long enough, so every time Philip cried, I nursed him. Whenever I put him down, he cried, so I spent all day and most of the night carrying and nursing him. To make things worse, the stitches that had been required when I gave birth, had become horribly infected. In order to alleviate the pain, I had to sit leaning to one side. It made nursing terribly difficult. Finally, using a mirror, I saw a huge grapefruit-sized abscess growing around my stitches. When I called the doctor, I was told to soak in a tub until the abscess broke. For three days I was in agony. I sat alone in that apartment, my breasts leaking milk, my son and I both crying. I desperately wished I had Mamaji with me to tell me what to do next. I wondered how I had angered God so much that He had taken her from me when I needed her so much. It was one of the lowest points in my life. I was terribly lonely and, during a time when most women would be celebrating, I was sad and depressed.

Before Philip turned two, I learned the hard way that I was still carrying anger from my past. When I reached out to hold Philip, he refused to come to me and when I insisted, he ran from me and hid his face in Mark's legs. The pent-up rage I felt toward Mama manifested into the poor treatment of my small son. My impatience and moods made him fearful of me. Through my tears, I realized I was not nurturing Philip. If he fell, I'd brusquely tell him to brush himself off and stand up. If he banged his knee and cried, I'd tell him to be brave and stop crying. I was tired from working nights and then staying up with Philip during the day. I lost my temper and shouted at him. Instead of being a mother to him, I was teaching him survival skills, and he learned that I was not his source of care and solace. It was a terrible realization and the guilt was more than I could bear. I tried to do the best I could to rectify the mistake I was making and resolved to learn how to nurture and comfort my son.

I spent many months thinking of what my life had been, and I realized the only way to stop being so angry was to forgive Papa and Mama. What had happened was in the past and while it had not been right or just, I needed to move forward. I had to stop hoping they would suddenly, magically become real parents. The process wasn't easy or quick. It was long and private but by the end of that year, I could call them without crying or feeling rage. I felt my heart open, my fists unclench, and I stopped holding my breath and exhaled. But I had to stop using the term, "Mama". I came to terms with the fact that she had could never be a mother to me, and avoided calling her Mama as much as I could when I saw her. There were still occasional moments when I was moved by something particularly unjust, but for the most part my life was happy and I took great joy in being a mother.

Two years later, when I gave birth to my second son, Samuel, in New Jersey, I had no more fantasies that suddenly Papa or Delora would behave as other parents did. I made the perfunctory phone call to Papa and told him he had another grandson. He made a comment or two, but as usual his conversation was a monologue in which he described how Joram who was still living at home, was now pursuing a graduate degree, and that he was wonderful, smart and successful. Surprisingly, Delora was much nicer and asked me about the birth process and also about Samuel and Philip. She offered some advice which was actually helpful. I wanted Philip and Samuel to have their own relationship with their Nana and Nani—one that had nothing to do with my memories. It wasn't the kind of relationship I dreamed of if Mamaji had been there, but my children had no idea of what my life had been and they enjoyed their grandparents. They even got birthday cards from time to time and could recall fond memories of Mickey Mouse pancakes, stuffed aloo parathas, and sleepovers in cartoon sleeping bags.

From Philip and Samuel, I learned what it felt like to love as a mother should and I reveled in showing them all the care and affection I wished I had experienced. It helped me move past my own childhood, and having a loving relationship with my sons saved me. I cherished being a mother and my children brought me more joy than I could have ever imagined. Because of my marriage I was able to learn so much about India and my past. Mark loved to travel, and we were able to fulfill my desires to see the world. The four of us traveled all over the globe, visiting countries I had only dreamed of. I learned that I was resourceful, smarter, stronger, and much more able than I had ever believed or had been told. My new life gave me the confidence to pursue what I loved—writing, travel, family and friends.

I also had the freedom to reconnect with what was left of Mamaji's family. I had lost Nani and Vera Masi by age 13. But I finally met Venetia Masi, and I felt I had connected with a part of Mamaji by meeting her sister. I also met my cousins Vimal and Premal and began a friendship with them. Tragically, Venetia Masi was murdered about ten years after I met her and this was a great loss. I met my cousin Joel and his father, my Vidyasagar Mamu, before he died. I traveled to UK and met Farina Masi and my cousin Anita and Sandeep. Sadly, their father, my Vincent Mamu, died of a sudden heart attack before I could meet him. All of Mamaji's siblings had also faced great tragedy or had died an early death.

Over the years, I tried to write about what had happened and how much I missed Mamaji, but I could never finish more than a page or two. The story was always untruthful—filled with excuses and half-truths. Even worse, as much as I tried, I could never find a way to fit Mamaji into the story since I knew nothing about who she had been. I felt it was a betrayal to tell my story without her. I wanted to know her. Sometimes, in the middle of the day, one of my boys would say something endearing or bring home a picture from school. Late at night, I sat in the dark, weeping that I could not tell Mamaji how wonderful her grandsons were. I could not even say, "I remember when she used to..." It wasn't the big days that bothered me—her birthday, the day she died, Mother's Day. It was always a small, seemingly insignificant event that would suddenly kick me in the gut with a deep longing to tell her that Samuel just lost his tooth or that Philip had learned to ride a bike, or that her all her grandchildren were amazing, wonderful, and accomplished people.

As the years passed and my boys grew into teenagers, my curiosity to know Mamaji faded. Many of my nephews and nieces were getting married. We organized family gatherings or met for weddings or graduations, but Papa and Delora never joined us. When Papa turned 80, we surprised him with a birthday party and all of us met in Burnsville. In total there were 73 of us—children, spouses, grandchildren, and one great-grandson. By Papa's 90th birthday both he and Mamaji had 22 grandchildren and 11 great-grandchildren. Sadly, Papa only really knew Joram's children as a grandfather should.

In 2010, my friend Nina Foxx asked me to contribute an essay for an anthology being prepared for Mother's day called *Letters for my Mother*. She asked me to write a letter to my mother. I am not sure why but, for some reason, all my past inhibitions were gone and I wrote furiously. I began to write without any embellishment or cover. I wrote long into the nights. I asked my siblings, my mother's friends, my Farina Masi, Papa, anyone who had known Mamaji, for more information. When I finished, I knew I could finally tell my story as it should be told.

David's 5th birthday Chandigarh, India 1963
(Back row left to right—Harold Mamu, Vidyasagar Mamu, Mamaji, Taj Chachi, Venetia Masi, Front row left to right—Emmanuel, Gideon, Hannah, Miriam holding Elisheba, Deborah, David with his cake, Joel, Vimal and Premal)

CHAPTER
EIGHTEEN

THE EARLIEST INFLUENCE in my life was from Mamaji but the longest was from Delora. There are studies done that prove a parent has the greatest influence on a child during the first three years of life. Even so, it stands to reason that when you are raised by someone, you would naturally learn to imitate, consciously or unconsciously, that person's value system and perhaps even some of their personality traits.

Even though Delora was not a mother to me, the impact she had in my life was still present. She did not love or care for me, of that I was sure. But she had taught me a great deal about what I wanted and didn't want to be. There were the inconsequential things that had been absorbed just from living with her for so long: sharp cheddar cheese on toast with bitter marmalade on top, British phrases, recipes for Indian-style goulash, and a matter-of-fact and practical understanding of treating ailments. But Delora's life made me sad, because in a way she had settled for less than what she could and should have been. At one time, as a single woman she was not only ambitious and intelligent but she had embraced a value system that was close to my own heart. Instead of chasing money or power, she had chosen to help those who had neither voice nor status. But once she stopped being Delora and became "Mama," it was as though a part of her died. She became cruel and petty. Sadly, she could only see me as a hindrance to her ultimate goal: complete control and power over what had become her small and limited world.

My fear that I would eventually become like Delora compelled me to have nothing to do with anything she had been and to overcompensate and be as completely opposite as I could. I gave away everything if it wasn't being used, storing almost nothing and creating a clutter-free environment. I rejected costly or expensive goods, and my favorite places to shop were neighborhood garage sales and thrift stores. I always bought plenty of groceries, feeding and overfeeding my children, friends, and even my children's friends. I trusted only a few people as friends but, at the same time, hosted huge parties and get-togethers with those I knew, as if each one was my last. When I found myself in a conflict, I abhorred silence and always sought to solve a problem and immediately wanted to talk about it. I absolutely despised being sick, and even when feeling poorly, I pretended and carried on as if I was at the peak of good health. But, most of all, I became fiercely independent to a fault. I saw the need for others as a great folly, and it took me years to realize how wrong that was. I had to learn to trust again.

But it wasn't enough that I didn't want to be like Delora; I wanted to be more than just an antithesis to her. I wanted to know and be like Mamaji, but I still had no real awareness of *having* her. She was a shadow, a vapor that existed only in my mind. At the time I began this memoir, I had a lofty aspiration that somehow the act of talking and writing about her, or just longing for her would bring her to me. That didn't happen. She is still almost as distant as when I started this project, and I know it will never be possible to really know her. All the tears and wishes and prayers would never allow me to really connect with her in any tangible way. She has been permanently lost to me and there is nothing in the world that can change that. Mamaji is a beautiful image that stares at me through dark, deep-set eyes from photos piled in a box. She was mine for a very short time, but no longer.

A romantic would tell me that I still have her letters and she is talking to me through them. Perhaps that is true, and in some ways, her words—penned in her scratchy, wavy scrawl, dark arrows scattered here and there and her use of numerous plus signs, showcased her casual and playful nature. She weaved lively stories when she learned of the affair between the housekeeper and the cook, reminisced about the rains in Mussoorie, painted images of quiet summer nights sleeping under a starry sky on the rooftop, recalled her delight in "restaurant surprise" (how I wish I knew what that game was!), gave vivid descriptions of fights between Papa and his family, expressed her disappointment in her own mother at times, anguished in dealing with Papa's irrational jealousy, described her deep loneliness, wondered if she should have married at all, and told of her wish to "just vanish." Her words made me laugh, caused melancholy, and brought me to tears. I rejoiced so many times at our shared feelings and even shouted for joy in some of her revelations, *I'm just like her!* But the realist in me knew that the letters were still only paper and ink—far from a real relationship between a mother and daughter.

The unfairness, the injustice of not knowing my mother, washed over me. Because I could see that my older siblings had a real, true connection to her. Evident, because I could see how Mamaji's value system and talents were present in them. She had always been devoted to Papa and his work and was his constant helpmate. She had written his monthly newsletters and completed his correspondence. She had not only supported his great ambitions, but was always encouraging him, even at the risk of her own health. At the end of her life, she verbalized her concern that Papa's work go forward. When I thought about how Miriam supported and loved Richard, I could not help but see this same trait of Mamaji's in her. Miriam had left her comfortable life in Minnesota to travel halfway across the globe to a faraway land.

When it came to the huge task of building the house, hiring employees to help with the household and Papa's work, Mamaji managed it all independently. She had kept the budget, paid the workers, made sure that deadlines were met, and managed a small staff. She was unrelenting that the four eldest children be allowed to attend the prestigious Woodstock boarding school. She visited the headmaster and not only arranged for admission for Miriam, Gideon, Emmanuel, and Deborah but also at a reduced cost. My older siblings fondly remember their days at Woodstock of horse-riding in the mountains, strict schoolmasters, and Mamaji's constant love and care. As a young man, Gideon, who had similarly learned his business savvy from Mamaji, had impressed the CEO and founder of his corporation so much that he eventually became his right-hand man and, later, started his own successful business.

Mamaji had a clear, simple and honest understanding of God. Rather than seeing God as a separate Being that needed to be compartmentalized in some way, God was ever-present in her life as someone she could talk to and share her joys and struggles with as a friend. All her children eventually learned this, but it was Emmanuel who had stalwartly followed this grasp of God. It had first manifested in his awe and love of physics and then in his decision to follow his call to be a pastor.

Mamaji was a truly generous person who gave of herself and anything she had to all those she knew without expecting in return. She saw the best in people and gave what she had to make them reach their dreams. Like Mamaji, Deborah has always been incredibly generous. Even in the days when she had almost nothing, she gave what she had—buying tickets to help celebrate my anniversary or giving me $50 to tide me over to the next month. Her heart is big and she always gives unflinchingly.

While it's relatively clear to see how Mamaji's influence was present in the Biggers, as much as I tried I could not find her in David, Hannah, or myself. Oh, there were things I attributed to her—perhaps my love of the written word, maybe Hannah and David's propensity toward cavities and the need for complicated dental procedures. Both of them are musically talented and, while Mamaji loved music, it was Papa who was more of the musician. But I wanted to have something of Mamaji that was real—something that manifested in my life in a way that I could point to and be proud of. But I couldn't really find that connection. People have said I have some of her features. They point out my forehead, hands, or sometimes even my eyes. But Deborah is the one that looks just like her. There really wasn't anything that I could definitively grasp and say *I got this from Mamaji.* The funny thing was that even though we Three Stooges lived with Delora the longest, none of us became anything like her.

We all had traits that didn't belong to Papa and didn't belong to Delora. Both of them were famous for holding a grudge. They didn't speak to relatives for years, because of some perceived slight such as not calling for a birthday or disagreeing on a political matter. Papa and Delora had almost no friends. They had work acquaintances, and when we were young even some friends, but soon those dwindled to nothing. But my siblings and I, even if we sometimes got irritated or annoyed with each other, made a pact long ago to never allow anger or pettiness separate us or create long years of silence. Having true friendships is one of the greatest blessings I have had in my life and I always have cherished and held them dear. My two closest friends, Annette and Carol, have been a source of support and love for more than 40 years.

I couldn't definitively say that I enjoyed entertaining or making friends because Mamaji did. Or that I worked hard at forgiveness and tried not to hold grudges because she also sought after peace and mended relationships. Or that my creativity came about because she was so artistic she could see beauty in something as simple as the Malta orange that grew in Dehradun. She hadn't taught me her ways, told me her thoughts or her dreams for me. She didn't have time to advise me on marriage, know my children or to encourage me in my role as a mother. We didn't have hours to discuss my struggles or fears or how I could improve. But even though I did not know Mamaji, somehow in an unexplained and mysterious way, I still became like her.

Occasionally, there were small moments when I felt connected to Mamaji in an indirect way. One of those moments was one summer when Miriam came to visit me in New Jersey. We were discussing my inability to make good chapatis. I had always had an aversion to making them because of the sheer amount that had been made back in Minnesota. For some reason, I could never get mine to puff with steam correctly. Miriam asked me how I had been making them, which was the method Delora had used. Miriam shook her head at me, "You're doing it wrong! That's not how you make them!"

Right there and then we went to the Indian grocery store and she showed me the correct brand of atta to buy, how to mix the dough, and the correct method for rolling and cooking chapatis. In about 15 minutes, I was making chapatis like an expert.

"I can't believe I've been doing this wrong my whole life. How did you learn how to make them like this?" I asked.

Without skipping a beat, Miriam looked up at me and quietly said, "Mamaji taught me how to make them like this."

It was as if I had drawn a complete circle back to Mamaji. Later, I was so excited to pass on her method for perfect chapatis to my own sons.

So despite what I did not have, there remained some kind of inexplicable connection between Mamaji and myself. Sometimes I felt like I understood her and how she would respond to my questions. In a small way, I heard her voice in my own. A voice that despite being separated for more than 50 years was still saturated and infused by her. I would presume that Mamaji would tell me to get on with life, to be grateful for all that I have, to love others as God loves me, to forgive those that have wronged me—because I will also have to ask others to forgive me, and to be strong and determined. She would tell me to remember the good and forget the bad, and look forward to many happier days. I would even indulge myself a bit further and steal a little of what she wrote in her letter to Gloria. I take her words and cherish them as if she had written them just for me.

My darling daughter, Elisheba,

It's so blessed to have good memories. There are memories of your childhood that are sweet and you always look at them with fondness and not regret as you know childhood cannot come back, so the memory is sweet. There are things that you remember and miss and know you can do them again—God willing. So you enjoy those memories too. Then there are memories of things and friends you have enjoyed and know could happen again, but know won't happen and that makes you sad. Do you understand what I mean?

Love,
Mamaji

THE END

Mamaji, Shimla, India
circa 1944

EPILOGUE

Burnsville, Minnesota, December 2014

I'M BACK IN Minnesota again. And for one of the strangest moments in my life. After a bad month at home, Delora died. The funeral home did not successfully put on her sari, but Deborah did an excellent job. Delora was always so careful with each pleat and her pallu lies perfectly. *What are you telling Mamaji right now? Is she asking you, "So? How are my children? Did you love them? Did Elisheba behave herself?"*

I want to say something meaningful as I see her, but I can't. Instead, I touch her hands—I have nothing to say. Delora's nieces and brother from Canada are here, but surprisingly her sister did not make the trip. They all recall wonderful memories of their aunt. Her home-aid arrives. She is dressed as if going to a dance club in a short, black, leather skirt and thigh-high, white, leather platform boots, but she begins to wail and cry loudly, "Mama was so good! She was a wonderful woman!" She tells me that Delora often spoke of all of her children. The funeral service is conducted by Emmanuel.

Papa looks so sad, so defeated. *He looks crumpled. How can a man outlive two wives and still manage to give a sermon?* But he does. He stands and tells of his life mostly, but adds in the story of how he first met Mamaji and then when he lost her and remarried. He talks about Delora's great sacrifice to leave her surgical career to be a mother to all of us. I can listen to all of this without even batting an eye. I look forward to a different and new relationship with Papa. Then Joram speaks and uses the term "my mother" while he talks. He says he loved her unlike anyone else in this world. *Joram knows he cannot say the words "our mother."*

I'm happy that for him that his children had a chance to know their grandmother. Afterwards, he invites only his friends and family to the house. I'm embarrassed by this because it's rude to ignore the few others in attendance. However, he made all the arrangements for the funeral and burial. Back at the house, it's like a party for all except for Papa who looks so handsome in his newly bought suit but can barely lift his head. I hate seeing him like this. Emmanuel, David, Hannah, and I stay until Papa is tired and ready for bed, and then we all go over to Deborah's house where we are staying. We talk and laugh but there are no tears. My emotions are for Papa and I wonder how he will manage without the daily fellowship and friendship Delora offered him.

The next day at the burial, I do cry. Not because I feel sorrow, but because I see Papa crying. But Joram and his wife do not shed even one tear. Joram bends and kisses the casket before it is lowered into the ground. I can't believe Delora is actually gone. *How can that be? Why did she just lay there? Why not get up and take control just like always?*

I remembered how I had always been so intrigued by her former life before marriage. She shared few details of who she had once been. Even when I had pressed and asked her for stories of this hidden self, she was reluctant to share and instead repeated old, safe stories. Maybe it was because even she could see that she had become only a dim shadow of the woman she had once been. There were so many times I prayed that God would take me, and sometimes I prayed that he would take her. And now that the day is here, there is something that is unfinished. But I don't know what it is.

It occurs to me that Delora showed David, Hannah, and me a side of her that no one else ever saw. The older siblings saw it sometimes, but they didn't get the full force of the dark side she had. How can someone who was a wife to Papa, a zealot in her love for Joram, a loving grandmother to her three grandchildren, an involved aunt to the Canadians, and a skilled surgeon to her patients be so evil, so cruel for so many years to the three of us? We knew a part of her that she didn't want anyone else to see. All of us have a side that we don't want others to see. Mostly, we hide it by smiling, clenching our teeth, or just pretending. But sometimes that side comes out. If we are pushed far enough, or put into a situation that demands more than we can handle, we are all capable of showing that dark and ugly side. I guess Delora had a deep need to show us her worst.

I am completely and utterly confused as to how and what I feel. Am I sad that Delora is gone? In an odd way I am, but I don't know exactly why. I'm sad because I love Papa and he will be lonely. I'm sad because in all the years, she and I became friendly but never friends and I think she realized she had not treated me right but had too much pride to tell me so. I'm sad because it's hard for me to see any justice in the way things turned out. I still think about her. I wish I could stop.

Crystal Lake, Minnesota, earlier, in January 2014

THERE IS A transfer belt hanging on the door of this room. It reminds me of my long-ago job in the Minneapolis nursing home. We had fastened them around elderly patient's waists in order to be able to firmly grasp them and move them from the chair to the bed or the wheelchair to the toilet. Back then, the transfer belts were made from plain oatmeal-colored material and the frayed ends fit through a hard, square metal buckle. But the one hanging on the door is patriotic with its red, white, and blue stripes. It has a rounded, brass buckle and looks almost friendly. But for all its fake cheeriness, I'm not fooled. What is it doing here in Papa's room?

From the outside, the rehab center looks typically institutional and my heart was heavy when I walked through its doors. But inside, it is surprisingly a pleasant-looking place. The large sitting area has a lovely glass cage with tiny live birds. I am grateful the expected smell of old urine is absent. Papa's room is right next to the nurse's desk and my heart quickens as I think about seeing him after his stroke. But he isn't in his room. His empty bed has a fake wooden headboard and footboard that barely disguises the hospital bed. Deborah, who still lives in Burnsville, has come over during her lunch hour with me. She surmises he must be in the dining room.

Oh, no, not the dining room! I don't want to see him there. I remember how my long-past, elderly patients had looked, their trays filled with pureed food, their eyes bleary, and bibs around their necks. They had always been "encouraged" to eat in the dining room instead of their own rooms, because it was supposedly beneficial for them to socialize. In reality, none of them spoke to each other, but sat in silence while spooning colorless mush into their mouths. And now Papa is in the same kind of room. I see the back of his head first. He had always been so fastidious with his hair and now I barely recognize it. Long, unkempt strands grow well beyond his ears. His wheelchair is just as I had imagined. Both its leg supports are missing and as I approach his legs are dragging. His tray has a cloth napkin and real china. As he looks up, he spoons bubble-gum pink ice cream from a small paper carton to his mouth. His eyes meet mine. They are not surprised, not happy, not sad—just nothing.

Deborah sits down and makes chitchat and I control my emotions; *not as bad as I thought*, I lie to myself. Hannah has visited Papa already, traveling from her home in Georgia, David from Florida, and Emmanuel had come from Massachusetts. Miriam is in India, and had seen Mamaji in the last stages of life and wanted to remember Papa as he had always been. Gideon had not left his home in Connecticut and had not verbalized the reason for his absence. Papa's speech is slurred, he goes in and out from confusion to lucid thoughts and, yet, I feel a wave of anger from him. He turns his head and only speaks to Deborah, barely acknowledging me. I am amazed and actually impressed that he even remembers enough to know he wants to be angry with me.

About 16 months prior to this visit, Papa and I had argued. He was angry at me because on my trip to Minnesota I had also seen Peter Chacha with whom he was not speaking. After reprimanding me, he launched into my long-ago past with Sunil for some unknown reason. He accused me of "running around" and "behaving shamelessly" with him. I defended myself and this led to a long lecture. Then, I proceeded to leave the house in exasperation. Afterwards, I was sorry and called him a number of times to apologize and hopefully mend our broken ties. Each time, I could feel he was still angry, but maybe just a little less than before. He needed to give me one more talking-to and get it out of his system and we would be good to go. But then he fell and injured his brain; a stroke they said. Or did he have the stroke first and then had fallen which subsequently injured his brain? Did it matter? All I know is that Papa is now confused and his usually sharp wit and intellect are not what they have been.

We wheel him into the sunroom where he asks to sit on the couch in the bright, warm dhoop. Deborah returns to work and suddenly I am alone with my angry father. I sit next to him and he doesn't move over to make a place for me. I take his hand and he pulls it away from me. I long for his confusion to clear so he can give me one of his good old lectures. I deserve it, after all. I could have been a better daughter. Did it matter that he had not loved me as he had loved Joram? Did it matter that he wanted his sons much more than his daughters? Did it matter that he had hurt me so deeply? It didn't, because he was my father and I had hurt him too.

Despite everything that I had said to him or he had said to me, I love him. I don't trust him, but as much as I had tried to stop loving him, I couldn't do it. I've learned something about my capacity to love by loving Papa for so many years. I found out that once I love someone, I can't just stop loving them. My love might change, but I can't turn my love on and off like a faucet. I still love Papa and I will love him until the day I close my eyes on this earth.

I start crying—the tears are uncontrollable, "Are you still angry at me?" I ask him in Hindi.

He looks at me and says, "Angry? You had to say your words and you said them."

His eyes are clear, "I'm sorry," I say.

He stares at me a moment longer and says, "Alright."

He moves over on the couch and makes room for me to sit down beside him. In the sunlight, thousands of dust specks move in rhythmic motion in a halo around his head. His hands are still beautiful. I have always loved them. His fingers are long and elegant with perfect half-moons on each of his nail beds. I hold his hand and this time he doesn't pull away. The skin is dry and I pull out a tube of hand lotion from my purse and massage gently. And then we hold hands silently.

It is a brand-new experience to sit with him and say nothing. In the past this would have been uncomfortable, and words would have filled the void, but now both our speech is limited. He cannot say all he wants and I do not want to say all I can. I still see him as Papa, who had always been in control of each and every person and thing in his life. I cannot fuse my strong, tall and handsome Papa with this man sitting in the wheelchair—not yet.

In his room, I help him stand so he can use the toilet. Even though he has full control of his bladder, they have put on a pair of Depends. He always bought his beloved cotton boxers in packages of three; he liked them big and roomy. I hate seeing the white plastic next to his skin. For a moment I panic. *Will I have to actually help him to use the toilet?*

Thankfully, Papa comes to my rescue and manages all on his own. After he finishes, I help him wash his hands in the sink. He looks up into the mirror and for the first time I see him as he is—not my Ricky Ricardo Papa, but a 93-year-old, gray-haired man. I can barely recognize him. Then he takes a comb and carefully parts his hair, holding the comb characteristically, with his pointer finger and thumb at the edge of the comb, in order to part his hair precisely in one straight line. That one gesture of his, which I know so well, reassures me. *This is my Papa!* A man I have known, loved, feared, disappointed, longed and cried for.

Papa is tired. I help him lay down in his bed and tuck his blankets snug around his chin and feet. He likes the feel of the soft velour blanket Deborah had brought for him around his face and snuggles into the lushness of the brown velvetiness. I read to him.

First, from the book of John and, then from the beginning chapters of the book he had been writing. I read slowly and deliberately. He stays awake for the first two chapters of John and falls asleep during the opening chapter from his own manuscript. As I sit next to him, I stroke his hand—it had dug in the dirt to plant a tree, supported him when he stood on his head for exercise, made wonderful curries, played the piano, written thousands of pages on yellow legal pads, gestured emphatically in sermons and talks, made long, smooth strokes while shaving, and layered soft butter onto warm fresh bread in the way only Papa could do. The clock ticks in the quiet room and marks every second with a loud click as it passes. Papa is getting older by the second and so am I. For now, I am the one holding his hand and helping him. But very soon, I will be lying in a bed, needing a hand to hold as my time ticks away. *When Papa is gone I will be a real orphan. And I'm up next.* When he wakes, he eats some barbeque chicken and then settles into bed.

The next morning when I arrive, he is already in Occupational Therapy, endlessly pedaling on a contraption with his hands. He looks up at me and smiles. For the first time in as long as I can remember, Papa needs me and wants me. He wants me to sit next to him, to take him to his room, to eat with him, to read to him. I make an appointment at the barber during his therapy and then wheel him to the salon. He perks up and directs the barber to cut it shorter, while watching from a mirror. During the shampoo, I ask the technician if I can massage his head. Papa closes his eyes and leans back while I give him a good old Indian-style mallish, as he had enjoyed so much in the old days. I dry his hair and he asks for the comb and styles his own hair.

In the afternoon, I slip out during his Physical Therapy to see Joram. When I return, Papa is in an agitated state. He is in the sitting area and asks a stranger, "What's going on here? What kind of place is this?" The orderly says he had become angry when offered a bath. I bring him over to the couch.

Papa is convinced someone is trying to hurt him and asks, "Do you really love me? Are you and Joram cooking up something to hurt me?" His eyes are huge and filled with tears.

He is so broken, so shaken that I begin to cry, "No, no, Papa. We all love you. We're here to help you."

After 15 minutes or so, we both quiet down and meet a friend and patient of Deborah's who is also in the sitting area with her seven-month-old baby, Ethan. The sight of the baby cheers and calms Papa. Back in his room, I read John chapter four to him. Then I lay down in his bed next to him. It is peaceful and quiet. We talk about life, growing old, and God. I play George Beverly Shea singing *How Great Thou Art* on YouTube and soon Papa feels sleepy and I tuck him in.

That night I say goodbye to Papa. I am getting on an early-morning flight. He is lucid, asking me when I will get to New Jersey, how long the flight is, and other details. I read aloud from Matthew, chapter nine in which Jesus heals the paralytic man. Afterwards, we pray together. In the past, when I had heard Papa pray, he had only prayed for Joram and his family by name. I was included generally along with, "the rest of the family." But, tonight, he prays for me by name and thanks God that I have been able to come and see him. We finish with the Lord's Prayer. When it is time to say goodbye, Papa hugs me tightly and kisses me two or three times.

I begin to cry and hug him back, "I love you," I say.

"I love you too," Papa replies, which only brings more tears.

It is time to go. I have not received so much affection from Papa since I was a young girl. I have been given a gift. It is the Papa I remembered from long ago—loving, caring, and vulnerable. He is the father I have longed for and want to remember.

AFTERWORD

IN MAY 2019, Papa died.
 I had been so happy because I had four years with him
alone—without the corrupting presence of Delora. Even though
Papa was older, he recovered from his stroke and was clear and
articulate, just as he always had been. I came to see him often in
Minnesota and spent weeks with him, cooking his favorite foods,
reading Mamaji's letters to him, looking at old family pictures,
and laughing about the good times. I was able to fully express my
feelings about missing Mamaji and the cruelty and ruthlessness of
Delora. I told him I felt abandoned by him. At first he was aghast,
almost not believing me, but then as I quoted some of Delora's
favorite phrases to me, he was quiet and agreed that what she had
done was wrong. We agreed never to waste our time together to
discuss Delora. Papa ceased referring to her as, "your mother"
when he spoke of her and instead used the term, "my second wife"
or, "Joram's mother." I was so grateful that in his old age, he made
that distinction. I read him what I had written after I visited him
at the rehab center and he was moved to tears, "Why didn't you
tell me you felt like that?" he asked me. On the morning he died,

Papa told me he was going to be in heaven that day. I asked him to please give my love to Mamaji and he agreed.

But when Papa's end had come and gone, Delora's hand reached out from her grave, using Joram as her mouthpiece. In 2000, Papa and Delora had signed a trust which specifically and intentionally excluded all seven of us and named Joram as the sole beneficiary. After Papa suffered his stroke, he was denied access to his own ample finances. During my visits, I was moved to tears at the poor care he was being given. Even though it was clear he was being neglected, he begged me to not say anything and promised to call me if things became unbearable. Joram and his wife shared the house with Papa and filled it with thousands of dollars of tasteless and garish art, watches, bulky statues and in their true redneck, provincial style, even a full-sized carousel horse. Papa expressed his dismay to me a number of times and finally became so desperate that he called Deborah and asked her to take him to a lawyer. Unfortunately, Joram eavesdropped on the private phone call and through shouting and fear intimidated Papa and Deborah so much that neither felt safe taking the matter further.

On the day Papa died, he tried to correct the mistake he had made 19 years ago by reminding us that he had two wives and eight children and that there "was enough for everyone." He implored Joram to not be greedy or selfish. But Joram was trained by his mother too well. He claimed he had taken care of Papa his whole life (although Papa was always independent and required only the care of a once-a-week health-aid), and felt he was justified in claiming all the inheritance as his own. I always found it amusing that this huge, overgrown, middle-aged man had depended on his parents his whole life, working full-time but never leaving his childhood home to pay his own mortgage, groceries, and utilities, or even perform simple adult tasks like cooking for himself. He had just one meek friend of his own age and finally resorted to finding both his wives in his late years by trolling the internet. Curiously, even after his marriages, he was unable to live self-sufficiently and lived with his parents. It was clear that Joram never viewed any of us as his siblings, and his actions at the end of Papa's life proved that Delora's love of money still lived deep in his soul. It was no surprise when Joram decided to cease all communication.

For me, Papa's actions from May, 2000 will always haunt me. On the one hand, he had done something so wrong by ultimately disowning all seven of us. But then I also had experienced too well the dark and wicked influence Delora had on all our lives, including Papa's. Even though he had tried to make things right, he had not done enough. His words from the trust opened old wounds, and I confronted ugly visages from my past once more. I had to begin the process of forgiving again. Although Papa and I had made our peace, I will always question his love for me. I am not really convinced of it.

I am certain Mamaji will be happy to know that even though her untimely death was a great tragedy, the loss has not conquered her children. As she told Venetia Masi long ago in her dream, we *are* fine and we have all found peace and love. We choose to live our lives embracing our good memories of Papa and following the example of Mamaji who taught us to value love, relationships, each other, and to live lives that please God.

Miriam splits her time between India and America and has three sons. She is a happy Dadhi to two delightful grandsons. Gideon lives in Connecticut and has a family of two girls and two boys. He has four adorable grandchildren. Emmanuel lives in Massachusetts and has three girls and a boy. He is Nana to five lively grandchildren. Deborah lives in Minnesota and has two sons. David lives in Florida and has four daughters. He is grandfather—or Papa as he is called, to his three beautiful grandchildren. Hannah lives in Georgia and has twin boys and a girl. I live in New Jersey and have two sons.

Mamaji truly loved me—and I miss her very much.

ACKNOWLEDGEMENTS

First, I must thank my sister, Hannah. She has read this manuscript about as many times as I have written it and I have even used her exact words in places. Thank you, Hannah Banana for your suggestions, corrections, criticisms, wit and encouragement. Oh, and DAAQBINGTA!

Doodh, Debbie, and Miriamah, thank you for reading this when it was just a chronological tally of events, and offering your never-ending inspiration, praise, and reassurance during the past seven years.

To my siblings—in essence we all wrote this memoir together and it belongs to all of us. You have all allowed me to write some of your memories and I am forever grateful to you for helping me through this project. We reminisced and cried but mostly we laughed like we always do. I love all of you guys, I would not be here without your strength and love. Stooges and Biggers—forever!

Thank you Farina Masi. Your stories and family history filled so many blanks for me; I would have never been able to piece my past together without you. I love you lots!

To my friend and editor Raquel—you believed in this story. Your insight and humor as we gorged on fries at the Tick Tock Diner made our "work" so much fun. Thank you!

Thank you to Walter Cummins at Serving House Books, for your guidance, kind patience and wisdom throughout the publishing process.

I also want to thank close friends and readers who read the manuscript in its infantile stages and provided so much valuable feedback—Annette, Carol, my niece Naomi, Vaishali, Maureen Chachi, Jackie, Abe, Wendy, Julie, Mike, and Liz.

DISCUSSION
QUESTIONS

1. Why did Papaji feel the need to remarry and return to "normal" as quickly as he did?
2. What was the moment in each character's life when they comprehend that their reality was not going to be what they had imagined? How did this awareness change them?
3. Once she began working full-time, what prevented Elisheba from leaving her situation and moving out?
4. Why couldn't the siblings simply refuse to give their checks to Mama?
5. Did you feel Elisheba was justified in making Mama's life difficult?
6. What were the coping mechanisms the characters used to deal with difficult life situations?
7. What were the life events that shaped each character's story?
8. How did cultural isolation play a role in the way Papaji parented? How did it impact the way each child related to his/her environment?

9. How did Mamaji's last requests relate to her fear that her children would not be well cared for and that they would experience cultural isolation? Was it selfish of Mamaji to ask Papaji not to marry again?

10. Was Papaji to blame for the way Mama treated the children because he trusted her too much? Or was he to blame because he was selfish?

11. Was Elisheba an active or passive participant in her life story? Do you feel this changed over the course of the narrative?

12. Keeping in mind that the Eastern and Western understanding of respect is different, how do Respect and Indian Culture play a role in this story?

13. Do you feel Elisheba is a reliable narrator of her story?

14. With which character in this story do you most identify?

15. Which character in this story frustrates you the most?

16. How do you relate to the examples of injustice, redemption and forgiveness demonstrated by the characters in this story?

17. Why are memoirs so popular? What are the benefits and drawbacks of sharing personal revelations?

AUTHOR
BIO

E LISHEBA HAQQ WAS born in Chandigarh, India, but was brought up in Minnesota, USA. She earned her MFA in Creative Writing from Fairleigh Dickinson University and currently teaches writing at Rutgers University. Her work has appeared in *A Letter for my Mother, Gateways, She.knows.com,* and *New Jersey Monthly.* An RN by profession, she has been published in *Creative Nursing* and *Journal of Nursing Education and Practice.* She enjoys unplanned travel, black tea, and printed books. Elisheba lives in New Jersey with her family and can be found online at www.elishebahaqq.com and on Facebook, Instagram, and Twitter.

CPSIA information can be obtained
at www.ICGtesting.com
Printed in the USA
JSHW020345230920
8161JS00003B/215